NELL

THE AUSTRALIAN HEIRESS WHO SAVED KERENSKY FROM STALIN & THE NAZIS

Heroic Nell Kerensky and her husband in Paris, America and Australia

SUSANNA DE VRIES

First published in 2020 by Pirgos Press
Updated edition published in 2021 by Pirgos Press
Bookshop distribution in Australia through Boolarong Press, Brisbane.
Digital distribution by Ebook Alchemy

ISBN 978-0-9806216-6-2 (p/b - b&w)
ISBN 978-0-9806216-7-9 (p/b - colour)
ISBN 978-0-9806216-9-3 (ebook)

Nell Tritton Kerensky, 1899-1946
Brisbane history, 1890-1926
Tritton's Store, George Street, Brisbane
Spanish influenza pandemic, 1919
Alexander Fyodorovich Kerensky, 1881-1970
Ford Maddox Ford, publisher
Jews, persecution of, in Tsarist Russia
'Lockhart plot' to assassinate Lenin
Robert Bruce Lockhart, 1887-1970
Marie Bakshirtskeff, artist 1858-1884
Vladimir Ilyich Lenin, 1870-1924
Josef Stalin, 1878-1953
Flora Benenson Solomon, 1895-1984
Nina Berberova, author 1901-1993
Stanford University
New Canaan, Connecticut, USA

Cover by Bernard Milford, Brisbane, using 1910 Baedeker map.

CONTENTS

Nell Tritton in a dress of white French lace photographed before her 21st birthday party. (From the collection of Mrs Lavinia Tritton)

CHAPTER ONE

A Brisbane Heiress & a Family Tragedy

Elderslie, Christmas, 1924.

For years Christmas celebrations at *Elderslie,* the Tritton's family home, had been subdued. This undercurrent of sadness was caused by the fact that two of Nell's siblings had died just before Christmas 1919, victims of the Spanish influenza pandemic that killed over 50,000,000 people worldwide.

Still in their early twenties, Charles, the brother Nell adored, and Lillian, her asthmatic elder sister, were victims of the influenza pandemic and died within weeks of each other. Their deaths were horrific and painful. The lungs of both siblings filled with thick viscous fluid due to pneumonia and they died painfully, choking for breath. Memories of their final hours haunted Nell's nightmares and her mother took years to recover from the deaths of two of her four children.

The coroner's report confirmed that Nell's elder brother and sister had died from pulmonary influenza, their immune systems and kidneys weakened in childhood by a lead-lined water tank and lead water pipes in the family's first home, a weatherboard cottage south of the Brisbane River. According to the coroner's report, lead in the water had a detrimental effect on the Tritton children's immune systems making them vulnerable to viruses and other diseases.

Doctors warned Nell's parents that eighteen year old Nell and her married sister Idie could also have been affected by lead poisoning. Nell learned from the coroner's report that her life could be curtailed by a weakened immune system which could cause kidney and heart problems.

A strong-minded intelligent young woman, Nell was determined that, if her life was to be brief, she would live it to the full. She had been promised a year in Paris but the outbreak war in 1914 made that impossible. In spite of this she was determined to fulfil her ambition, spend time in France and learn to speak French like a Parisian.

Nell was unusual for a girl of her era. She became a prize-winning rally driver partnered by her brother and one of his school friends at a time when few women drove cars. She defied the system, wanting a career at a time when marriage was seen as the only career suitable for a woman.

After two years as Brisbane's first female cadet journalist she became a journalist in Sydney but never abandoned her dream of spending a few years in Paris.

Nell was in her mid-twenties when returning home for Christmas she broke the news to her parents that she was going to fulfil her dream and spend a year in Paris. Her mother expressed disappointment having hoped Nell was about to announce her engagement to her rally driving partner. But when he proposed marriage Nell had told him gently she liked him as a friend but not as a husband.

When her mother realised Nell was determined to spend a year overseas rather than accept the marriage proposal, she pointed out that eligible men were in short supply as so many of them had died in the Great War. Leila Tritton said it was time for her independent-minded daughter to marry and settle down rather than go gallivanting around Europe.

Nell replied she would only marry someone she loved passionately but as yet she had not met the right man.

His youngest daughter's wish to live overseas worried Nell's father. He had never forgotten the deaths of his two oldest children from the Spanish flu pandemic. On a business trip to Europe, her father had spent time in Paris and knew of artists living in rat-infested studios with only buckets for toilets. This was not something he wanted for his adventurous daughter.

Nell's father realised his daughter could not be dissuaded and told her that having turned 25, she had access to her share of the family trust he had established after Charles' death to safeguard the future of his children and grandchildren. She should use trust money to rent a comfortable apartment in Paris, rather than a chilly studio with primitive plumbing. He was concerned that should Nell become ill overseas, she would have no family to care for her.

Nell was touched by her father's concern, only too aware that his own childhood had been difficult. Her grandfather, William Tritton, had lost his job due to lung disease and due to his father's ill health Fred Tritton had to leave school before completing his education. The fact Nell's father had no money and no parental support had been the spur that drove him to become a success.

As a migrant Fred Tritton had worked hard and eventually became Queensland's wealthiest businessman, widely respected for his probity and his generous contributions to charities.

William Tritton, Nell's paternal grandfather, had left the small French-speaking island of Jersey to work as an Inspector of Weights and Measures in London before his illness forced him into retirement. In his fifties, with four teenage sons, William Tritton had been warned that foggy London air could lead to tuberculosis which, before the discovery of antibiotics, was a death sentence. He was advised to move to a warmer climate and decided to immigrate to Queensland. This pioneering state in 1889, was offering grants of bush land to adult migrants of good standing. William Tritton hoped this would result in a better life for his sons.

In the late 1880s the four Tritton boys and their parents made the 10,000 mile voyage aboard the migrant ship the SS *Sirsa.* They landed at Townsville where William realised that work opportunities for his sons were limited so decided the family should remain on board and land in Brisbane, the capital of Queensland. Arriving there the Tritton family were given temporary accommodation in a government hostel. Charles Tritton, Fred's elder brother, was offered a job with good prospects in Sydney which he accepted.

Under the terms of the Crown Lands Act, William Tritton was entitled to a 'selection' of virgin bush. However all land grants had to be cleared of trees and fenced within twelve months of receiving them. The Tritton land was situated on what is now Blunder Road, Oxley, then on the outskirts of Brisbane. Nell's grandfather was not strong enough to help with the hard physical work of clearing the bush so his young sons Frederick (Fred)Tritton and his brothers Joe and Jack built a small cabin and lived rough while they cleared the trees and fenced the land.[1]

Having secured their sole asset, Nell's father, Fred, found a job as a warehouseman. He was determined to set up his own business, but needed capital. Aged 21, with the consent of his family, Fred Tritton used the Blunder Road land as security to obtain a bank loan. With the money, he leased commercial premises in South Brisbane and opened a shop selling furniture and home wares. He imported household items from England as there was very little manufacturing in Brisbane which was still a large country town lacking sewerage and other amenities.

Frederick Tritton soon opened a much larger shop on South Brisbane's Russell Street and married his 19 year-old sweetheart Eliza

(Leila) Worrell, in Woolloongabba's Church of the Holy Trinity. His young bride had migrated to Brisbane with her parents from the north of England. The couple had met through their local Anglican church and fallen in love.

The newly-weds had very little money so their first home was an old weatherboard cottage on the south side of the Brisbane River. The cottage came with a lead-lined water tank which Queensland building regulations permitted as normal practice. Unfortunately, at that time, no-one knew the dangers lead poisoning posed to the immune systems of children. In 1899 when Nell was born, doctors were not aware that lead poisoning could occur and worse still, cause irreversible kidney damage.

Nell and her elder siblings, Charles, Lillian and Idie spent their earliest years in the weatherboard cottage near the Brisbane River which flooded during heavy summer rains. In one severe flood when their father was at work, Nell remembered huge tree trunks flying downstream, carried by the raging waters of the swollen river. Leila Tritton and her children had to be rescued by boat.

Line engraving of Brisbane in time of flood after a drawing by the nineteenth century Brisbane artist Joseph Clarke (Author's collection)

Baby Lydia Ellen (Nell) Tritton and her siblings, Idie (left), Charles and Lillian. (Courtesy Mrs Lavinia Tritton)

Elderslie in Adelaide Street, Clayfield, during Nell's childhood. (Courtesy John Oxley Library, State Library of Qld)

The rear of Tritton's store on Brisbane's North Quay during Nell's school days. The 'talking machines' advertised were radios and gramophones. Larger windows were eventually installed when the rear of the building was modernised. (Author's collection)

The fact his wife and children had been exposed to danger in two major floods made Fred Tritton determined to move to a flood-free area. He had already lost stock and machinery due to flood damage but had prudently insured his furniture factory and his department store against flood. With the aid of insurance money he was able to restock quickly and resume trading.

Due to successful advertising and hard work from Nell's father Tritton's store prospered and he was able to purchase a newly-built house named *Elderslie* at No 151, Adelaide Street, in flood-free Clayfield. This broad, tree-lined avenue with large homes set in spacious gardens was regarded as one of Brisbane's most attractive streets.[2] Believed to have been designed by the prestigious architectural firm of Richard Gailey and Son, and completed in 1904, the wide verandas of *Elderslie* provided the perfect outdoor living area for the Tritton family during Brisbane's hot humid summers.

This attractive Federation era home had unusually large bay windows and well-designed reception rooms with handsome pressed metal ceilings. The building of *Elderslie* had been commissioned by Edgar Harris, a wealthy Brisbane merchant, who named it after a family home in England. The first owner had spared no expense in its construction but due to financial setbacks, Edgar Harris was forced to sell his beautiful home soon after it was completed.

The Tritton's moved to *Elderslie* shortly after Nell's sixth birthday. Nell and her two older sisters, Lillian and Idie, were delighted when they found they were to have their own bedrooms. Nell loved her attractive new home with its big rambling garden and the lush fernery under the house which provided a cool retreat on Brisbane's hot summer days. Part of their large garden was left as bush land while closer to the house scarlet poincianas, purple jacarandas and crimson and pink bougainvillea were planted.

Several of *Elderslie's* six bedrooms had French doors opening onto broad verandas. There were two outdoor toilets as Brisbane still lacked a sewerage system and instead had what were known as outdoor 'dunnies' in garden sheds. Necessary visits resulted in frequent shrieks of horror when the sisters found they were sharing the 'dunny' with large hairy spiders and the occasional snake or green tree frog.

Every night Nell's mother read aloud to her children. For clever six year-old Nell *Elderslie* was a magical place. Her mother had furnished *Elderslie* with Tritton's quality furniture made in their factory, using Queensland's native timbers. Curtains of imported brocade hung in the living areas with attractive floral chintz curtains in the bedrooms.

By 1905, regulations mercifully prohibited the use of lead linings in water tanks. This meant the two youngest Tritton children, Cecil and Roy, both born at *Elderslie*, were not exposed to lead as Nell and Idie had been in their previous home.

As his own education had been cut short, Fred Tritton was determined that his children would receive the best education money could buy. Nell and her elder sisters were educated privately at the Brisbane High School for Girls on Wickham Terrace before the school moved to its present location in South Brisbane and was renamed Somerville House where Nell enjoyed her final year of school and left with a report saying she had been an outstanding student.

At Somerville House Nell had problems with maths but excelled in anything to do with writing and literature. She enjoyed French lessons and was determined to speak French perfectly, inspired by a family legend that told of an aristocratic French ancestor who married a Tritton after escaping from the French Revolution. The aristocratic young woman, whose parents had been guillotined, hired a fisherman to take her by boat from the Normandy coast to Jersey. On this tranquil island she found refuge on the Tritton's farm and eventually married a member of the Tritton family.

Somerville House School for Girls, Brisbane
The new school building which Nell attended after it moved to these handsome premises from the inner city. (Private collection)

Nell, like many of her classmates from Somerville House, was expected to be presented to Queensland society at a debutante ball at Government House on Fernberg Road. (Photo by Jake de Vries, taken at Government House when the author received an Order of Australia.)

Nell, (christened Lydia Ellen, names she disliked and never used) as a romantic teenager, loved the idea of an aristocratic French ancestor. She hoped to become a writer and planned to use the pen name 'Nellé (Ellen spelt backwards with an acute accent to make it look and sound French).

At school Nell wrote a couple of short stories as assignments but her French pen name provoked malicious comments from girls in her class who were envious of her family's wealth. They whispered behind Nell's back that the Tritton's were not 'old money' like them and merely *nouveau riche* immigrants from a small island.

Nell's motto was 'Rise above it'. An extroverted happy girl who found it easy to make friends, Nell dealt with her critics by saying she would rather be noticed for doing something unusual than be ignored for being colourless and boring.

Nell enjoyed a happy secure childhood and adolescence in a beautiful home with a tennis court and an athletic elder brother to partner her in doubles matches. She became a good tennis player, competed in the school tennis team and headed the swimming team. She topped her classes in English, French and history but continued to hate mathematics, for which she always received very poor marks. She enjoyed ballet and ballroom dancing and won prizes for both.

Nell's French teacher encouraged her plan to study in Paris and suggested she could attend the Alliance Française language school in Montparnasse. It was funded by the French government and had an excellent reputation. Nell's father agreed she should go there and he would pay her fees and accommodation.

While still in his twenties, Fred Tritton had been astute enough to realise that the growing city of Brisbane needed a department store selling household goods to newly-arrived migrants who built homes as soon as they had money. He expanded Tritton's store at 260 George Street onto land on North Quay, decades before Myer and David Jones opened department stores on Queen Street. However by the mid-twentieth century these stores started taking business away from Tritton's which meant it closed its doors in the late 1970s.[3]

Much of Fred Tritton's success lay in his skilful use of advertising. He paid a fee to the Brisbane City Council to have slogans advertising Tritton's George Street store printed on every tram ticket and advertisements for Tritton's on the back of each bus and tram.

The slogan *TRITTONS STANDS BEHIND THE PRODUCTS WE SELL* was something most people remembered when they saw it on the back of a bus. It became a joke in Brisbane with buyers of double beds that a member of the Tritton family would arrive with each bed and stand behind the buyer on the first night it was used.

In his furniture factory south of the river, Fred Tritton employed experienced British-trained cabinet makers who crafted the beautiful native timbers of Queensland. Their reputation for quality furniture and good service helped make Tritton's a household name in Queensland. Many clients travelled long distances to shop at the crowded department store for furniture, rugs, lighting and other household goods ensuring the business prospered.

Nell's parents could now afford to employ a cook and a succession of country girls to help run the household efficiently after the birth of two more boys, Roy and Cyril.

In the school holidays, to keep his young family occupied, Fred Tritton commissioned a large rectangular swimming pool with several changing rooms attached and a hard-surface tennis court. An area of the lawn was reserved for games of croquet. Nell was the most athletic of the three girls and enjoyed partnering her brother Charles in the friendly tournaments that took place at the Tritton home on Saturday afternoons.

Before the onset of World War One, family life at *Elderslie* revolved around tennis and croquet parties each weekend with Nell and her sisters playing in long white tennis skirts. Lillian, Idie and Nell learned how to be good hostesses by helping her mother serve afternoon tea with assorted home made cakes to their guests on the wide verandas of *Elderslie.*

In this traditional household, every Sunday morning the family were driven in their imported silver Buick to the local Anglican Church where their father was a churchwarden. Fred Tritton read the lesson from the Old Testament or King James Bible whose richness of language impressed Nell. Sunday school followed morning service and the family then drove home for a large Sunday lunch. This usually consisted of roast beef or lamb with home-grown vegetables, and a trifle or apple crumble. The afternoons were devoted to reading and family games of croquet.

A devout Anglican, Nell's mother was active in charities associated with her local church. Leila Tritton's pet project was Coorparoo's Queen Alexandra Home for Children, which provided a home for orphaned and abandoned children and the children of single mothers, well before the government took any responsibility for them.

In recognition of her work and dedication, Nell's mother was elected head of the Management Committee.

Leila Tritton worked hard to raise money to expand this privately-funded home for which Tritton's were the main benefactors.[4]

Fred Tritton paid for each abandoned or orphaned child to receive generous birthday and Christmas gifts and a new school outfit each year. In addition to money provided by the Tritton family, Nell's mother worked hard organising 'bring-and-buy' sales and other fund-raising events to cover staff wages and other expenses.

In spite of their wealth, Nell's parents lived relatively modestly and without ostentation. Their attitude to money had a profound influence on Nell who was raised to be generous to those in need. Her parents were careful not to spoil their six children who were expected to earn their pocket money by doing chores and helping the gardener and the domestic staff.

Once they were old enough, the four eldest children, including Nell, were taken to Tritton's store by their father to help in the busy pre-Christmas rush. The girls worked behind the scenes wrapping parcels while Charles was attached to a department manager to gain first-hand experience as one day he would be running the business. Even Roy and Cyril, the two youngest boys, both born at *Elderslie,* were given small tasks to perform.

Nell's mother frequently reminded her children to 'count their blessings.' Neither she nor her husband had been brought up with money. Leila Tritton pointed out to her children that they were extremely fortunate so must do whatever they could for those less fortunate than themselves. For the rest of her life Nell remembered her mother insisting that what counted in life was not what you possessed, but what you could do for those in need and she took this to heart.

Leila Tritton was always accompanied by her daughters on her regular inspection visits to the Queen Alexandra Home. She insisted they donate some of their toys to the orphaned and abandoned children who lived there. She left her daughters to make friends and play with the children while she discussed practical issues with the Matron, inspected the kitchens, and visited the dormitories.

In addition to Fred Tritton's vital financial support of the Queen Alexandra Home and Orphanage he supported the Salvation Army and was an active member of his local Rotary Club. This organization provided generous support to local schools and charities.

Nell's father was a motoring enthusiast and had a large turntable set into the floor of his garage so that his expensive imported silver Buick could be left on the turntable and then easily driven out of their garage front first.

Nell's elder brother Charles, a motoring enthusiast like his father, gave Nell her first driving lessons as a teenager in the grounds of *Elderslie.* Later she was given driving lessons by her father's chauffeur-handyman.

Like her father and elder brother, Nell was fascinated by fast cars. She became an excellent driver and mastered the complicated procedure known as double-declutching which was standard on cars made in the 1920s, a process which defeated many novice drivers. Partnered by either Charles or by one of his school friends, Nell became the first Queensland woman to win prizes for rally-driving and became a champion driver in what was at that time an exclusively all-male sport.

When Nell left Somerville House, the Great War of 1914-18 was raging in Europe and attending university was still not considered suitable for young women from affluent families who were expected to marry rather than pursue a career. The fledgling University of Queensland, established in 1910, initially located in the city before moving to the St Lucia campus, was run by men and very few places were allocated to women. Cambridge University allowed women to attend arts lectures but refused to grant them degrees, as Nell discovered when she investigated the possibility of going to study in England.

Academics and doctors, most of whom were male, were reluctant to concede that women should have the benefit of a higher education. They claimed the role of women was to support a husband and bear his children. The reactionary Dr Henry Maudsley (1835-1938) as editor of the *Journal of Mental Health* (later the *British Journal of Psychiatry*), made the outrageous claim that because women's heads were smaller then those of men, women's brains must also be smaller. This, Dr Maudsley postulated, made women incapable of rational thought.

Until they married, girls were expected to remain at home, help their mothers run the household and look for a husband. The only socially acceptable work outside the home for women was to act as a volunteer for selected charities.

At school Nell had won a prize for a poem describing the awe-inspiring beauty of the Glasshouse Mountains where she loved going bushwalking and climbing with her brother and his friends. At the time this was a dangerous pastime as the mountains were isolated and serious climbing accidents were not uncommon

Nell, although very feminine in looks, was a tomboy. Unlike Nell, her sisters Idie and the asthmatic Lillian were not interested in bush walking. They remained at home helping their mother. To Nell, the idea of being a lady of leisure appalled her. She longed to be a writer and have an interesting career among creative people and was looking forward to her year in Paris.

In 1914, the outbreak of what became known as the Great War against the Kaiser's Germany made this plan impossible. Nell would have to stay in Brisbane a little longer.

CHAPTER TWO

The Spanish Flu Pandemic & Nell joins the Red Cross

In 1914, when the German army invaded Belgium, Britain and France declared war on Germany. Tsarist Russia, having signed a defence agreement with France, stipulating that each country would defend the other in time of need, entered the war on the side of Britain, France and their colonies. Thousands of young Australians enlisted as volunteers along with New Zealanders to defend the 'mother country' and were proud to be known as Anzacs. They joined the Allied forces, and were sent overseas to fight along with a few nurses to care for them. In this sexist era, women doctors who wished to enlist were turned down by the British War Office, being told they were not strong enough physically or mentally to deal with battle conditions.

Standing on the corner of Queen and Edward Streets Nell watched sun-tanned young men in uniform as they marched past her. They were looking forward to adventures overseas. Nell's favourite cousin, young Corbett Tritton had enlisted as a volunteer. Later that evening in her bedroom at *Elderslie,* Nell wrote a poem about brave young men prepared to die for their country. She wanted to help the war effort and the Anzacs in any way possible.

Lady Goold-Adams, wife of the Governor of Queensland, Sir Hamilton Goold-Adams, sat on a charity committee with Nell's mother. Over morning tea the Governor's wife asked Leila Tritton if part of their substantial home could be made available for Red Cross volunteers who needed a packing depot for gift parcels to be sent to soldiers. The parcels would include hand-knitted socks, mufflers and balaclava helmets for Anzacs facing the bitter cold winter of the trenches.

Nell's parents were happy to have the Clayfield Red Cross unit based at *Elderslie.* Volunteers used the large kitchen to bake fruit cakes and Anzac biscuits using oats, flour, treacle or honey and flakes of coconut. These ingredients were selected as they would not turn mouldy on the long sea voyage from Queensland to France where in 1915 Australians were manning the trenches along the Somme River valley.

Nell left Somerville House in 1917 at the age of eighteen. Her promised year in Paris to finish her education was now out of the question. She joined her mother and her elder sisters working as volunteers with the Clayfield branch of the Red Cross based at *Elderslie.*

Nell worked hard and was made supervisor of the Clayfield Red Cross packing division. She hoped one of these food parcels might reach her cousin, Lieutenant Corbett Tritton, (who she called Corby) who she knew was risking his life in the trenches on the Somme.

In wartime, Tritton's furniture factory had converted its machinery to manufacturing items needed by the troops. Charles Tritton intending to take over once his father retired had become a senior manager in the family business. Charles had wanted to volunteer like his cousin Corbett but Fred Tritton pointed out that his heir was already doing essential war work. He had a pregnant wife and a young son to consider and was needed helping his father run their department store and factory. So many men had enlisted and been replaced by unskilled women that good management was vital.

Each morning Nell and her sisters scanned the casualty lists in Brisbane's *Daily Mail,* dreading they might find Corby's name or those of other young men who had attended those carefree pre-war tennis parties at *Elderslie.*

The Great War with its huge death toll and rationing of various items seemed as if it would never end. But eventually an armistice was declared and a peace treaty signed at Versailles in 1918 optimistically described as 'the war to end all wars'.

Life in Australia slowly returned to normal. The Anzacs came home, many of them crippled and psychologically damaged by the horrors of the first war to involve machine guns. As Brisbane settled back into its pre-war routines, women who had taken over men's jobs during the war had to return to what were known as 'home duties'.

Nell was thrilled when she and Charles, Lillian and Idie received a gold-embossed invitation to join their father at an investiture to be held at Queensland's Government House where their mother was to be awarded an MBE from Buckingham Palace. The day after Leila Tritton's investiture Fred Tritton arranged a family celebration at *Elderslie.*

The first warning of a dangerous strain of influenza, known as Spanish flu (although later it was believed it had been brought to Australia by returning troops) was published on 3 May, 1919 in *The*

Brisbane Courier. The article reported a dangerous strain of influenza which developed rapidly into pneumonia and resulted in the deaths of thousands. In New South Wales, hospitals were full and tents set up to serve as hospitals. It was feared that once the pandemic spread across the border to Queensland it would cause chaos in Brisbane's hospitals.

A tented hospital was set up on the Exhibition showgrounds as well as in schools and children sent home. The help of volunteers to act as nurses was sought, with many cases of influenza in Brisbane and surrounds. As more and more patients died, civilians were urged to wear face masks. [5]

During the Spanish flu pandemic in 1919 hospitals were overcrowded and temporary tented hospitals constructed in which patients were nursed by volunteers. In Brisbane a tented hospital was erected on the Brisbane Showgrounds. (Private collection)

For reasons unknown, this virus rarely attacked the elderly. Instead, it affected young men and women who after a brief illness died painfully, unable to breathe, from pneumonia. There was no cure or vaccine against this lethal strain of flu. [6]

Brisbane's hospitals soon overflowed with influenza patients and many sick people lay on stretchers in hospital passageways due to the bed shortage. Medicines ran out and a long queue of horse-drawn and mechanised ambulances lined up outside the Royal Brisbane Hospital waiting for vacant beds so their patients could be admitted.

Soon influenza cases were so numerous they had to be nursed by volunteers, as the nursing profession was overwhelmed by the flood of patients wanting admission to the Royal Brisbane Hospital and then to all the smaller private hospitals. Business suffered and some shops ran out of essentials. Several tram routes no longer operated as their drivers had died from Spanish flu.

During the first week of September 1919, the asthmatic Lillian, whose health had been affected by lead poisoning in childhood, became feverish. She collapsed with a high temperature and was put to bed.

Brisbane's hospitals could not cope and as many influenza patients were turned away, Lillian was nursed at home. Idie, Nell and their mother took turns to sponge Lillian's feverish body with cold water to bring down her temperature. This proved futile as the lethal flu virus had attacked Lillian's heart, liver and kidneys. Despite treatment from leading specialists, with her weakened immune system she failed to respond and developed pneumonia. Gasping for air as her lungs filled with fluid, Lillian died on 19 September 1919, two weeks after showing the first symptoms of the Spanish influenza virus.

Nell and her grief-stricken family were in shock, stunned by the rapidity of her sister's death. Lillian's funeral was attended by family and friends and she was buried in the Tritton family plot at Dutton Park Cemetery. They were all in mourning when Charles, heir to the business as Fred Tritton's only son, developed the same ominous signs as his late sister. Nora, his young wife, was heavily pregnant with their second child and was clearly at risk. The hospitals were still overcrowded so Fred Tritton rented a private ambulance and had his heir moved to *Elderslie* to be nursed by his mother and sisters who risked their lives to nurse him without protective clothing but were warned to wear masks.

The family doctor and a senior physician from Wickham Terrace made daily calls. But like Lillian, Charles failed to respond to treatment. He lapsed into a coma and died on Christmas Eve 1919, with a painful death similar to that suffered by his sister.

Nell, who had been as close as a twin to her brother during their teenage years, was devastated by his death. Charles had been her partner in tennis tournaments and in bush walks and climbing expeditions to the Glasshouse Mountains before his marriage. Now Charles was dead and the Tritton money had been unable to save him.

It seemed incongruous amid so much grief that *Elderslie* was decorated for Christmas with brightly coloured paper streamers and wreaths of artificial holly. A pine tree covered in tinsel and glittering ornaments flanked by brightly-wrapped presents stood in the drawing room. Her brother and sister's deaths shook Nell's faith in God. In spite of all their prayers, the Almighty had allowed her siblings to suffer terribly and die cruel painful deaths.

Despite the humidity and heat of sub-tropical Brisbane, Charles Tritton's funeral had to be delayed until after the Christmas holiday. He was buried at Dutton Park cemetery in the same grave as his sister.

Their death certificates cited the cause of their deaths as 'Bubonic influenza and chronic nephritis' a diagnosis which puzzled Nell's family until the autopsies revealed kidney and liver damage. It became clear that the lead lined water tank at the family's first home had been responsible for lowering their children's immune systems and causing their premature deaths.

Nell's parents were shocked and naturally worried that she and Idie could also have been affected. Nell, when told of the coroner's report, reacted by becoming determined to make the most of her life since it might be cut short.

For Leila Tritton, the loss of two of her children within a month of each other was devastating. Nell's mother, previously a very active woman, suffered terrible depression. She lay in bed with her face to the wall, refused to get up and ate very little. Idie was distracted by preparations for her grand white wedding, so it fell to Nell to care for her mother and the house.

Nell proved herself capable and hard-working. She took over the running of the house and staff, helped Idie with her wedding preparations and supervised her younger brothers, Roy and Cyril, ensuring they did their homework. Nell replaced her mother and acted as hostess at her sister's wedding to the architect, Roy Ashley Shore. With financial help from Frederick Tritton, the young couple bought a block of land in Ascot where Idie's husband designed them a comfortable home.

The two sisters were very different. While Nell had no wish to marry and dreamed of becoming a writer, Idie had always looked forward to marriage and children and had no wish to have a career or travel abroad. But in spite of many visits to medical specialists Idie remained childless.

Nell's dream, once her mother had recovered, was still to spend a year or more studying in Paris. She longed to speak perfect French, write a book of short stories or a novel and find a publisher. This was impossible in Brisbane for even though the capital of Queensland, it was still a big country town.

France took a long time to recover from extensive war damage to its road and rail transport and food was still in short supply. Nell's father said it was not a good idea to spend a year in Paris yet. She should go there when France had been able to rebuild and recover its former prosperity.

Fred Tritton knew he must run the family business until one of his younger sons was experienced enough to take over his role. In spite of the fact Nell was intelligent and good with people in a male-dominated world, Nell's father never considered her for a management position in the family company.

This decade known as the Jazz Age or the 'roaring twenties' was a time of financial recovery which helped Tritton's department store grow in size as Brisbane's population increased rapidly. George Street became the commercial hub of the city and Fred Tritton became the leading light of Brisbane's business community.

However Tritton's store was cramped for space. The George Street entrance was partly obscured by billboards advertising a pawn shop and a tobacconist. It badly needed a more impressive entrance and much more floor space.

Nell's father decided to borrow from the bank and build a handsome new extension facing North Quay. He already owned the land where he had built Queensland's largest department store. The yard behind the store was still used for delivery carts with stables for the cart horses that pulled them. Part of it was now used for the new extension with an enormous sign saying TRITTONS in letters two metres high on the roof of the building.

From the profits of his enlarged store, Fred Tritton bought blocks of suburban land which increased in value and he would eventually open a second store in the sugar milling town of Nambour.

Tritton's original entrance on the corner of George and Adelaide Streets, now the site of Brisbane City Council Library Headquarters. Staff are sitting outside the store in the bus hired for their annual picnic day holiday. (Photo courtesy State Library of Queensland)

Tritton's logo was placed on all items of hand-made furniture (Private collection)

Some of Tritton's best clients were wealthy pastoralists from the Darling Downs and other parts of Queensland. They visited Brisbane each August for the annual Agricultural Show or 'Ekka' held at the Exhibition Showgrounds in Bowen Hills. Graziers brought their wives to town, exhibited their cattle sheep and livestock to the public and spent their profits in Brisbane's shops. A tradition still alive and well in the 21st century.

Fred Tritton realised he needed to attract affluent buyers so provided limousines to bring graziers and their wives to his store on George Street during the show. Their purchases however were still despatched by horse-drawn drays to properties on the Darling Downs, central and western Queensland and even to parts of northern New South Wales.

Soon the big Percheron cart horses stabled in the yard behind the new extension to Tritton's department store were replaced by motorised vehicles. Brisbane was modernising as the Queensland capital increasing in size.

On the advice of Nell and her fashion-conscious mother, Tritton's stocked a range of attractive gifts, electrical equipment and what became known as 'talking machines'. These first radios, gramophones and black Bakelite discs called records proved profitable for Tritton's as Queenslanders eagerly embraced the latest technological advances.

Fred told Nell and her younger brothers they would be entitled to a share in Tritton's profits once they turned 25 years of age and were deemed capable of handling money wisely. He had set up a family trust in memory of Charles and Lillian to ensure Charles' young son received a good education and to provide financial security for Charles' widow and for Nell, now his only unmarried daughter in case she never married, though this seemed unlikely.[7]

Idie, happily married to an architect, was still hoping to have a family, the ambition of most girls of her era. But Nell was determined that if her life was to be short, it would be exciting and include a period living in Paris. Marriage and settling down in Brisbane rated low on her list of priorities. As soon as it was possible to go to Paris, she wanted to be there.

CHAPTER THREE

Dancing with the Prince of Wales

Living at home in post-war Brisbane without a job to occupy her and Paris out of the question, Nell became bored and restless. Reluctantly her parents agreed to allow her to apply for a cadetship with the main local newspaper. But on one condition; Nell had to make her debut into Queensland society at the next summer ball held at Brisbane's Government House.

The Governor's summer ball had not taken place during wartime. This traditional occasion was resumed in June 1920 when Nell was twenty-one, by which time many of her school friends were married. Nell protested she did not want to 'come out into society' and did not want to marry until she was at least 25. But her mother was firm. Her one remaining daughter must attend the summer ball with them.

To please her mother Nell agreed to a compromise. She would make her debut at the ball as long as she could go overseas as soon as France had recovered from the severe damage caused by the war.

The June 1920 debutante ball, traditionally hosted by the Governor of Queensland and his wife, had been renamed the Jubilee Ball to coincide with a visit to Brisbane of the popular young Prince of Wales. His tour of Australia and New Zealand was arranged to thank both countries for the sacrifices made by so many Anzacs in the recent war.

Edward, Prince of Wales, the handsome playboy heir to the throne (known as David to close friends) had unwillingly agreed to undertake this long overseas tour because he dreaded the prospect of a long separation from his mistress, Mrs Freda Dudley Ward, with whom he was passionately in love. The vibrant and attractive Freda, married to a senior member of His Majesty's Government was several years older than the Prince of Wales. Although the heir to the throne refused to accept this, Freda had no intention of divorcing her admittedly dull husband to marry a wilful and at times childish young prince.

The situation was even more complicated as Freda Dudley Ward's husband was a King's Privy Counsellor. The socially prominent but ill-matched couple were official guests at functions at Buckingham

Palace.[8] King George V and his wife, straight-laced Queen Mary, feared a major scandal should the press learn of their heir's clandestine romance. By sending the Prince of Wales on a long overseas tour the King and Queen hoped to end his unsuitable relationship with a married woman and on his return marry him off to a suitably virginal bride.

The Prince of Wales was known to love parties and dancing. Aristocratic English girls competed for his attention as they fancied the idea of becoming the queen and were unaware of the Prince of Wales' secret liaison with Freda Dudley Ward.

Queenslanders were excited by the prospect of a visit from the handsome bachelor heir to the throne. which was to take place from 25 July to 5 August 1920. Brisbane's Government House was re-decorated and invitations to the first ball to take place since the war were greatly sought after.

Nell photographed professionally in her romantic pink Juliet dress trimmed with roses. On the night of the July 1920 ball she substituted the pink velvet bandeau seen here for black pearls woven into her hair. (Courtesy Mrs Lavinia Tritton)

Frederick Tritton and his wife were pleased to receive invitations to the summer ball along with Nell, their unmarried daughter. Instead of the standard parade of debutantes in white ball gowns and long white gloves the Governor and his wife decided to hold a ball in which fancy dress was optional, with a competition for the female winner. They hoped to make the ball very enjoyable for the fun-loving Prince of Wales, who was known to become bored by formal events.

Nell and her mother were driven by their chauffeur to Sydney to buy suitable outfits at David Jones' Model Dress Department and matching silk shoes as *haute couture* clothes were unavailable at that time in Brisbane. Nell and her mother chose a romantic ball gown of soft rose-pink silk, ornamented with pink and white silk roses. Nell had decided she would attend the fancy dress ball as Juliet Capulet, the tragic heroine of Shakespeare's play *Romeo and Juliet.*

On the day of the ball, the hairdresser wove Nell's black pearl necklace into her glossy chestnut hair. She wore the sapphire necklace and matching earrings her parents had given her on her eighteenth birthday, telling her they had chosen sapphires as they highlighted the blue of her eyes.

On that memorable night for Nell, Queensland's Governor, Sir Hamilton Goold-Adams, awarded her the prize for the best costume, a silver dressing table set. Lady Goold-Adams formerly presented Miss Nell Tritton to the Prince of Wales who looked handsome in dark evening suit, with dazzling white dress shirt and military medals. He bowed formally and asked Nell for the next waltz.

Protocol ordained the heir to the throne must first dance with the wives of local dignitaries. But this unconventional Prince of Wales believed in doing things his own way. Ignoring protocol, he asked Nell for the pleasure of a second dance. They remained on the dance floor joking and flirting until the music struck up again. He and Nell made a handsome couple as they both loved dancing and became the centre of attention. Elderly ladies whispered this could be the start of a royal romance and the young Tritton girl could be a future Princess of Wales and Queen of England.

Little did they realise the Prince's brief flirtation with Nell was designed to deflect press attention from his passionate love affair with Freda Dudley Ward. Every day the Prince of Wales wrote passionate letters to his married mistress. They were sent to England in the diplomatic bag so there was no risk compromising letters could fall into the hands of journalists. For several years the heir to the throne had implored Freda to run away with him to a ranch he owned in Canada. The prospect of being king once his father died filled the Prince of Wales with dread, Unknown to anyone except his mistress he feared he might be impotent and incapable of siring an heir, the chief task of any Prince of Wales.

Freda Dudley Ward had no intention of causing an international scandal by running away with the heir to the throne, even though her marriage had soured.[9] She was devoted to her two young daughters and knew their lives would be ruined by the scandal of a divorce.

To throw the press off the scent during his Australia-wide tour, the heir to the throne chose to flirt with the most attractive girl in the room at each function he attended. He was very attentive to Nell and they made such a handsome couple that other dancers stopped dancing and applauded.

When the music stopped after their second dance, the Prince of Wales thanked Nell for being such graceful partner and as they left the dance floor together with all eyes upon them.

But contrary to the gossips who had regarded two dances in a row with the Prince of Wales as the start of a royal romance, Nell never heard from the heir to the throne again. The idea of becoming part of the constrained life of a member of the royal family was the last thing Nell wanted.

She was flattered by the Prince of Wales' attention but disliked the gossip and speculation his attention had provoked. What Nell wanted was to see Europe, have a career and become financially independent.

CHAPTER FOUR

Pioneer Female Journalist & Award-Winning Rally Driver

'Miss Tritton was dazzlingly attractive and a talented writer'
Nell's former mentor who later worked for *The Sydney Morning Herald* wrote this under the pseudonym *'WFW'*

Each year the *Brisbane Courier,* (forerunner of today's *Courier Mail)* offered a cadetship to a male candidate with outstanding writing ability. Women had never dared to apply. Remembering the proverb, 'Nothing ventured, nothing gained', Nell decided she would apply.

After interviewing her at length, the editor of the *Brisbane Courier* described Miss Tritton as the most outstanding applicant. He said he had no hesitation with creating a precedent and doing something unheard of, awarding the coveted cadetship to a young woman.

Nell received a letter from the editor confirming she had been awarded the cadetship. In the Queen Street office she would receive practical training in journalism with a senior journalist as her mentor. As she was still under 21 she needed her parents' permission to accept this position with the *Brisbane Courier. (*In 1933 the paper would merge with *The Courier Mail,* both owned by media tycoon, Sir Keith Murdoch, father of today's Rupert Murdoch).

Nell's parents were grateful that she had taken charge of the house when her mother was suffering from depression. Since taking up the cadetship meant she would remain living at home in Brisbane, they agreed to her doing this.

A senior male journalist was selected to act as Nell's mentor, who wrote under the pen name of 'WFW' and whose full name was never revealed. The male journalist described Nell as having great charm and 'dazzlingly attractive'. He praised her intelligence and said she had 'the biggest blue eyes he had ever seen'.[10] He taught Nell interviewing and writing techniques, developed her writing style and gave her confidence in her ability to empathise with people and communicate their stories in prose people enjoyed reading. He was a perfect mentor.

Nell enjoyed the challenge of reporting on events, interviewing people, undertaking research and writing stories. Her charm, good looks and genuine empathy encouraged those she interviewed to trust her.

Nell and her mentor were commissioned to write a story about the arrival in Brisbane of a huge German tank called Mephisto (The Devil) written on it.

Captured by Queensland troops at the battle of Villers-Bretonneux in the final year of the Great War, the German tank had been shipped to Australia via London. It took a year to arrive in Brisbane and was displayed outside the Queensland Museum. Mephisto became an object of fascination to Nell's young brothers, Roy and Cyril who implored Nell to take them to see it after reading the lively article Nell and WFW had written describing Mephisto's unveiling ceremony.

After receiving praise for their Mephisto article, nervously Nell showed her book of published poems to her mentor, asking if he considered any of them good enough to be published in the paper's weekly poetry column. She was delighted when two of her poems were published but when she thanked the editor he warned Nell it was impossible to live from writing poetry alone. She should stick to journalism for which she clearly had a talent or think about writing a book.

Nell asked her mentor how to get a novel or a book of non-fiction published. WFW warned Nell that publishing was a male-dominated field. An attractive young woman like her would find the price some male publishers demanded one she would not be prepared to pay. He didn't elaborate further and Nell was unaware that sexual harassment was something she would encounter later in her career. He advised her to write romances as these were always popular with female readers. She should send a synopsis and the first three chapters of a romance novel to a London publisher called Mills & Boon as they specialised in publishing romances and paid extremely well.

WFW suggested Nell work on a novel about an orphaned English governess who takes a job on a large Australian sheep or cattle station and falls for the handsome eldest son of the owner. She would have no difficulty finding material for this type of saleable fiction as he understood some of her friends at Somerville House had married the sons of cattle station owners.

Nell thanked him for his advice but told him she did not want to write soppy romances. She hoped to write short stories with a twist in the tail like the spy stories of Somerset Maugham which she enjoyed.

Her mentor didn't give up on her. He advised her to submit her short stories by post to the editors of American magazines. The Americans paid far better than British or Australian magazines, but it was hard for female authors to be taken seriously so writing short stories and submitting them by post was a good alternative for her. Nell noted his advice for the future.

After working for almost three years at the *Sydney Daily Mail* covering weddings and women's fashions but with no opportunity to cover political or current events, Nell decided to apply for a job with the *Sydney Guardian.* She hoped that working on a smaller paper she would be given more interesting assignments. Maybe she would get the chance to cover political events.

Nell wanted to live independently but the 1920s unmarried girls needed permission from their parents to leave home. Nell obtained her parents' agreement on condition she shared a house with a girl from a respectable family and would return to *Elderslie* for family reunions at birthdays, Easter and Christmas.

In 1923, having turned 23 the previous September, Nell moved into a rented apartment in Elizabeth Bay in Sydney's Eastern suburbs with a female journalist slightly older than her. Nell was determined to live on whatever money she earned so she did not have to ask her father for money. Fred Tritton, who had made his own way in the world, was impressed by his youngest daughter's determination to be financially independent and told her so.

Working at the *Sydney Guardian* Nell was disappointed and frustrated that once again she was not given more serious topics to investigate. Instead of political assignments she was confined to what the male journalists mockingly called the 'hens' corner,' covering the latest fashions, social events and society weddings.

Once again Nell dared to ask the editor if she could write about politics. When this suggestion fell on deaf ears she handed in her notice and looked for another position.

Nell started working as a freelance journalist for *The Triad,* a beautifully produced arts magazine, for which she reviewed the latest plays and books. Under her contract with *The Triad* magazine Nell was allowed to submit articles or review books for other publications. She longed to write a book of her own, but she knew that for a woman to have a book published in Australia was very difficult. She enjoyed working for *The Triad* with talented people who loved art and literature and learned a great deal. The elderly owner published the magazine as a retirement hobby and when he died from a heart attack his executors showed no interest in keeping it going. It was put up for sale but there was little interest from buyers due to high production costs and the magazine had to close.

Left without the job she enjoyed, Nell saw this as her opportunity to spend the year in Paris she had been promised in return for attending the debutante ball at Government House. She planned to take an intensive course at the best language school in Paris, learn to speak French fluently and dress like a Parisian.

Her resolve to go to Paris was strengthened by reading the diary of a Russian girl who had gone to Paris to live which had intrigued her with its glimpses of two cultures, so unlike Australia and the world she knew.

CHAPTER FIVE

A Diary Inspires Nell's Extended Stay in Paris

I long to see everything, know everything, learn everything.
Marie Bashkirtseff, *Journal*

In a second-hand bookshop in the centre of Sydney Nell had found a battered copy of the diary of Marie Bashkirtseff, an aristocratic Russian girl who had moved to Paris to study art. Marie had succeeded in exhibiting and selling her paintings at a time when art was a male preserve and 'women's art', like women's writing was regarded as inferior to that of men. Nell had heard her French teacher at school praising this journal and had always wanted to read it.

Nell started reading the book that evening, found she could not put it down and stayed up most of the night in order to finish it. She felt as though Marie was speaking directly to her with some uncanny similarities in their lives. Like Nell, Marie had a medical problem. She had been warned by her doctor that she had a weakness in her lungs and could die young of tuberculosis. Like Nell she was determined to cram as many experiences as possible into her life if it was to be cut short. Marie had wanted to travel, become an artist and live life to the full, as in the nineteenth century there was no cure for tuberculosis from which she had been diagnosed.

Marie had been born in the Ukraine in 1858 to a wealthy aristocratic Russian couple. They owned an estate in an area forcibly incorporated into the Russian Empire by Empress Catherine the Great.

The marriage of Marie's parents was unhappy, due to her father's constant womanising. When her father moved his pregnant teenage mistress (daughter of a local peasant), into the family home Marie's mother decided to leave her husband and she was lucky to retain control of her dowry money. Most wives lost control of their money and had to hand money or any property they possessed to their husbands when they married.

Marie's mother took her twelve-year old daughter, young son, several of her domestic staff and her personal physician and moved to the large estate of her widowed mother near St Petersburg. Marie loved the magnificent river city with its canals and balmy summer evenings when everyone took advantage of the long twilights which lasted until midnight, known as the 'white nights' of St Petersburg.

When she died Marie's grandmother bequeathed the major part of her fortune to her favourite granddaughter. Marie knew that under Russian law this rich inheritance would automatically become the property of any man she married. She did not want to lose her independence, having found a career she loved. Marie had been assured by her singing teachers she had a beautiful mezzo-soprano voice and could become an opera singer. In spite of fears that singing might prejudice her health Marie wanted to turn professional even though it involved a long training. Opera as a career was open only to exceptional women who could both sing and act. It offered them fame, glamour and international travel, in an era when very few women were able to have careers.

Her mother, now legally separated from Marie's father, sold the family estates and took her family and entourage of servants, including Marie's French governess and a family doctor to Europe. With this money Marie's mother was able to take suites in the best hotels in Vienna, Rome, Paris, Baden-Baden and Nice. These cities had excellent opera houses where Marie watched the world's best singers perform and mother and daughter could visit art galleries.

Marie, tall and slender with waist-length red-gold hair, was turning from a girl into a beautiful young woman. Her teachers at the Conservatoire praised her acting ability, an important talent for an opera singer and her slender figure was an added bonus. For Marie, the possibility of a career in opera was a more exciting prospect than marriage, which she knew had brought nothing but unhappiness to her mother.

After constant travelling Marie's mother decided to settle in Nice which had a mild Mediterranean climate, elegant shops, art galleries and an opera house with a winter season attended by foreign royalty. Marie and her mother attended royal gala evenings where her mother paid for a box so Marie could watch the performances at close range.

For the next three years, Marie took singing and music lessons with leading teachers and also learned to play the piano and the harp to concert standard. As a Russian heiress she and her mother were always dressed in the height of fashion from the House of Worth, the leading Paris couturier who dressed the royal families and the aristocracy of Europe.

At seventeen, Marie Bashkirtseff was deemed to be of marriageable age and a prize on the marriage market where young heiresses were in demand by aristocrats, some of whom were desperate to marry for money. Marie's mother received several proposals for the hand of her beautiful daughter from Russian and French noblemen and weeded out suitors who she believed to be fortune hunters.

Marie's mother consulted the Almanach de Gotha, the Bible of the aristocracy, and found entries for every unmarried prince or Romanov grand duke of the right age to marry her daughter. Her mother favoured the suit of a handsome Serbian prince until his betrothal to a princess was announced in the press.

Her mother's second choice was a Romanov Grand Duke, the Russian equivalent of a prince. The young Grand Duke arrived with flowers, jewels and a leather-bound book of poems by the romantic poet Pushkin. It was not the jewels which aroused Marie's interest but the fact he read aloud in Russian several of Pushkin's poems. She was pleased he had found out what appealed to her, as other suitors had not bothered to do this.

As an heiress, her reputation had to be carefully guarded as virginity was greatly prized in brides, so Marie was never allowed to be alone with the Grand Duke. Her governess or her mother chaperoned all their meetings and, as a result their conversations were stilted. Marie was persuaded by her socially ambitious mother that the Grand Duke would make an ideal husband and her position in society would be an enviable one.

Marie was alerted to her handsome suitor's real character when watching from an upstairs window as he walked back to his carriage. The Romanov Grand Duke roused his sleeping coachman by kicking him so hard that his spurs drew blood from the unfortunate man. Marie was horrified. The servant could not defend himself or retaliate in any way or his employer would have had him whipped or killed for insulting a member of the Russian royal family.

Marie decided that the title of 'Grand Duchess' was not worth a miserable life with a husband capable of such cruelty. It was safer to remain single. In her journal she made the telling entry, *Let us not expect anything from men other than lies and deception. Let us love dogs! Men and cats are unworthy creatures.*[11]

Marie continued her voice training and acting lessons and was promised a brilliant future by her teachers. But shortly after her nineteenth birthday her doctors' fears came true. Marie developed a cough so severe that there were days when she could not speak. Diagnosed with a tubercular lung, Marie realised that she would never become an opera singer. In her diary Marie described her distress, *My God! What a voice I had. It was powerful, dramatic, captivating, and gave listeners chills down their spine to hear it. And now I have nothing, not even a voice to speak with.*

Instead of giving way to despair, Marie developed a new ambition. She had always enjoyed visiting art galleries and painting in watercolours, deemed a suitable occupation for ladies. She decided to move to Paris, learned to paint in oils and become a professional artist at a time when art was a profession reserved for men.

Marie's mother worried about her daughter but wanted her to be happy in the short time left to her. She leased a mansion at 77 rue des Champs Elysée, at that time the most elegant street in the centre of Paris. This spacious house had an attic with a large skylight which admitted plenty of natural light so it could become Marie's studio.

Marie took a portfolio of her drawings to the Académie Julian in Montparnasse, the only art school that accepted female students and they immediately enrolled her. Other famous students from the art school included Edouard Vuillard, Pierre Bonnard and Henri Matisse.

Marie enjoyed her art classes, writing in her journal how '*I long to see everything, know everything, learn everything*'. Attending art school meant rising early each morning and being driven from the centre of Paris to Montparnasse. She attended morning classes at the *atelier* or workshop, with a short break for lunch followed by afternoon study, returning home by horse-drawn carriage. She had an early dinner with her mother and her entourage before exhausted by the day's exertions, Marie retired to bed.

When she felt well enough, she would return to the Académie Julian for an evening class. But on some days she suffered from such intense pain in her chest and lower back she had to stay in bed.

The next day, if the pain had abated, Marie would be back to her studies. She learned to draw in pen and ink, pencil, charcoal, and pastels. The Académie Julian was unusual in providing a teacher of anatomy to help the life-class students make accurate portrayals of the human figure. But drawing from nude male models was considered far too daring for female students and they were only allowed to draw female models.[12]

One of Marie's paintings depicted a life class of female students who were drawing a nude female model and Marie painted it as a protest at the restrictions imposed on female art students. Her painting would eventually be regarded as an important pictorial record of the way women artists were treated in the nineteenth century.

Marie Bashkirtseff was awarded the Académie Julian's annual medal for her artistic skills and her original subject matter. Her work was admired by Manet, who was seen as the leader of the group of *avant garde* artists who would call themselves the Impressionists. Like them she was inspired to paint realistic street scenes by reading the novels of Zola. Marie's oil painting *The Meeting* was a realistic work with a very unusual composition regarded as so good it was bought by the French Government to hang in an art museum. She also enjoyed a literary flirtation exchanging chatty letters with the celebrated short story writer, Guy de Maupassant.

Marie's journal fascinated Nell who found parallels in it with her own life. Marie's final entry in her journal written just before her 27th birthday would haunt Nell for years. Before she died of tuberculosis Marie wrote, *I have reached an age when I can talk about death. I'd like to see everything, embrace everything and die in ecstasy, experiencing the last mystery, the end or a divine beginning?*[13]

Reading Marie's journal strengthened Nell's resolve to write a novel or a book of short stories. Like Marie, Nell also wanted to '*see everything, embrace everything.*' Nell hoped that in Paris she might experience a great and passionate love, marry and live happily like her parents.

However Nell dreaded having to break the news to her parents that she had booked her passage to London, aware of the sense of loss her parents felt over the absence of her dead siblings. She knew they would worry about her health alone in a foreign country and would miss her, but it was time to leave if she ever wanted to fulfil her dreams.

On Christmas Eve 1924, which was the anniversary of Charles Tritton's death, the Tritton family went to Dutton Park cemetery to lay wreaths on the graves of Charles and Lillian. Nell, sensitive about her parents' feelings after this emotional visit for all of them, waited until dinner was served to break the news that *The Triad* magazine had folded so she was going to Paris. She added she had been lucky to obtain a cancellation for an outside cabin on a P&O liner sailing to London.

Marie Bashkirtseff's painting 'The Meeting' 1884 was painted from sketches made in the streets of Paris. Her depiction of street urchins in ragged clothes and scuffed boots is brilliantly realistic. Marie's painting was shown in public at a time when women artists rarely had their work exhibited and was subsequently bought by the French Government., Nell saw it in the art gallery beside the Luxemburg Palace.[14] *(Photographed by Jake de Vries in the Musée d'Orsay.)*

Her mother had hoped Nell was going to announce her engagement. She was very disappointed to learn that Nell had turned down a proposal from a young lawyer, a friend of Nell's late brother. Her mother told Nell she would be sorry if she stayed away for too long or another girl would snap up her suitor. Again she reminded Nell that due to the high death rate in the war, eligible men were in short supply. If Nell waited too long, she could be left on the shelf and end up a spinster living with a cat and a canary.

Nell's father had a different view to his wife. As a teenager Fred Tritton had crossed the world seeking adventure and saw something of himself in his youngest daughter's determination and strength of spirit. However he was concerned about Nell in France. Her father warned his favourite daughter that most French tap water was polluted, contaminated by typhoid and other diseases. She must always drink bottled water including using it to clean her teeth.

He advised Nell that as she was over 25 she could receive money from the family trust he had set up for all his children and grandchildren. He warned her that with access to money in a family trust she could be a target for fortune hunters.

Nell could not help laughing at this warning. She insisted she was nothing like those silly young women in the novels of Henry James and Edith Wharton who fell in love with handsome men who married them for their money. She assured her father she would be very careful who she associated with on board the ship.

Fred Tritton was proud of the fact Nell had supported herself for years as a journalist and never asked him for a penny. Her Christmas present would be a left-hand drive car suitable for driving in Europe He would arrange for the car to be waiting for her when she landed in France. Always a canny businessman her father explained doing this meant she avoided paying tax on the car.

With a twinkle in his eye her father added there was a condition to his generosity. In return Nell must visit Selfridge's, London's largest and most profitable department store. She must write a report telling him which household goods were selling well and obtain copies of Selfridge's mail order catalogues. These catalogues had made Gordon Selfridge so successful that her father wanted to be the Gordon Selfridge of Brisbane. Selling goods by mail order in Queensland with its vast distances would open up new business for Tritton's.[15]

Weeks later, the Trittons travelled to Sydney to see Nell off. They waited in front of the Maritime Terminal at Sydney Harbour, watching porters carry hundreds of trunks up the gangplank of the huge ocean liner. Nell's young brothers were impatient to get on board and explore the ship. This kept them happy until an announcement was made over the loudspeaker that all visitors must disembark.

Before her family descended the gangplank there were many kisses and repeated assurances from Nell that she would write frequently. Nell gave her father a special hug and whispered in his ear that in Paris she hoped to meet an exceptional man like him.

The liner's siren sent out a long wail that it was about to sail. The engines were turning and the enormous propellers churned the water as Nell stood on deck for a last look at her family.

As the ship slowly moved away from the quayside, the passengers threw down coloured paper streamers to be caught by family and friends in the traditional Australian ritual of farewell.

As the red and orange streamers linking her with her family tightened and snapped, Nell realised that at long last she was embarking on the adventure for which she had longed for so many years.

Ocean liner departing from Circular Quay with colourful streamers connecting the passengers with loved ones on the quay below. Nell sailed to London's Tilbury docks calling at Colombo and several other ports en route. (Private collection)

Lithograph by Thea Proctor showing an elegant Australian girl going overseas in 1920. This was a period of relative affluence after World War One when Nell finally attained her dream and left for Paris. (Author's collection)

CHAPTER SIX

April in Paris, 1925

I will make Paris the most beautiful city in the world
Napoleon Bonaparte

After an uneventful six-week voyage with its highlights of a tour of Ceylon's tea plantations and a visit to the Naples art museum, the P&O liner docked at Tilbury. Nell's fellow passengers had been elderly couples or honeymooners with a few widows and married women travelling alone. She did not meet any dashing fortune hunters against whose wiles her father had warned her. The few single male passengers seemed more interested in each other.

The ship's officers were handsome in their white tropical uniforms, but Nell found them blasé and poorly educated, accustomed to success with bored married woman who wanted the thrill of a shipboard affair. When they employed the same tired old seduction routines on Nell, she disliked their shallow compliments and repulsed their advances. One officer who pursued her boasted how on a previous voyage a married woman travelling alone had been so keen to have sex with him she had bribed the steward to let her into his cabin and she was there waiting for him when he came off duty.

As a child growing up in Australia at a time when there were few Australian books for children Nell had read a great deal about England. She was looking forward to the sight of the famous white cliffs of Dover. She was disappointed when the P&O liner took a different route and berthed at Tilbury where the docks were as drab as Brisbane's wharves.

Nell was met by her aunt and uncle and her cousin Anne who was a year younger than Nell and unable to drive but wanted to accompany her to Europe. After collecting Nell's shipping trunk, they drove to the home of her mother's relatives in the north of England.

The following weeks passed in a whirl of meetings with more relatives and sightseeing trips to London visiting places she had read about in books. In Kensington Gardens she saw the statue of Peter Pan, visited the Houses of Parliament and heard Big Ben chime. The mummies in the British Museum fascinated her, as did Charles

Dickens' Old Curiosity Shop where his character 'Little Nell' had lived and over whose sad death as a child Nell had wept. The National Gallery and Nelson's column in Trafalgar Square were highlights of visits to London.

Mindful of her promise to her father and in order to buy presents for her aunt and uncle, Nell visited the Selfridges department store in Oxford Street. As promised she prepared a detailed report for her father. She told him which household goods were selling well and new lines she thought Tritton's should carry. She added names and addresses of manufacturers so that he could import them and enclosed Selfridge's latest mail order catalogues.

At Selfridge's she saw stylish young women wearing the new season's clothes and Nell realised that Australian shops were a year behind the London fashion scene. She realised the new clothes she had bought in Australia were very dated. As she did not want look like a dowdy colonial she and her cousin went shopping for the very latest fashions. They had shorter skirts than she had ever worn in Brisbane and the new length showed off her long slender legs. Visiting Harrods in Knightsbridge Nell had her hair cut in the latest short bob which, she was delighted to discover, really suited her.

After seeing young women wearing lipstick and eye shadow in the daytime, something 'nice' girls in Brisbane only wore in the evening as it was considered 'fast', Nell became more daring in her use of make up. She bought a pair of black velvet evening trousers which would have been considered *risqué* at home.

It had been agreed that Nell and Anne would make a brief visit to southern France and northern Spain. The cousins caught the ferry at Dover and crossed the English Channel arriving at Calais where Nell found that her father had kept his word about getting her a new car. They were met by a Renault representative with a brand new left-hand drive car who suggested he take Nell for a test drive. He had no idea Nell had been a rally driver in Australia, as so few young women drove cars at the time and was surprised at how quickly and skilfully she was able to drive the new Renault with all the latest modifications.

The cousins headed south-west to Bordeaux and were struck by the beauty of the city with its handsome stone buildings facing the river. Nell left the Renault with the owner of their small hotel. She and her cousin enjoyed a boat trip down the Garonne River stopping at several wineries to taste the finest wines of the Medoc and St Julien vineyards. For Nell this was another change as her parents rarely had alcohol on the table at *Elderslie*.

Nell did all the driving as they drove south to the seaside resort of Biarritz. This elegant resort was where the late King Edward VII had spent his summer holidays with his last mistress, Mrs Alice Keppel.

They spent the following night at the picturesque fishing port of St Jean de Luz, where they were the only foreigners before they crossed into Spain at the French frontier town of Hendaye, with Irun on the Spanish side where Nell tested a few Spanish phrases from her guide book. The frontier guards were young and joked and flirted with the two attractive young women.

Taking the coast road, Nell drove to Santander, the exclusive holiday resort where the Spanish royal family had their summer palace overlooking the Atlantic.

Extremely wealthy Spanish families owned beautiful summer villas facing the Playa de Sardinero. Each morning the long white sandy beach was freshly raked and umbrellas and deck chairs were put out for hire. Nannies in uniforms with stiffly starched white aprons walked their little charges along the beach or along the paved promenade. It was all so different from the wild beach at Redcliffe in Queensland where the Tritton's had their holiday home. In the centre of the city, Nell was shocked by the sight of blind beggars and vendors of lottery tickets dressed in ragged clothes, indicating the vast gulf that separated the rich from the poor.

In the 1920s, few Australians visited Spain. A hotel concierge, keen to practice his English, asked Nell whether it was true that in Australia kangaroos hopped down the main streets and said it must be exciting to live in such a young country. He would love a chance to go to Australia. Nell was pleased by his enthusiasm for her homeland. This was a pleasant change from the British who tended to regard Australia as a land populated by convicts and regarded themselves as superior to any Australian they might meet.

Although the sun was warm in March the sea was still too cold to swim so the girls decided to drive across the interior to Madrid. The landscape with its parched red earth dotted with gum trees was an unexpected reminder of outback Australia.

In the spring of 1925, Spain was a tranquil country but tensions were simmering under the surface. Workers were poorly paid and often lived in terrible conditions with poor sanitation. The rate of exchange was such that for foreign visitors everything was cheap. Nell and Anne bought beautifully tailored suede jackets, the softest of leather handbags and almond-toed shoes with slender heels.

In the palatial Prado Museum the cousins saw a magnificent collection of paintings by Velasquez of young princesses called *infantas* in huge balloon-like dresses. She was fascinated by Goya's portraits of Spanish grandees and his satirical portraits of the Spanish royal family and was horrified by his painting titled *The Fifth of May* recording the shooting of Spanish patriots by French invaders.

Nell had set herself a goal of learning ten new Spanish words each day. By waving her hands around and adding a few French words she was able to make herself understood by the locals. She made them laugh when she used the Spanish phrase '*Yo soy Australiana de la tierra de los kangaroos'*, 'I am an Australian from the land of the kangaroos,' and mimicked the jumping of kangaroos.

In the evening after dinner the cousins watched flamenco dancing. In the street they were pursued by ardent Romeos uttering extravagant compliments known as *piropos* with much use of the word *guapa* which according to Nell's Spanish dictionary meant 'beautiful' or 'desirable'.

At first these encounters were flattering but the novelty soon wore off. Nell realised that all foreign women travelling alone no matter how plain, were seen as targets by Spanish men. Spanish girls were strictly chaperoned when they were allowed to emerge from their homes, always accompanied by their parents or an older female. She realised that this cloistering of Spanish girls accounted for men pursuing all foreign girls who ventured there alone.

As March was nearly over and the days became longer, Nell realised that it would be springtime in Paris and April was the time to be there. Nell and her cousin arrived in Europe's most elegant capital city, as the chestnut trees lining the *quais* began to flower. Waiters were putting out tables and chairs on the pavements in front of cafes to take advantage of the mild spring air.

They stayed in the Hotel Sophia, a small hotel off the Boulevard Raspail in Montparnasse, close to the language school where Nell's French teacher had advised her to enrol. The Alliance Française had excellent teachers as it was under the direct control of the French Ministry of Culture. Nell checked in and was made to sit a language test to assess her competency in French. She was pleased with the score she achieved and was placed in one of the higher level language classes.

Term started the following week and Nell and her cousin spent the rest of the week sight-seeing with her Baedeker guide. They went first to the Eiffel Tower and took the lift to the top. Wandering along the Quai de Montebello facing the great tower and the famous Rose Window of Notre Dame, Nell was delighted by the many stalls selling books and prints.

Quai de Montebello and Notre Dame where Nell bought prints of Paris for her apartment, photographed in the early 1950s. (Private collection)

Nell instantly fell in love with Paris with its blue-grey shuttered windows and wrought-iron balconies and the graceful bridges which spanned the Seine. The girls wandered through the gardens of the

Tuileries with their formal clipped box hedges and green lawns. They took rides on the *bateau mouches* or river ferries and Nell photographed enchanting private courtyards bright with plants in terracotta pots.

Nell loved the wide choice of small cosy *bistros* and elegant *brasseries* with large gilt framed mirrors and was surprised to find they were open all day and late into the evening, unlike Australia where everything closed early. They bought delicious cakes packaged individually in small decorative boxes or consumed them in the *patisserie* with a glass of champagne.

Nell took her cousin to the Champs Elysées where decades earlier the mother of Marie Bashkirtseff had leased a mansion which Nell was disappointed to find had been demolished and replaced by offices. They spent a fascinating day in the Louvre, with so much to see that Nell knew she would spend days there in the future. As Anne knew so little about art they took a guided tour of the Denon wing with its masterpieces of French art and in the Grand Galerie they saw Leonardo's Mona Lisa surrounded by visitors, many of whom expressed surprise it was so small. Like Nell they had only seen it in books so had no idea of its actual size.

In Montmartre after watching artists at work in the Place du Tertre they climbed a long flight of steps and visited the basilica of the newly-built Sacré Coeur, which commemorated the young men who had died so tragically in what was known as the 'war to end all wars'.

Nell hoped to buy one of Marie Bashkirtseff's paintings to remind her that it was Marie's journal that had made her so want to live in Paris. Visiting a few commercial art galleries, Nell was thrilled to find an oil painting by Marie Bakshirtskeff; a portrait of a blonde girl holding a spray of lilacs. Aware prices for art are always negotiable Nell bargained and ended up paying a price she could afford. She was thrilled to have bought a painting by the brilliant young artist whose life she saw as an inspiration.

On Anne's final days in Paris they explored the Left Bank as Nell wanted to rent an apartment in Montparnasse within walking distance of her language school as parking in Paris was a problem.

After some last minute shopping for presents for her aunt and uncle in England, Nell drove her cousin to the Gare du Nord railway station. They found a porter to carry Anne's suitcase, heavy with purchases, said their goodbyes and promised to write.

Nell set out to find a studio apartment to rent on the Left Bank. Montparnasse was full of young people who wanted to forget the horrors of war and enjoy life. The majority were Americans from wealthy families who were glad to escape the puritanical conventions of prohibition in America. They spent their days sightseeing and sitting in cafes and their evenings in cabarets and jazz clubs drinking wine.

Artists and writers from all over the world flocked to the bohemian Left Bank. Nell loved this area with its cafes where artists and writers met, considered the centre of intellectual life in France. Bleak attics in Montparnasse, renamed 'studios' were leased to aspiring foreign artists and writers. She soon discovered these studios were the real estate agents' term for former servants' rooms in the attics of four storey houses. But the little windows set into their slate roofs provided good light for artists.

St Germain des Prés was full of publishing houses, bookshops and jazz cellars while the Latin Quarter to the west of Montparnasse had acquired its name when the first students at the Sorbonne, France's oldest university, had their lectures delivered in Latin. Nell learned from her guidebook that in the Middle Ages Latin was a universal language all over Europe.

At first Nell stayed in a small inexpensive hotel while being pursued by a persuasive letting agent trying to lease her a studio. She discovered studios were cheap because most of them lacked running hot water and only had a cold tap and a smelly toilet shared on each landing which was emptied every morning by the night-soil man. The artists had to use the public baths.

In compensation for poor sanitary facilities, many Left Bank studios had breathtaking views over blue slate rooftops or overlooked a cartwheel pattern of cobbled streets. Several studios Nell was shown had distant glimpses of the Eiffel Tower but she still hesitated to sign a lease.

The streets of Montparnasse had a distinctive smell of black tobacco from Gauloises cigarettes and the wonderful aroma of freshly-baked bread with an occasional whiff of expensive perfume. Less attractive was the odour that came from the cast iron *pissoirs* on the boulevards where men relieved themselves inside basic round metal structures, open at top and bottom.

Nell decided her father had been right about France having poor sanitation and decided to go for a better grade of accommodation since she would be in Paris for at least a year or even longer. She would take up her father's offer and use money from the family trust to rent an apartment with a proper bathroom. The romantic *vie de Bohème* Nell had read about in books was not nearly so romantic in real life.

It took Nell several days before she finally saw an apartment she loved. The elderly concierge showed Nell and the agent into an apartment that occupied part of the second floor of a converted mansion built by an aristocratic family in the eighteenth century. The building was surrounded by high walls, built to provide privacy and to protect its owners from thieves and ruffians.

For Nell it represented everything she dreamed about in Paris. The apartment was small but very attractive on a narrow cobbled street called the rue de Regard on the edge of Montparnasse and St Germain.[16] The agent assured her that this was one of the most beautiful and unique streets on the Left Bank.

Nell's new apartment had elegant proportions as it had been part of the formal entertaining area of its aristocratic owners. Tall windows framed by shutters were painted the distinctive shade of blue-grey only found in France. Each window had a narrow wrought-iron balcony and Nell noted how each balcony had a different design in the wrought iron.

Nell also like the area which included the long winding rue de Vaugirard, now an émigré Russian quarter with boarding houses with signage in Russian and Russian teashops. It adjoined the picturesque rue de Cherche-Midi full of second-hand bookshops and those selling *brocante.* This was a word Nell did not know. She searched her dictionary and found it was translated as 'junk'. But the *brocante* shops of the rue de Cherche Midi were far more exciting than the junk shops in Brisbane's Woolloongabba.

The area was now quiet and tranquil but the high walls remained, guarding the big interior courtyard. The agent told Nell the sons of the original family who had built the mansion in the eighteenth century and whose descendants had occupied it ever since, had been killed in the 1914-18 war leaving the family with no young heirs. They sold the enormous residence to developers who divided the mansion into tasteful apartments each with a bathroom and small kitchen. They had also installed a lift.

The mansion in the rue de Regard where Nell lived was entered through a massive stone archway with the coat of arms of the first owner carved into the stone lintel. These former family residences had heavy wooden doors tall enough to admit a horse-drawn carriage and were unique in this part of Paris.

Nell rented an apartment in one of a row of converted mansions in the rue du Regard. Over each arched doorway was the coat of arms of the first owner of these magnificent mansions with their heavy wooden doors and paved interior courtyards. (Photographs by Jill Richardson)

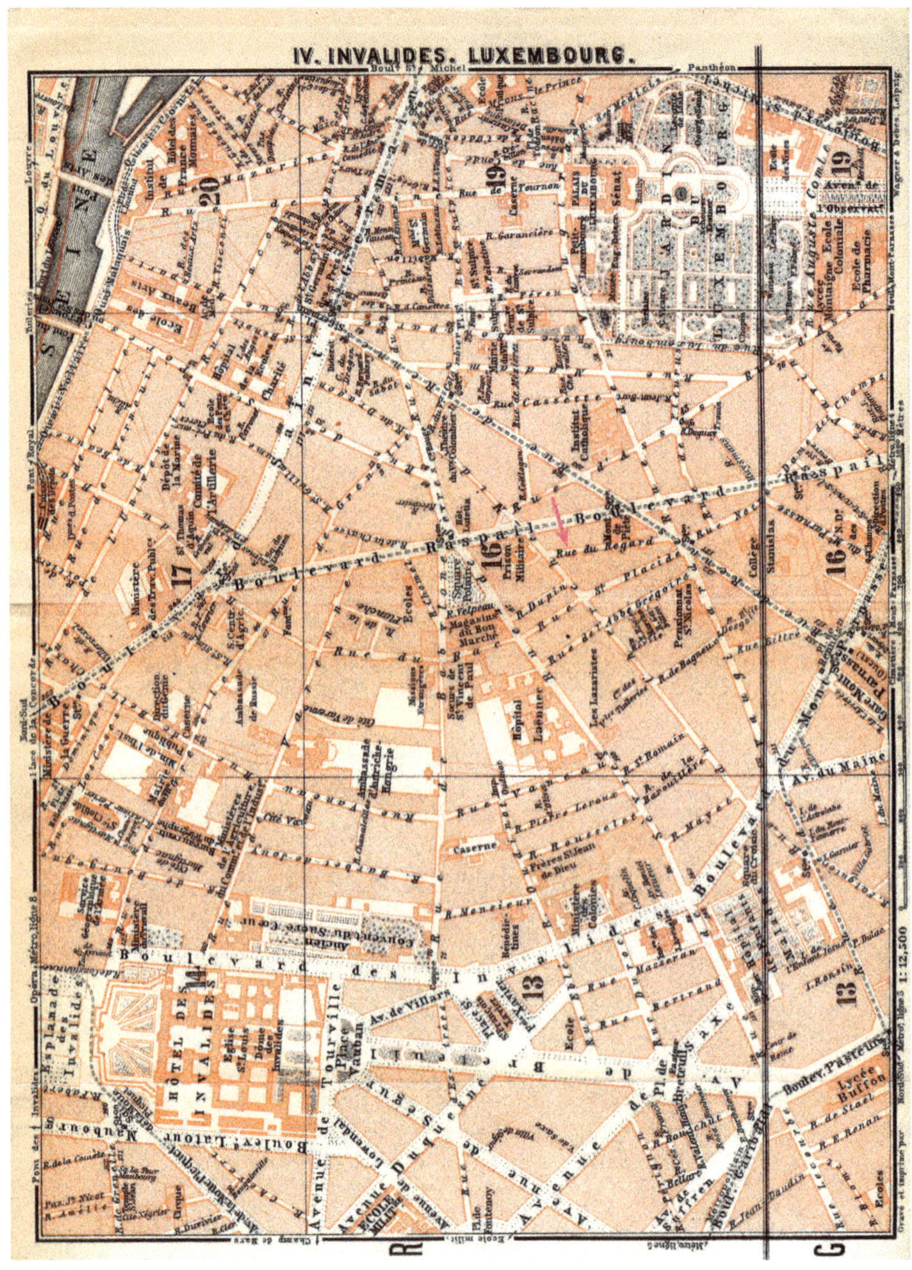

The apartment in the rue du Regard (see arrow on map) had such atmosphere Nell decided it was worth the extra money in rent she would have to pay.

The combined living and dining area had a parquet floor and beeswax perfumed the room with its scent. The white marble mantelpiece was set into a wall lined with bookshelves. Nell intended to buy colourful rugs, cushions and framed prints of Paris from the bookstalls that lined the *quais*.

Madame Dupont, the *concierge,* explained that if Mademoiselle Tritton wanted to return after midnight she must ring the brass bell by the door. She would hear it and let her in. Madame Dupont showed Nell a heavy iron key hanging from her belt with which she opened the tall wooden doors early each morning. She did this to admit a farmer bringing milk from goats that he had milked in the street outside.

Nell was intrigued and made a point of going to watch the goatherd deliver the milk in a metal churn he handed to Madame Dupont. She poured the still-warm milk into numbered jugs that she would deliver to each apartment early in the morning. She charged a small monthly fee for this service. Madame Dupont had advised Nell to shop in the market on the neighbouring Boulevard Raspail for fresh fruit and vegetables at good prices. The small shops on the boulevard also sold fresh fish and meat. She recommended the *boulangerie* at the far end of the rue du Regard which opened at seven every morning and sold *baguettes* and *croissants* fresh from the oven.

During her language classes at the Alliance, one of Nell's professors explained how the Left Bank was known for its struggling artists who would later become famous: Picasso, Modigliani, Chagall, Cocteau, Soutine, and Giacometti as young men had rented studios in Montparnasse in the days when they could scarcely afford a square meal.

Famous writers Jean-Paul Sartre, Simone de Beauvoir and James Joyce lived on the Left Bank as did the English writer and publisher Ford Maddox Ford. Several of them, including the young Ernest Hemingway who had just had a novel published to great acclaim in New York, rented studios in the rue Notre Dame des Champs, only two minutes' walk from the rue du Regard. Nell was thrilled to think she had chosen a corner of Paris dedicated to the literati.

Nell asked the elderly professor why so many Russians had taken over the neighbouring rue de Vaugirard, now full of lodging houses with Russian names. He told her they had fled to Paris during the Russian Civil War which erupted after Lenin's October revolution of 1917. She was warned not to refer to them as refugees, a term they disliked. They called themselves *émigrés*.

He continued that in Tsarist Russia these *émigrés* had been wealthy but everything had been confiscated by Lenin's Bolshevik government and they were lucky to have escaped being sent to concentration camps known as *gulags*. Hundreds of thousands of Tsarist Russians had fled to Paris while others had sought refuge in America.

When Lenin died prematurely his younger colleagues, Stalin and Trotsky, battled for supremacy and Stalin prevailed. The Russian dictator exiled Trotsky and Alexander Kerensky, who had taken over as Prime Minister after the Tsar abdicated. Kerensky had tried to introduce democratic reforms but had fled to Europe in fear of his life after the Russian Revolution. Lenin and his ruthless assistant Stalin had put a price on Kerensky's head.

This was all news to Nell who had only heard positive things about the Russian Revolution. In Brisbane, no one knew about the *gulags* where so many Russians and Eastern Europeans had died and Russia was often described as a workers' paradise rather than a regime of terror. Clearly she had a lot to learn about Russia. She was grateful to the professor for setting the record straight for her. Little did she know this was just the beginning of her lifelong interest in Russian history and involvement in its politics.

Nell enjoyed her first year at the language school. She and her fellow students, mainly Americans, often met at the café-restaurant *Closerie de Lilas* whose entrance was planted with mature lilac bushes. The proprietor allowed the students to sit there for hours over cups of coffee discussing art, music and the latest books.

The bomb damage to France's roads and railways had been so great that German war reparations did not cover the cost of reconstruction. The French franc had to be devalued which resulted in Paris becoming the cheapest city in Europe. Americans flocked to the French capital in droves as their dollars went further there than in any other European city. With her wealthy American student friends, Nell went dancing in smoky jazz cellars and visited the Folies Bergères where statuesque showgirls with legs to their armpits danced in huge ostrich feather head dresses and little else.

Nell was shocked to see hundreds of ex-soldiers hobbling around on crutches or begging for small change on street corners. Special seats on the Metro were reserved for *'les mutilés de la guerre'*, a term to describe disabled ex servicemen, often with limbs missing.

Life on the Left Bank was cheap for anyone with foreign currency and it had quickly become a colony of students and artists. Introductions were not needed to strike up a conversation with neighbours sitting at the next table in a pavement café so for an attractive outgoing young woman like Nell it was easy to make new friends.

As a former journalist, Nell enjoyed meeting students from many different countries and conversing in French and she soon acquired a circle of acquaintances from a range of countries. Nell's language classes took place in the mornings which gave her plenty of time to explore Paris in the afternoons when she enjoyed passing time in cafes like le Dome, le Jockey and La Rotunde.

Her first European summer in Europe was spent away from the humid heat of Paris at the magical Isle of Capri where, through mutual friends, she rented a villa with the English novelist Francis Brett Young and his wife. Mrs Brett Young was convinced of the innate superiority of the English over mere colonials and tried to patronise Nell, who was amused by her pretensions.

Nell did all the shopping in local markets as she had picked up some Italian. Mrs Brett Young liked the fact Nell's family had money and told a visiting journalist they were sharing a villa with an heiress. This resulted in Nell's photo appearing in the *Sydney Morning Herald,* on the beach under a parasol, with a story about an Australian heiress enjoying a holiday on the island of Capri. [17]

Through the Brett Youngs Nell attended parties thrown by several British authors who owned villas on this beautiful island. She was fascinated to learn from the writer Compton McKenzie that the Roman emperor Tiberius when exiled from ancient Rome, had built a villa on Capri and the many gardens were a treasure trove of Roman statues commissioned by Tiberius.

She particularly enjoyed the company of Compton Mackenzie, and his wife Faith. Compton was well-read, amusing and a brilliant jazz piano player. The couple were childless and Faith McKenzie became fond of Nell, perhaps looking upon her as the daughter they never had.

When the snobbish Brett Youngs returned to England, Nell stayed on in Capri as a house guest of the Mackenzies. Compton Mackenzie was a historian who had worked for British Intelligence in the war and was now writing spy novels. He was a worldly man with a dry wit and spent hours discussing books and writing with Nell. He encouraged her to start work on a novel set in Montparnasse and promised to critique her manuscript. If he liked it he undertook to send it to his literary agent on her behalf.

CHAPTER SEVEN

The Perils of Publishing for Women Writers

Returning to Paris, Nell was determined to keep fit despite the delicious smelling food in local cafes and restaurants that she found so irresistible. She took a brisk walk each morning to the nearby Luxembourg Gardens where tree-shaded avenues were lined with marble statues of gods and goddesses. She walked as far as the artificial lake in front of the Luxembourg Palace, originally built for Queen Marie de Medici, and now home to the French Senate.

Nell often visited the small art museum attached to the Luxembourg Palace where she was able to admire Impressionist paintings.[18]

In one of the galleries she was thrilled to discover her favourite painting by Marie Bashkirtseff; the brilliantly realistic *The Meeting,* and she returned time after time just to look at it. Nell remembered that the sale of this painting to the French government was mentioned in Marie's diary as her first great success.

On sunny days Nell sat on a bench in the gardens overlooking the shallow lake where children paddled and sailed their toy boats. She enjoyed talking French to whoever was seated next to her in order to improve her command of the language. She wanted to learn to speak French perfectly.

One morning Nell started speaking French to the mother of a sweet little girl. The mother replied in French but her Australian accent gave her away. Both women burst out laughing on realising they were fellow Australians.

The young woman's name was Stella Bowen and she told Nell she came from Adelaide. Her art teacher had recommended that the orphaned Stella travel overseas to further her artistic studies and her trustees had agreed to let her use money inherited from her deceased parents to study in London.

'L'Australienne'. A portrait of Nell by the Australian artist Ethel Carrick Fox who Nell met in the Luxembourg Gardens. Carrick was painting nursemaids and children in the gardens as she couldn't afford to pay for models. Carrick painted Nell in the garden of her Montparnasse studio. (Author's collection)

With an annuity paid by the trustees of her parents' estate Stella was introduced to the famous novelist and publisher, Ford Maddox Ford who was from an older generation and had been badly wounded in the trenches in the Great War. Stella had fallen in love with him and left art school in order to nurse Ford back to health. They had lived in a cottage in the British countryside and Stella explained how Ford had taught her a great deal about art and literature. As soon as he was well enough, he started publishing a literary magazine called *The English Review,* which was prestigious but made very little money.

Stella and Ford and their young daughter moved to Paris as the devalued franc made the cost of living in Paris cheaper than England.

Nell realised that Ford had used Stella's money to bring out an Anglo-American literary magazine called *The Transatlantic Review* which published works by clever young writers such as James Joyce, Ernest Hemingway and Scott Fitzgerald.

When Ford was away on an American author tour his replacement as editor at *The Transatlantic Review* was Ernest Hemingway. The young American journalist turned novelist and his wife rented a studio over a noisy sawmill at No 113, rue Notre Dame des Champs, a few doors away from the much larger studio rented by Ford and Stella.

Hemingway's wife Hadley and Stella had become good friends as they both had young children. The used to meet in the Luxembourg Gardens so the children could play together. Ernest Hemingway's novel set in Montparnasse and Pamplona had been published in New York, received good reviews and sold well. *The Sun Also Rises* went on sale in Paris at Shakespeare and Company, the shop run by American expatriate Sylvia Beach and aroused great interest from American expats. As yet Nell had not read it.

Over many months Nell and Stella became good friends and Nell admitted she was working on a book of short stories provisionally titled *Tales from the Left Bank* and was looking for a publisher. Stella said she would be happy to show the first draft to her husband as the *Transatlantic Review* was to start publishing books about Paris. Nell placed her typed pages in a folder and gave it to Stella who said she would pass the folder on to Ford to read.

On their morning walks, Stella explained that Ford was busy getting the next edition of *The Transatlantic Review* to the printer but would read Nell's stories as soon as he had time. He said he would get back to her but never did.

One morning Nell found Stella shocked and upset. She had received a letter from her friend Hadley Hemingway, who had discovered that Ernest, the husband she adored and had supported financially while he wrote his first novel, was unfaithful. He was having an affair with *Vogue* journalist Pauline Pfeiffer, a stylish young woman with a wealthy family in Arkansas. Pauline Pfeiffer had claimed to be Hadley's best friend and had joined the married couple on holiday in the South of France.

Exposed as an adulterer, Hemingway had suggested he divide his time between both women, which Hadley, the mother of their little boy, refused to do. She felt betrayed by Pauline who she had regarded as her best friend. Hadley still had an income from her family and lawyers advised her that a clean break was the best solution.

Ernest agreed to give his wife the royalties from *The Sun Also Rises* as she had supported him financially while he wrote his first novel without realising it would become a popular book and film.

The rue de Furstenberg, an area Nell thought so attractive she made a detour and passed through it on her way to see publisher Ford Maddox Ford. (Private collection)

In the 1920s divorce was considered shocking. The news that Ernest and Hadley were divorcing was the hot gossip of Montparnasse café society. Many people were surprised at the news having regarded the Hemingways as a devoted couple. Most people took Hadley's side, seeing Pauline Pfeiffer as a marriage wrecker who had seduced Ernest. Bets were being placed that Pauline would insist Ernest marry her once Hadley had divorced him.

When next Nell and Stella met in the Luxembourg Gardens, Stella told Nell that Ford could see her at the office of *The Transatlantic Review* on Friday afternoon. He would be finished by six o'clock. If the receptionist had gone home, Nell was to walk past the reception desk, go down the passage and find Ford in his office.

Friday afternoon was unseasonably warm. Nell chose a cotton

dress with short sleeves and flat shoes to walk past the rue de Furstenburg, one of her favourite places on the Left Bank. It was so hot that she rested there on a park bench, thinking how lucky she was to be in Paris.

As it was getting late, Nell feared Ford might think she had forgotten their appointment and leave his office. She walked quickly to the Odeon Metro station and caught a train which took her across the river to the centre of the city. She climbed the steps close to the Louvre and turned into the quiet side street where Ford rented an office for *The Transatlantic Review.* [19] The main door was still open but the receptionist had already gone home. Following Stella's instructions, Nell walked down a passage to Ford's office and knocked on the door.

He called out 'Come in' and she found the publisher seated behind an imposing desk. He heaved his bulk out of his chair to welcome Nell and gestured for her to sit beside him He poured her a glass of wine from a bottle in front of him, said he had enjoyed *Tales from the Left Bank* but parts of the text needed careful editing which he would be happy to do. She would have to write four more stories to have enough material for a book. If she did this, he would be happy to do the editing, write an introduction and publish her stories as a book. His office had typesetting facilities and he could publish a small English edition which would sell in Paris and he would sell the British rights to a London publisher himself.

This was good news. As Ford moved his chair closer, Nell began to feel uncomfortable. His breath reeked of stale tobacco. He rested a hand on her shoulder as he indicated which parts of her typescript needed cutting. Nell wondered if she was over-reacting or was Ford merely exhibiting an avuncular interest?

As his hand slid down her bare arm and cupped her breast she realised her first instincts had been right. For a moment she froze then her shock turned to anger that Ford was attempting to deceive Stella who had spent her inheritance on establishing Ford's literary magazine.

Nell was furious that Ford had assumed that in order to get published she would deceive her friend by having a sordid affair with him. Nell stood up, pushed Ford's hand out of the way, grabbed her typescript and made for the door.

Ford tried to bluster his way out of the situation, saying 'Nell, don't be stupid. If I tell friends in publishing I've rejected your work, no one will touch it.'

Nell no longer cared. Her cheeks burning with rage she stormed out of his office.

Back in her apartment she poured herself a large glass of wine and paced the room until she felt calmer. She realised her refusal of Ford's sexual advances could be the death knell for her literary ambitions. Ford had the power to damage her by claiming her writing was mediocre. London publishers would accept his opinion of her work and would not bother to read anything she submitted to them.

Nell decided to keep quiet about what had occurred. For her friend Stella to learn of Ford's advances when she had invested all of her money in his magazine and was now almost penniless with a child to support, it would be almost impossible for her to leave. Ford's literary magazine was not doing well so he lacked money to pay child support. Stella would find it hard to survive if she left him.

Ford could also claim Nell had fabricated the story of his unwanted advances out of spite because he had rejected her manuscript. It was her word against his. Stella was in love with Ford and would take his side. Her friend would regard Nell as a troublemaker and their friendship would be over.

Nell realised she was in an unwinnable situation. She recalled her journalist mentor in Brisbane who had warned that publishing was dominated by men who sought sexual favours from female authors. He also claimed American women's magazines had enormous circulations and they paid better than their British or Australian counterparts. What a good idea to sell in her stories in America. Sexual harassment was not possible if all negotiations took place by post.

Nell airmailed her short stories to three American magazine editors and waited.

Weeks later she received a reply from an editor in America who offered a generous fee for stories about young Americans in Paris. He regretted Nell could not publish under her own name. She must write her material as 'An American Girl in Paris'. Stories about exiled Russians living in poverty would not interest his readers but he did want more stories about Americans in Paris. So Nell continued writing short stories for American magazines under a pen name. [20]

Just before Christmas 1926 *The Transatlantic Review* published a book of short stories by a former nightclub dancer named Jean Rhys. Ford was quoted on the back cover as the editor, claiming Rhys as his literary discovery.

The Left Bank and other Stories by Jean Rhys was set in a similar area to Nell's book *Tales from the Left Bank* but the night club dancer's story was far more salacious and many of her stories featured prostitutes engaged in loveless sex. Ford used his contacts with male publishers to sell the overseas rights for Jean Rhys' book to London's Jonathan Cape and New York publishers Harper and Rowe.

Out of interest, Nell bought a copy of Jean Rhys' book about prostitutes, pimps and men who paid for sex as seen through women's eyes, which Ford's introduction claimed was 'something very new in literature' and she could see why it was selling so well .

Much later Nell would learn that Ford had made the same unwritten contract with Rhys as he had suggested to her. When short of money Jean Rhys had been invited to stay with Ford and Stella in their large-open-plan studio in the rue Notre Dame des Champs. Jean had slept on a small bed in the corner of the studio and Ford and Stella had their double bed at the other end of the large room. Stella cooked dinner for them each evening and then Ford worked with Jean Rhys, editing her diaries and turning them into a book of short stories.

Stella was kept busy with her painting, looking after her little daughter and doing the cooking and shopping. Ford retired to their double bed with her but after she was fast asleep, he padded across the studio and climbed into bed with Rhys as part of their unwritten contract to publish her book.

Stella saw Ford through rose-coloured glasses and had no idea that he was a sexual predator.

Jean Rhys hated sex with the obese Ford and told her Montparnasse friends Stella knew exactly what was happening in this strange *ménage à trois*. Stella simply turned a blind eye to preserve her relationship with Ford and chose to keep quiet about his sexual peccadilloes.

Jean Rhys banked the cheque she had received as an advance for the British edition of *The Left Bank and Other Stories* which Ford had sold for her.

Some months later she went to London with the typescript of a second novel she had based on her experiences with Ford in Paris and gave it the title of *Quartet*. Thirsting for revenge she found a London agent to handle the sale of this second novel. *Quartet* was the story of a wealthy married man (Ford) who demands sexual favours from an out-of-work actress (Jean Rhys) in his family home where she is a guest in his spare room. In return for her sexual favours the obese powerful man secures the actress a lucrative part in a new play in London's West

End and the wife ignores the situation.

Quartet became one of the most successful revenge novels of all time. In the novel, Mrs Heidler (Stella) is the complacent wife who enjoys the financial benefits of marriage but dislikes sex with her obese husband. She encourages his adultery with his protégé as a way of keeping the marriage together.

After *Quartet* was published it was humiliating for Stella that readers who knew them believed she had encouraged Ford's sexual activities with Rhys. As a result of the gossip Stella left Ford and went to London taking their daughter with her.

When Ford first met the young Stella she had been a naïve but wealthy art student just arrived from Australia with money in the bank from her deceased parents. Stella spent most of her inheritance backing Ford's failing literary magazines. So when she finally left him after his infidelity with Jean Rhys she had to support herself and her daughter by painting portraits. In her memoirs *Drawn from Life* written years later, Stella blamed herself for wasting her money on Ford.

Ford's womanising was confirmed by Violet Hunt, Ford's resident mistress before he lived with Stella Bowen. The vengeful Violet Hunt told the press Ford had left his wife and children for her and used her money to fund his first literary magazine, *The English Review* which had not been financially successful. Ford's wife was a Catholic who refused to divorce him so he had never been able to marry Violet Hunt or Stella Bowen and lived a life of pretence with both of them.

Nell felt sorry for Stella. She only claimed to be Ford's wife to protect their young daughter from the scandal of illegitimacy. However Ford, the ultimate womaniser, soon found another young woman who believed Ford was a literary genius.

On an American book tour Ford had met Janice Biala, a romantic girl who liked the idea of living with a great writer and dedicated her life to caring for the narcissistic Ford. Meanwhile Stella struggled to bring up their daughter on very little money. [21]

CHAPTER EIGHT

Meeting Nina Berberova

Nell was as beautiful as Anna Karenina, calm, wise and intelligent. Nina Berberova in her memoir *The Italics are Mine,* published in America in 1993.

Living in Montparnasse, Nell rose early and walked along the cobbled rue de Regard to buy a *baguette* from the local *boulangerie* for breakfast. A row of customers waited patiently in a queue for the crusty loaves and golden-brown *croissants* to emerge from the ovens at the rear of the bakery.

On several occasions Nell had noticed an exotic-looking young woman waiting in the queue reading a book. The title was in a foreign script that Nell guessed must be Russian. She was tall and slender with a high cheekbones, enormous dark eyes and very short jet black hair. Every now and then the girl raised her head from her book. Nell saw her face was very pale. Her black woollen coat was worn and frayed at the cuffs but she still managed to look distinguished.

Nell was intrigued. As the queue moved forward, she was pushed against the young woman. In French she apologised and asked if the girl was Russian. Nell knew from reading Marie Bashkirtseff's diary that educated Russians spoke excellent French having learned it in childhood but very few of them knew any English.

The young woman smiled. She said her name was Nina Berberova, she was from St Petersburg and was a writer. Nell explained she was an Australian journalist from a town called Brisbane and was studying French at the Alliance Française and hoping to write a book.

As they waited in the queue they continued chatting in French. By the time their *baguettes* arrived, they were on first name terms. Nell was fascinated to learn that Nina was writing a biography of the Russian composer Tchaikovsky, including his private life and his disastrous marriage. She was clearly a writer of some importance but had to do factory work to survive as an émigré in Paris.

Nell suggested they continue their conversation over a *café au lait* at the Closerie des Lilas, which was only a short walk from the *boulangerie.* They found a quiet table in the sheltered courtyard and Nell ordered two cups of *café au lait* while they continued their conversation uninterrupted.

Apologising for her lack of English, Nina answered Nell's questions in perfect French and told Nell about her life in St Petersburg. Nina's father was a senior government official while her mother acted as an accompanist for a leading opera singer. Nina's parents had supported the enforced abdication of Tsar Nicholas II in favour of the Provisional Government that replaced the Tsar, led by Prime Minister Alexander Kerensky, a former barrister who Nina liked.

Nina told Nell that her father had admired the reforms Kerensky had carried out as Justice Minister. These reforms included abolishing the Tsar's brutal secret police and establishing freedom of religion in Russia. Her father believed that the Romanovs had spent so much money on palaces and art collections that their extravagance combined with Russia's war with Germany had drained the Russian Treasury almost dry.

Nina's father was unusual as he believed in higher education for women. Convinced his daughter had a gift for writing, he had paid for Nina to study Russian literature at the University of St Petersburg where she won several prizes before she and her husband managed to escape to Europe.

Nina told Nell it was hard to make a living from writing. She had hoped to complete a post-graduate thesis, become a teacher in a Russian school and write novels in the school holidays. The Russian Revolution of October 1917 had changed her life. Lenin had ousted the Kerensky Government and moved the seat of government from St Petersburg, now renamed Petrograd, to Moscow. Nina's father, as a government employee and her mother, were made to move to Moscow while Nina remained in St Peterburg which Lenin had renamed Petrograd as he did not believe in saints.

Nina's family's apartment had been requisitioned to house three families of workers and the brutal official who did the rehousing turned Nina out of her home, telling her she was eligible for a cheap rented room in the Writers' House. This was a former mansion confiscated from a wealthy family. Its magnificent ballroom had been turned into a canteen serving inexpensive meals to the resident writers.

At the Writers' House Nina met her future husband, tall handsome Vladislav Khodasevich, the famous poet who was in residence there. She fell hopelessly in love with him when she heard him reading his poems. Their relationship deepened, they became lovers and planned to marry once the famine which was devastating so much of Russia and the Ukraine was over.

Nina had volunteered to teach a class of illiterate manual workers to read and write and managed to obtain a grant to write a biography of Russia's great composer Pyotr Ilyich Tchaikovsky, regarded as an important literary project. Nina was allocated the famous writer Nikolai Gumilyov as her mentor. He encouraged Nina to write about Tchaikovsky's passionate relationships with handsome young men which had inspired him to write many of his early compositions. Up to now this had been a banned subject. Nina's biography revealed how the great composer had yielded to pressure from his widowed father, and married the neurotic Antonina Miliukova. She had pursued him for years but Tchaikovsky was unable to consummate the marriage.

Nell realised Nina was a serious literary writer struggling to complete an important project. Her tragedy was that her husband was now too ill to work and Nina was the breadwinner. To pay the rent she worked for several days a week on an assembly line in the outer suburb of Billancourt, an area full of impoverished Russians.

These Russian *émigrés* provided abundant material for the short stories Nina wrote for the Russian language newspaper *Poslednie Novosti.* Unfortunately the newspaper could only afford to pay her a pittance as a writer. Nell admired the way Nina adapted to the huge change from her former comfortable life in Petrograd to poverty in Paris. It made her feel guilty she had money in the bank and a nice apartment while Nina was reduced to working in a factory twice a week to earn money.

From the pallor of Nina's face Nell believed Nina did not have enough money to eat properly. She wanted to buy a good lunch for the two of them and get to know Nina better. She needed to be discrete so as not to embarrass Nina, who would hate to feel she was an object of charity.

Nell made the excuse she needed to go to the cloakroom. On the way she ordered two *filet mignon* steaks with *pommes frites*, green salads and a bottle of Veuve Clicquot. She told the waiter not to bring the account to the table as the luncheon was a surprise for her friend and she did not want her to pay. She gave him a large bank note adding that he could keep the change.

When Nell returned to the table she, told Nina it was her birthday and she had been longing to invite her for a celebration lunch. The

Closerie de Lilas was the ideal spot for two writers to celebrate as Emile Zola, Simone de Beauvoir, Jean Paul Sartre and Ernest Hemingway had all eaten here.

When their meals arrived it became obvious Nina was hungry. Wanting to help her new friend financially but afraid of offending her, Nell asked if Nina would consider giving her tutorials in Russian literature. She had always wanted to read the work of the great nineteenth century Russian novelists and discuss them with an expert. She would pay Nina the university lecturers' rate for doing her a favour. She would also be grateful if Nina, who spoke excellent French would correct any faults in her pronunciation. They could meet at the Closerie des Lilas each week and of course lunch would be included in the fee.

Nell thought this scheme would kill two birds with one stone. A regular source of income from teaching would release Nina from the drudgery of the factory assembly line and provide Nell with additional tuition in French. She only hoped Nina would not feel she was being patronised and refuse.

However at the idea of teaching Russian literature Nina's face lit up with pleasure. She would be delighted to do this. She suggested Nell read an English or French translation of a selected Russian nineteenth century writer before each tutorial. They could then discuss the way these authors handled plot, writing style and development of their characters and dialogue.

They agreed it would suit them both to meet at the Closerie de Lilas at the same time every Tuesday. This was the day Nell's classes at the Alliance ended early and Nina was also free. They parted with a promise to meet the following week.

****

After a couple of months of tutorials Nina's reserve had vanished. Eventually in answer to Nell's questions, Nina explained why she and her husband had become disenchanted with Lenin's Russia and had fled. Instead of the man they had idolised, Lenin had become a brutal dictator ordering the execution of anyone he perceived as a political enemy.

As the famine in Russia grew worse and countless thousands died of hunger, writers and journalists were forbidden to mention the famine or report the deaths which had resulted.

Nina also told Nell of her horror on learning that Lenin had issued orders that her admired mentor Nikolai Gumilyov and his friend were to be shot by a firing squad. He had defied orders and written about the famine, the failure of Lenin's collective farms and the *gulags* or slave labour camps where Lenin's political enemies were forced to build steelworks for the new industrial Russia. Nikolai Gumilyov continued to ignore the directive to have his writing censored before it was published. He had written with sympathy about the *kulaks* (hard-working peasants who owned their own farms). When ordered to send their livestock to Lenin's huge collective farms many of them had slaughtered their animals, rather than relinquish them. In revenge Lenin had them sent to *gulags* or had them shot by firing squads.

Gumilyov was a distant cousin of Nina's mother and due to the fact he had been paid to mentor Nina and oversee her biography of the great composer, they had become good friends.

For her part Nina had become very fond of the great writer and traveller and in Petersburg they used to meet over meals in the canteen of the Writer's House. Due to the famine, meat and tea were no longer available so they were given an unpalatable meat substitute made from baked acorns, ground to a powder and mixed with boiling water. Nina pulled a face remembering its bitter taste and trying to eat it with boiled carrots and potatoes, the only available vegetables. However they were lucky to have something to eat as the majority of the population of Petrograd were starving. Housewives boiled up grass and tree bark to make soup for their families in a desperate attempt to survive.

The great expatriate Russian writer Maxim Gorky was distraught by the news that his friend Gumilyov was to be shot. Gorky was unusual, being the only major Russian writer allowed to leave the Soviet Union with official permission. Gorky lived in a Berlin mansion bought out of his foreign royalties, which he had turned into a writer's commune.

Maxim Gorky had returned from Europe to Petrograd to plead with Lenin for the lives of Gumilyov and his friend Utompsky on hearing these two major Russian writers were to be executed by firing squad. However Lenin refused to see Gorky and they were both shot.

Khodasevich and Nina attended a memorial service for Gumilyov to show support for his family. At the cathedral they watched members of Lenin's secret police photographing everyone attending the service and demanding their names. Nina realised she and her poet fiancé were now on a list of suspect writers and would have to be careful what they wrote or they too could end up facing a firing squad. [22]

Nina and her fiancé attended a talk given by Maxim Gorky at the Writers' House. Gorky recognised Khodasevich and invited him and Nina to join him over a bottle of vodka. Food was short supply while vodka was plentiful.

Gorky revealed he was worried by the way the Russian revolution had turned out. It was meant to have been the people's revolution. But while Lenin and his cronies were living in luxury in villas, once owned by members of the Romanov dynasty, the workers had not gained the land promised to them by Lenin. Many were starving or had died in the famine.

Khodasevich admitted to Gorky that he and Nina wanted to leave Soviet Russia. Khodasevich's doctor had told him he had a chest complaint which could lead to tuberculosis. He would receive better treatment if he could get to Germany where medicine was more advanced than in Russia.

Khodasevich would be able to receive an exit visa on medical grounds and once he and Nina were married, she could apply for a student visa to study German literature in Berlin. Gorky had invited Khodasevich and Nina to stay as his guests in his writers' commune in return for which Khodasevich would do some editing on Gorky's latest project. This was a history of world literature intended to be read by the newly literate Russian workers.

Nina told Nell they had been lucky to be granted their exit visas. They had married in a registry office and took a train from Petrograd to Berlin and freedom. Nina was deemed to have broken her agreement to produce a biography of Tchaikovsky so had re-written it in French and a French publisher had expressed an interest in publishing it.

****

By now Nina had come to trust Nell completely. She was grateful for the money Nell paid her for lessons in Russian literature.

On the first evening when the Russian couple arrived to have dinner with Nell in her Paris apartment, Nell saw why Nina had fallen for Vladislav Khodasevich. With his aristocratic good looks, shoulder-length black hair and dark eyes he reminded Nell of the famous portrait of Lord Byron. They made a distinguished couple. Nell knew that Khodasevich's chest complaint was getting worse and felt desperately sorry for her friend. His medical expenses would be huge if tuberculosis was diagnosed.

Unlike Nina who wanted to be known as a literary author which meant a limited readership, Nell wanted to write a popular novel or a book of short stories that would have a wider appeal.

One evening over dinner, Nina confided she had been marginally involved in a spy plot that would make a wonderful book. Would Nell be interested in being its joint author? Nina's name could not be on the cover as the author or the Russian Government might try to silence her for ever. Based on actual events, the story revealed the British Government's attempt to kidnap and assassinate Lenin which they were determined to cover up as it made them look foolish and inept.

Nina had heard the extraordinary story from a friend, Baroness Moura Budberg, at that time the lover of Robert Bruce Lockhart, a British diplomat and spy. He told Moura he had been fooled by the Russians into handing over a million pounds in gold bullion to a Russian agent working for Lenin's secret police. Nell couldn't help laughing saying it sounded more like a film script than a novel.

Nina believed that Nell's journalist background made her the ideal co-writer for this thrilling spy story of love and espionage. Nell could submit it under her name to a London literary agent or publisher. They would split the proceeds and Nina would be the silent partner.

Nell thought about the idea. She had enjoyed John Buchan's popular spy novel *The Thirty-Nine Steps* which had the attempted assassination of a Greek Prime Minister as its plot. *The Thirty-Nine Steps* had been a huge success and was being filmed by Alfred Hitchcock who had added a love story to make it more appealing.

Nell knew that British publishers were looking for spy novels as her friend Compton Mackenzie was writing his second story of espionage and intrigue. Nina had repeatedly refused financial help from Nell so writing a joint novel and sharing royalties would be an ideal way of assisting her friend without offending her.

Nell needed more information about Nina's sources and asked whether Moura Budberg was credible. Nina said Baroness Moura Budberg, former wife of a Russian diplomat, had a degree in literature from Cambridge University and came from a titled Russian family with connections to the Romanovs.[23] Later it would be found these credentials were far from the truth.

Nell asked how Nina had met Baroness Budberg. Nina told her that she and Moura had been living in a writers' commune in Berlin, funded by the well-known Russian writer-in-exile, Maximilian Gorky.

When Nina and her husband were guests in Gorky's writer's commune, Moura was Gorky's personal assistant, English translator and resident mistress. However she had refused several times to marry Gorky telling him she had already had one elderly husband and did not want another.

When Moura became seriously ill with influenza, Gorky who was desperately in love with her, feared she might die. He begged Nina to nurse Moura who had become delirious with fever. From Moura's feverish ramblings about a British diplomat named Bruce Lockhart, and their involvement in a plot to kidnap Lenin in 1918, Nina pieced together a remarkable story.

The plot failed but had cost the British Government a great deal of money and forced Winston Churchill, at the time a Cabinet Minister to Prime Minister Lloyd George, to recognise the new regime led by Lenin. The former terrorist and assassin had ousted the government of Prime Minister Alexander Kerensky and tried to have him assassinated.

Nell found this story fascinating and ideal material for a spy novel. She and Nina agreed Nell would do the actual writing in English based on notes Nina had to translate from Russian into French for Nell as she had made them when she was acting as Moura's nurse. Moura's delirium had loosened her tongue and she had told Nina a great deal about her previous life which up to then she had kept secret. They agreed to split the profits of the book Nell would write and Nina would receive a major share of the royalties.

Nell, raised in Australia, had grown up respecting the British. She was shocked by Moura's story revealing that the British Government would stoop to kidnapping and assassination. She wanted to help Nina make money and at the same time fulfil her ambition to write a novel.

She found the story irresistible.

CHAPTER NINE

Nell & Nina's Banned Spy Novel

A lie told often enough becomes the truth. Vladimir Lenin.

Nell learned that the kidnapping of Lenin and Trotsky had been scheduled to take place at the end of August 1918 at a Soviet Party Conference to be held in Moscow. Lenin and his deputy were due to leave the Kremlin, guarded by the tough Latvian Rifle Brigade, known for being crack shots. Their leader, Colonel Edouard Berzin, a ruthless Latvian military man and womaniser, had a reputation for enjoying the high life.

It had been arranged with the British Foreign Office who were behind the kidnapping, that Moura and the young British diplomat, Robert Bruce Lockhart, who was now her lover, would run into Colonel Berzin in an expensive nightclub he frequented in Moscow. Countess Moura spoke some Latvian and would work as Lockhart's interpreter in this delicate approach to set up the plot.

A waiter had been bribed to place Moura and Lockhart at an adjoining table to Colonel Berzin who would be accompanied by his latest girl friend, a nightclub hostess. Moura would start talking to Berzin's girlfriend, and then turn her charm on Berzin. At this point Lockhart was to join the conversation, wave a bottle of the best French champagne and invite Berzin and his girlfriend to join them in celebrating their fictitious engagement. The four of them would spend the evening drinking and dancing and hopefully arrange to meet again. Lockhart would then reveal to Berzin he could obtain money for the Latvians from the British in return for a favour.

The Foreign Office plan, codenamed the 'Lockhart Plot', succeeded at first. The two couples struck up a friendship and spent several evenings drinking in nightclubs and gypsy taverns. Colonel Berzin, with encouragement from Lockhart and Moura, explained how the Latvians had been conquered by the Tsar's armies and wanted freedom from Soviet Russian domination.

Latvian freedom fighters therefore needed gold bullion to buy armaments to rebel against their Russian controllers. Gold bullion would be harder for Russian authorities to trace than cash sent through banks. At this point Lockhart revealed to Berzin he was a British diplomat and would put the idea of helping the Latvian freedom fighters to the appropriate department in the Foreign Office if Berzin would help with a plan to kidnap Lenin and Trotsky. Berzin considered the offer and agreed.

Lockhart reported his successful meeting with Berzin to the Foreign Office in London, telling them he was confident of Berzin's interest in helping.

In wartime, Britain and Tsarist Russia had been allies but they now feared Lenin and Trotsky would ferment revolution in Britain and the British Government wanted them removed. They were delighted that Colonel Berzin, when his forces were guarding Lenin, would, in return for a substantial payment in gold bullion, be prepared to turn a blind eye to a British attempt to kidnap the Russian leader. It was a mutually attractive deal.

Nina explained to Nell that Robert Bruce Lockhart, Moura's lover, had led an amazing life. He had twice saved the life of Prime Minister Alexander Kerensky and smuggled him out of Russia on a Swedish cargo boat. Lockhart enjoyed what he called 'cloak and dagger work' and as the front man for the plot, would deliver the bribe of a large quantity of gold bullion to Colonel Berzin via the British Embassy in Moscow.

The American Consul in Moscow put up some additional money as the American Government also distrusted Lenin and wanted him removed from power.

For some time the British Government had regarded Lenin and Trotsky with suspicion. Trotsky was known to be trying to export Marxist style revolution to Britain and France via militant trade unions. The British Cabinet feared a general strike would cripple the British economy and Britain's trade unions would impose Communism on Britain. Britain's largest landowners, including several dukes, were terrified of a Marxist revolution having seen what had happened to major landowners in Russia, who were arrested, imprisoned, and used as slave labour in *gulags*.

British soldiers were still stationed in Russia, many at Murmansk, as Britain and Russia had been allies in the 1914 war against the Kaiser's Germany. They would be brought to Moscow to act as official guards at the Conference along with the Latvian Guard commanded by Colonel Berzin.

The British guards were to snatch Lenin and Trotsky as they arrived at the Soviet Party Conference and 'dispose of them' so they ceased to present a threat to the West. How this was to be done was of course never put in writing.

Lockhart took delivery of the shipment and duly delivered it to Colonel Berzin. It had been shipped to Lockhart in Moscow by the British Foreign Office as crates of gold bullion sent to Lockhart in his name.

Unknown to the Foreign Office and to Lockhart, Colonel Berzin was working closely with Lenin's secret police and would double-cross them, handing over the gold bullion to his secret police handlers.

To make matters more complex, another plot to assassinate Lenin was under way, planned by MI6, who were working independently of the Foreign Office.

MI6 saw themselves as experts in espionage and subversion and were annoyed the Foreign Office seemed to be taking over their role. They arranged for a shady Russian arms dealer named George Relinsky to return to Moscow and organise the assassination of Lenin in such a way that Lenin's death would not have links to the British Government.

Relinsky stood to make a lot of money from a dubious arms deal if Lenin was assassinated. He had claimed in an interview with Churchill that once Lenin was dead, the ambitious Boris Savinkov, an elected member of Prime Minister Alexander Kerensky's government, should replace Lenin rather than Kerensky, a former barrister and not nearly tough enough to deal with the brutal Bolsheviks.

Arriving in Moscow with a passport in the name of an Irishman named Sidney Reilly, Relinsky searched for a suitable assassin. He was put in touch with a young anti-Lenin activist called Fanny Kaplan, who was already under suspicion and had previously been arrested and tortured by Lenin's secret police.

The handsome and charming Reilly spent time grooming Fanny and giving her presents. She was flattered by his attention and quickly fell in love with him. One of Reilly's 'presents' was a Browning pistol as he told her she needed to defend herself. Tutored by Relinsky, masquerading as Sidney Reilly, Fanny Kaplan was persuaded to assassinate Lenin in revenge for being tortured by Lenin's secret police.

Meanwhile Reilly had been informed of Lockhart's plans to assassinate Lenin by his MI6 controller when he made contact with the British Embassy in Moscow. He was introduced to Lockhart and

Countess Moura, but did not reveal the MI6 plan for Kaplan to assassinate Lenin as he was convinced the Lockhart plot would fail. He regarded the Foreign Office as bunglers and amateurs in the field of espionage which he considered should be left to MI6. [24]

On 30 August 1918 Reilly drove the gullible Kaplan to the armaments factory that Lenin was due to open. He stationed her close to the path Lenin would take to open the factory. Unfortunately, in choosing Kaplan as his assassin, Reilly was unaware that her eyesight was poor and vanity had prevented her wearing her glasses in front of the man she wanted to impress.

Hustled into position by Reilly she fired, but her three bullets lodged in Lenin's neck and shoulders rather than in his head. Lenin fell to the ground apparently mortally wounded. He was rushed to hospital but contrary to all expectations, survived.

Kaplan was arrested and tortured by Lenin's secret police but never betrayed Reilly aka Relinsky, the man she loved. She didn't want to believe he had used her and after prolonged torture, when she still refused to name anyone, she was shot and her corpse burned.

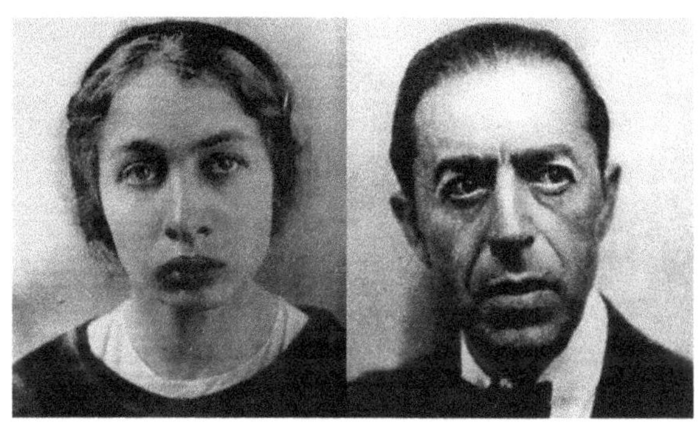

Identity photographs of Fanny Kaplan and Sidney Reilly

Lenin's secret police, the Cheka, had known all along about the 'Lockhart Plot' involving the British Embassy from the double crossing Colonel Berzin. On 30 August 1918 after Fanny Kaplan's assassination failed, the Cheka arrived at the British Embassy, arrested Moura and Lockhart, and took them to the grim Lubianka jail.

Lockhart and Moura were interrogated individually by the vulpine Jacov Peterss, second-in-command of the Cheka. To soften them up psychologically he made sure they could hear the screams of fellow prisoners being tortured. Peterss told Moura they had been betrayed by Colonel Berzin who was working with the Cheka and that she and Lockhart would be shot by firing squad the next morning.

Moura, realising the situation was desperate, pleaded for her lover's life. Using all the feminine allure she could muster she succeeding in striking a deal with Jacov Peterss. He said he would not force her to have sex with him but if she agreed to it, and would become a spy for the Cheka, she and Lockhart would be released. Lockhart would be exchanged for Maxim Litvinov, a senior Russian diplomat caught spying in London.

Countess Moura kept her Faustian bargain with Jacov Peterss. After having sex with her in his office, he promised her ten minutes alone with Lockhart in his cell after he had spoke to Lockhart himself.

Lockhart, whose life she had just saved, told Moura he loved her and that he was to be sent back to England the following morning. The faithless Lockhart promised to send Moura a visa that would allow her to join him in London when he would divorce his Australian wife and marry her. A promise he failed to keep.

The Russian secret police released Moura with just enough money to get to Germany. She arrived penniless but ever resourceful, found a job working for the writer Maxim Gorky.

The failure of the Lockhart plot and the loss of the gold bullion to the Russians ended Lockhart's career as a diplomat. The British Government, appalled at the loss of a million pounds to Lenin's secret police, insisted Lockhart had acted on his own initiative and denied any knowledge of this plan code-named the 'Lockhart Plot'.

Lockhart therefore became an embarrassment to the British Government and was forced to resign from the diplomatic service. Had he not agreed to do so, he would have been sacked.

The British Cabinet wanted to hide the fact that huge sums had been wasted on a plot to assassinate Lenin. They feared that if the press got hold of the story, the Liberal Party under Prime Minister Lloyd George could lose the next election.

Soviet Russia's secret police had played the British and American Intelligence services for fools. An enormous amount of money had been lost. This was a secret that could not be made public under any circumstances.

Lockhart became an inept merchant banker and lost the bank's money as well as his own. He left his long-suffering Australian wife and child but decided that Moura no longer appealed to him.

When finally Moura arrived in London and met her former lover

Lockhart, he told her they were from different worlds and living together would never work. He assured Moura he would always be her friend but was no longer in love with her. His brutal rejection after she had saved his life by having sex with Jacov Peterss taught Moura never to trust a man again.[25]

Nina Berberova, Nell's best friend in Paris who recounted Moura Budberg's story and would be co-author of the spy novel they would write about the Lockhart Plot. Nina eventually emigrated to America and was discovered as a literary author by Jacqueline Kennedy with prize-winning novels about Russian émigrés in Paris. (Photograph from one of Nina's book covers)

After being made to resign as a diplomat and failing at merchant banking, Lockhart found employment as a journalist with the media empire of Lord Beaverbrook. Twenty years later, during World War Two, he returned to espionage at which he was very successful. In return for keeping his mouth shut about the Lockhart Plot he received a knighthood and the impressive title of Sir Robert Hamilton Bruce

Lockhart at an investiture at Buckingham Palace.

The British Government claimed the plot to kidnap and kill Lenin was merely anti-British propaganda invented by the Russians in order to damage the British Government. All documentation was filed under the Official Secrets Act. Writing or broadcasting anything about this was now a legal offence for which those who contravened the Act could be jailed as a matter of national security.

****

Arriving penniless in Germany, Countess Moura gained a job with Gorky's publishing house by falsely claiming she had received a degree in English Literature from Cambridge, when she had only completed a short language course for foreigners. Quickly Moura established herself as Gorky's resident mistress and secretary in the writer's commune. This was where she and Nina met, and Nina learned of the failed Lockhart Plot, which Nina relayed to Nell.

Living in Gorky's writers commune and residence in Berlin, Moura's relationship with her elderly employer was manipulated on her own terms. To obtain an Estonian passport to visit her children, the widowed Moura used money given to her by the besotted Gorky to make a marriage of convenience to an Estonian aristocrat, the dissipated Baron Budberg, who need money to support an expensive gambling habit. The day after her arranged marriage to Baron Budberg, Gorky, consumed by passion for Moura, welcomed her back to the commune.

Living in Gorky's writers' commune, Moura had a one-night stand with the celebrated British author H G Wells before he returned to Britain. She had another fling with the charismatic Alexander Kerensky, the former Prime Minister of Russia, who in exile was running an anti-Communist newspaper in Berlin before he departed for Paris.

Bruce Lockhart had already saved Kerensky twice from Lenin's assassins while working at the British Embassy in Moscow. It was entirely thanks to Lockhart's bravery that Kerensky made it to Berlin in 1918.

So by a strange co-incidence the lives of Lockhart, Kerensky, Nina and Nell would become interlinked through writing their spy novel.

****

In Jazz-age Paris Nell and Nina gave their spy novel the working title of *To Moscow with Love*. Countess Moura would become a fictionalised character called Countess Natasha Kirov. Like Countess Moura, the fictitious Countess Natasha enchanted everyone around her when she sang Russian ballads accompanying herself on the guitar.

In the novel Nell gave Robert Bruce Lockhart the fictitious Scottish name of David Campbell-Boyd. Georgy Relinsky, the MI6 secret agent with the forged passport under the name of Sidney Reilly became Sean O'Connor. In reality Relinsky, like Lockhart, had been sentenced to death *in absentia* by the Russians. But unlike Lockhart had foolishly returned to Russia with the promise of a lucrative arms deal, and was immediately arrested and shot by the secret police.

Nina had an unexpected meeting with Moura, in a café on the rue de Rivoli as Moura, now working and living with the wealthy H.G. Wells, was on a shopping trip to Paris. Nina remembered that Moura had had a brief affair with Wells in Berlin.

Moura travelled to England and contacted Wells with whom she had had a one night stand while living with Gorky in Berlin. In no time Wells was besotted by her and ousted his girl friend so Moura became the resident mistress of yet another ageing but wealthy author. Moura was now spending Wells' money shopping in Paris.

Over several cups of coffee Moura filled in missing details in her story. She explained that as Gorky's European royalties had dried up, he was enticed back to Soviet Russia by Stalin's promises of an apartment in Moscow, the Presidency of the Russian Writers' Association and a handsome annual income. Moura had refused to accompany Gorky to Russia as she did not trust Stalin's promises.

Moura confided to Nina that H. G. Wells had named her as his heir. He was now in poor health and had not long to live. Using his money wisely she intended to set herself up in London as a literary agent and become her own boss as she was tired of taking orders from men.

The joint novel based on information Nina had received from Moura and related to Nell took her many years to write, as both of their lives became increasingly busy and complex.

CHAPTER TEN

A Russian Romance in Montparnasse

The romance that Nell had dreamed of finding in Paris began soon after she first arrived in Paris and moved into her apartment. She met her neighbour, Countess Yevgenia, in the vestibule, while waiting for the lift. The Countess had a shopping bag in one hand and several books in the other. She dropped a book and Nell picked it up, helped the elderly lady into the lift, carried her shopping bag to her apartment and was invited inside for a cup of Russian tea.

They introduced themselves and the aristocratic Russian insisted that Mademoiselle Tritton must have some genuine Russian tea. Settling Nell on her sofa she disappeared into her small kitchen. Nell looked around the apartment which was similar to her own in layout but much smaller.

A bookcase lined with Russian books occupied one entire wall. On a large round table were photos in ornate silver frames. One of them showed her hostess standing beside a distinguished looking senior officer in uniform who Nell thought must be the Countess's husband or her brother.

Nell's neighbour returned with a tray with two glasses in ornate silver holders, a silver sugar bowl and a saucer with thinly sliced lemons. Sitting opposite to Nell, she gave Nell her full Russian family name which was long and complex. Seeing the expression on her young guest's face, the older woman laughed and suggested Nell call her Countess Yevgenia. Her family name was unpronounceable to English speakers. She apologised that her English was poor as in Tsarist Russia they always had French rather than English governesses.

As she poured the tea from a silver samovar they chatted away in French. Detecting a trace of an unfamiliar accent in Nell's French, the Countess asked where she came from and was intrigued to learn Nell came from far distant Australia.

Nell explained she was studying French at a language school and asked her hostess who were the two handsome young men in military uniforms in photographs in silver frames on the table. With a catch in her voice Countess Yevgenia said they were her sons, both officers in the Tsar's army, shot by the Bolsheviks along with their father. They died in the Crimea where the Tsar's army had been forced to retreat and most of them were slaughtered by the Red Army.

After suffering heavy casualties senior officers of the Tsarist White Army surrendered. They handed over their guns, trusting Lenin who had given them his word of honour that they would receive an amnesty and be pardoned. But the deceitful Lenin had lied. He ordered the massacre of 50,000 members of the White Army, including Countess Yevgenia's sons and her husband. Her voice faltered as she told Nell how they had been shot by Bolshevik firing squads. The massacre lasted several days and the Crimean fields ran red with blood.

Countess Yevgenia pointed to another framed photograph of two men in uniform, one with greying hair and the other young and handsome. The photos were of her brother, Ivan and his son Nikolai, both cavalry officers in the Tsar's White Army. Captured by the Bolsheviks her brother and his son had been transported to one of Lenin's *gulags* or slave labour camps. Their journey in a cattle truck took three days without enough drinking water so that many of the prisoners died of thirst before they reached Siberia.

Realising that Nell knew little about the horrors of *gulags,* Countess Yevgenia explained that the word was an abbreviation for *Glavnoe Upravlenie Largerie.* These slave labour camps had been set up by Lenin and continued by Stalin to imprison those who they declared were 'class enemies of the revolution'. This included Tsarist army officers, priests, monks, nuns and aristocrats or anyone critical of the regime, all sent to the *gulags* along with thieves, murderers and rapists.

Nell apologised for her ignorance of the dark side of the Russian revolution. What she knew of Russia came from reading the diary of Marie Bakshirtskeff who had died years before the Bolshevik revolution. In Australia, newspapers had been sympathetic to the Bolsheviks, who had now changed their names to Communists.

Countess Yevgenia's commented dryly that Lenin's propaganda machine was promoting a false image of the Soviet Socialist Republic as a workers' paradise. Admirers of Soviet Russia were kept ignorant of the fact that Lenin and Stalin ordered the killings of hundreds of thousands of innocent people. Westerners invited to visit Soviet Russia were given plenty of vodka and caviar, shown handsome new schools, factories and steelworks. They were given guided tours by communist stalwarts who made sure journalists new nothing of *gulags* and the high death rate of the prisoners. They were not told these buildings were built by slave labour. Thousands had died building them and many were buried in the foundations.

Nell sometimes went shopping for her elderly neighbour and when she returned they enjoyed cups of Russian tea together. Nell enjoyed Countess Yevgenia's stories about her life in St Petersburg during the reign of the Tsar.

She learned that the Countess had escaped from the horrors of Soviet Russia where landowners or anyone with money was shot by the police or sent to work in a slave labour camp.

Countess Yevgenia showed Nell a photograph of herself in formal court dress. On her upswept hair she wore a diamond and sapphire headband known as a diadem with matching sapphire and diamond earrings. Wearing a diadem for evening functions at the court of the Tsar was obligatory.

Before leaving Russia Countess Yevgenia had a jeweller dismantle her tiara. As a precaution against theft Countess Yevgenia had sewn the jewels from her tiara into the seams of her bodice and skirt. Her French governess had taught her to sew and embroider; skills which saved her from starving when she arrived in Paris almost penniless. She unpicked the jewels and sold individual diamonds, sapphires and pearls to a jeweller in the rue de la Paix.

With money from her jewels the countess was able to buy a small apartment in the rue du Regard. She explained that she felt safe in this beautiful old building. So many Russian aristocrats were living in terrible conditions and generals and admirals were working on assembly lines in the Citroen and Renault car factories on the outskirts of the city.

Countess Yevgenia was grateful for the meagre payment she received for embroidering fabrics with delicate *petit point.* These commissions came from an *atelier* established by the Countess Yevgenia's friend, Grand Duchess Maria Pavlova. She supplied the fashion houses of Worth and Chanel with embroidery to adorn opera cloaks and evening dresses of aristocrats, actresses and film stars.

Like her fellow students at the Alliance Française, Nell dressed in black polo neck sweaters and slacks, even when visiting Countess Yevgenia who in Russia would have been shocked by her informality. But because the countess was lonely and Nell brought the older woman gifts of flowers and her favourite chocolates they chatted together over cups of Russia tea about St Petersburg all formality forgotten.

From questions about Nell's life in Brisbane the countess realised Nell's family must have money. As Nell had no regular boyfriend and was so interested in Tsarist Russia the countess suggested she accompany her to the annual ball to celebrate the birthday of the Grand Duke Gabriel Konstantinovich Romanov. He was one of few members of the Imperial family to survive the Russian Revolution which her handsome nephew, Captain Nadejine would be attending. Like Nell he enjoyed dancing and she would be delighted to introduce them.

Nell did not realise that Countess Yevgenia, having learned she had family money, was determined they should meet in a romantic situation. Her plans for her nephew's future hinged on his marriage to someone with money.

Each year the Grand Duke's wealthy supporters contributed to making this annual ball a big event. Aristocratic Russian émigrés, some in fancy dress, forgot their straightened circumstances and enjoyed themselves as they recalled the glorious days of St Petersburg under Tsar Nicholas II.

Nell was thrilled when her Russian neighbour invited her to the birthday ball of the Grand Duke. Knowing that Nina disapproved of the Tsar as a spendthrift who had drained the Russian Treasury with his extravagance, she did not tell Nina she was attending a Tsarist function. Nell bought a blue silk ballgown from the House of Chanel that fitted beautifully and would look perfect with the sapphire and diamond necklace and earrings that had been her twenty-first birthday present from her parents.

On the night of the ball Nell shared a horse drawn *fiacre* with the countess to the large house on the Isle de St Louis, near Notre Dame owned by the Grand Duke. Servants relieved them of their evening cloaks. Countess Yevgenia led Nell to the long line of guests waiting to be presented to the Grand Duke, his wife and their guest of honour, Prince Lobanov-Rostovsky.

Nell and Countess Yevgenia were joined by a handsome, dark-haired young man who the countess introduced as her nephew. Captain Nikolai Nadejine looked glamorous in his white jacket with a scarlet and gold braided collar and matching cuffs, tight trousers and black leather knee-high boots. He reminded Nell of Prince Andrei Bolkonsky in *War and Peace,* her favourite Tolstoy novel.

Captain Nadejine took Nell's hand, raised it to his lips and asked her to dance. When she replied in French he looked relieved as like his aunt, he spoke very little English.

Apart from duty dances with his aunt and her elderly friends, Captain Nadejine spent the evening at Nell's side. The countess was correct, he was an excellent dancer and had beautiful manners and made her feel special.

At the midnight buffet Nikolai suggested she try the Beluga caviar. He made his way through the guests crowding around the table and presented her with a plate of *blinis;* small Russian pancakes topped with caviar, sour cream and dill. He handed her a glass of champagne and led her to a seat. When they had finished, he returned to the buffet for plates of a spiced apple cake called *sharlotka* and diamond-shaped *paklavas* made from thin pastry filled with ground almonds and soaked in a honey syrup.

Nikolai collected another two glasses of champagne and led Nell away from the crowded dining room into the much quieter conservatory. They ate their desserts and sipped the Grand Duke's excellent champagne. Nell found Captain Nikolai far more interesting than the young men she had danced with in Brisbane. He made her laugh when he confessed that the uniform she admired so much dated from the Napoleonic wars and had been borrowed from a theatrical costumier. When arrested by the Red Army he had been stripped of all his possessions including his boots, his warm coat and gold watch.

Nell was impressed by his honesty and by his description of St Petersburg as the Venice of the North with its canals, palaces and handsome stone houses. During what he called St Petersburg's 'white nights' it never got dark and a long silvery twilight enveloped the city.

Nikolai described his family's town residence which overlooked the wide River Neva. Like everything else his family possessed, the house had been confiscated by the Bolsheviks and was now a worker's hostel. Nell knew from the countess that their family estates on the Volga River were now run as an inefficient collective farm with poor distribution of food, which had contributed to the famine that had enveloped Russia in the early 1920s.

****

The next morning, Nell could not stop thinking about the ball and Nikolai who she found charming and disturbingly attractive. He had admitted he was working as a café singer and part-time waiter. His father, General Nadejine, the former Russian military attaché to the Imperial Russian embassy in Switzerland, was now a taxi driver.

Nikolai suggested that one evening Nell might like to visit the café where he sang Russian ballads to an audience composed mainly of tourists. So Nell walked to the café located near the Place de la Contrescarpe. She entered, found a vacant table, and ordered a glass of white wine. She listened spellbound as Nikolai accompanied by an accordionist sang Russian ballads in his pleasant baritone voice.

Nell was embarrassed when gazing directly at her, Nikolai announced that his final number, another love song, was dedicated to *La belle Australienne.* His announcement made patrons turn around and stare at Nell.

After Nikolai finished his performance and changed into ordinary clothes, he worked a short shift as a waiter. When he had finished, he joined Nell's and said he would like to take her somewhere special. To a place where she would find the real Paris. He took her arm, hailed a cab and told the driver to take them to Les Halles. He told her the all night cafes at the vegetable market were famous for their bowls of delicious French onion soup eaten by market porters and all-night revellers. Seated at one of the round metal tables with porters in their faded blue overalls and late night party goers in evening dress, Nell and Nikolai talked until dawn.

Nell was fascinated by Nikolai's Russian childhood which was so different from her own early years in Brisbane. Nikolai talked about their apartment in St Petersburg overlooking the Neva River and their country estate and how much he loved his first pony, which he had learned to ride at four years old. His father, the general, was away for long periods in the Tsar's army so he was close to his mother. His parents spoke French at home but spoke in Russian to family retainers and the local peasants.

From an early age Nikolai had loved riding and won prizes for show jumping. He was not academic but wanted a career that involved riding and training horses. When he turned nineteen, his father had bought him a commission in the most exclusive regiment in the Imperial Cavalry. He loved life as a cavalry officer and was promoted to the rank of captain in his mid-twenties and told he had a good career ahead of him.

Young cavalry officers were considered highly suitable by many major Russian land owners as husbands for their daughters. When stationed in St Petersburg, the young officers in Nikolai's regiment were invited to grand balls held in the palaces that lined the River Neva. They were entertained in elegant homes where parents of eligible daughters sought out suitable husbands. However Nikolai managed to avoid such an arranged marriage because he had a jealous married mistress.

Nikolai explained to Nell that Lenin had broken his promise to give the peasants land and did the exact opposite. All land was confiscated.

Nikolai's family estate on the Volga River was confiscated by the Bolsheviks who would soon style themselves as Communists and it was now part of one of the enormous collective farms set up by Lenin and run by men from the city who knew nothing about farming. Distribution was slow and inefficient so most of the food had rotted by the time it reached the towns and cities where people were starving.

While Nikolai and his father were fighting with the Tsar's army, his mother, who was left in charge of their country property, was declared an enemy of the state. She was arrested and transported in a cattle truck to a slave labour camp or *gulag*.

Nikolai and his father were captured by Lenin's Red Army and eventually ended up in prison in the same *gulag* as Nikolai's mother. where she had been held in an area reserved for female prisoners. In midwinter, when temperatures fell below zero, prisoners slept in freezing cold huts on wooden shelves without mattresses. Fed on thin gruel made from rotting cabbage leaves and animal intestines and one slice of black bread a day, prisoners were made to labour until they became so weak they could no longer meet their work quota. Their meagre rations were then withheld so that they died from malnutrition.

They were lucky that Nikolai's father, General Nadejine, had served as the Tsar's Military Attaché in the Tsarist Russian embassy in Switzerland before the Great War. In Berne, General Nadejine had played bridge every week with three Swiss friends, one of whom had been appointed to a League of Nations committee at the end of World War One. General Nadejine's former bridge partner was in charge of locating German prisoners of war who had been sent by the Russians to *gulags* in error.

On a League of Nations inspection visit his former bridge partner had recognised General Nadejine among the line of starving prisoners. and used his diplomatic status to have Nikolai and his father released. He claimed they had diplomatic immunity so imprisoning them in a *gulag* contravened the Geneva Convention on the treatment of prisoners of war.

Thanks to his former Swiss bridge partner, General Nadejine and Nikolai were lucky enough to receive League of Nations passports and rail tickets from Russia to Paris; two of very few prisoners to leave a *gulag* alive.

In Paris Nikolai and his father were met by members of ROVS, the organisation that looked after former White Russian officers, located their relatives and found them work. They shared a cramped spare bedroom in the Countess's small apartment. Soon ROVS found General Nadejine a job as a taxi driver. Other former generals worked as waiters or doormen or on the assembly lines of the Citroen and Renault car factories.

Nell was horrified by all of this and Nikolai then told her the saddest part of his story. He revealed how in the women's section of the *gulag* his half-starved mother had died from pneumonia without any medical attention. He had been forbidden to see her when she was dying or to attend her burial. Later he learned that her body had been thrown into a mass grave by soldiers. As he told Nell this part of the story Nikolai's voice shook with emotion.

Nell took his hand realising how easy her life had been in comparison with his. He held her hand in his saying how wonderful it was to talk to someone who was so understanding. As dawn broke he insisted on escorting her to the main door of her apartment block. He behaved like a true gentleman and made no attempt to kiss her which she found disappointing and they arranged to meet the following evening.

From then on they saw each other every day. In the evenings after Nikolai's performance at the café, they met other homesick Russians like Nikolai. She loved their romantic evenings together when they went to Russian cabarets in Montmartre and danced cheek to cheek on tiny dance floors.

After drinking vodka Nikolai always became emotional and started calling Nell '*Moya dusha,* (my soul mate). He admitted that having been lonely for so long and now having met Nell, he could not bear to live without her. When they went for walks along the *quais* that bordered the Seine Nikolai became possessive and jealous and stared down any man who looked with admiration at Nell.

As Nikolai had very little money after paying his rent, they often ate in Nell's apartment and she learned to cook some of the Russian dishes that he liked. On special occasions they ate in the courtyard of the Closerie de Lilas, Nell's favourite café. It was only a short walk from there to the Bal Bullier where drinks were cheap. As it was popular with Nell's fellow students they spent many happy evenings there dancing and talking to friends.

Countess Yevgenia had found her apartment too small to accommodate Nikolai and his father, General Nadejine so they had to move to a cheap room in a damp basement in one of the lodging houses in the rue de Vaugirard. Nell was appalled at how they lived. She brought blankets and a big armchair with cushions to brighten up their room and warm overcoats to survive the damp cold of a Paris winter.

Nell had fallen hopelessly in love with Nikolai fully aware he was completely penniless and twelve years older than herself. But this was the first time she had been in love and full of compassion for how life had treated Nikolai, she was blind to his faults.

Nina told her she was making a big mistake if she married Nikolai who had confided to her that he was hoping to become an opera singer. Nina thought Nikolai did not have the talent to succeed in the competitive world of opera. His fondness for alcohol was a problem shared by many of his former military colleagues.

Nina warned Nell she should be careful about getting involved by a man who spent so much time drinking with his former army colleagues. But Nell, carried away by love, did not want to listen.

Returning to her apartment in the early hours of the morning in a horse-drawn cab with Nikolai's arms around her, it was only a matter of time before they spent the night together. From there it was a short step to him staying overnight regularly and leaving clothes in Nell's apartment.

Before long they were regarded as a couple by Nell's fellow students. Always generous, Nell wanted to pay for the singing tuition Nikolai needed to gain a place with a major opera company.

Nell installed a small grand piano in her apartment and paid a former opera singer to give Nikolai voice-training lessons. He gave up singing ballads to tourists but instead of using the time to study opera scores and do his vocal exercises, Nikolai spent time drinking at the headquarters of ROVS with fellow Tsarist officers.

A dinner given by Nell to introduce Nikolai to Nina's husband, Vladislav Khodasevich, the famous poet, was a disaster. Nell had assumed that as both men had lived in Petersburg they would have plenty to talk about but failed to realise their political views were poles apart and this would cause problems.

Nina, a member of the *haute bourgeoise,* whose family had supported Kerensky's government, told Nikolai that the Tsar's failure to introduce vital reforms meant he had been the architect of his own downfall and deserved to be deposed.

Nikolai was furious at these comments and a heated argument developed. After Nina and Khodasevich had departed, Nikolai made it clear that he disapproved of Nell's friendship with Nina.

Nina was horrified at Nikolai's outburst. Nikolai had moved into her friend's apartment. She saw Nikolai as a hopeless case, a former Tsarist officer who did nothing but sit around with his army friends reminiscing and drinking vodka.

Nina still doubted Nikolai had the talent to succeed as an opera singer and seemed happy to live off Nell's money. Once again Nina tried to warn Nell not to get involved with a man with an alcohol problem.

Nikolai convinced Nell that her rented apartment in the rue de Regard was too small for both of them and his grand piano. He persuaded her to rent a much larger apartment at No 15, rue de la Santé. It lacked the charm of the rue du Regard but was larger which enabled Nell to organise musical soirees and invite those who could advance Nikolai's career in the world of opera. Nikolai was given several auditions but failed to secure a contract at the Paris Opera or any other opera company.

Nina had been right about Nikolai's drinking. It was getting worse. He would return from the ROVS headquarters after drinking sessions consumed by rage over what Lenin and the Bolsheviks and done to his family. On several occasions he had lashed out in rage at Nell.

The next day, once again, he was repentant, covered Nell's hands and face with kisses, begged her to forgive him and told her how much he loved her. Nikolai persuaded Countess Yevgenia to give him one of her remaining rings, a large opal between two diamonds, which he gave to Nell as an engagement ring. Nina warned her friend of the proverb that opals brought bad luck to those not born in October.

Coming from subtropical Queensland Nell hated the winter cold in Paris and missed the sun. She loved Capri and had an open invitation to stay at the villa of her friends, Compton and Faith Mackenzie. The successful Scottish novelist and his wife had visited

Nell in Paris and he encouraged Nell to show him the novel she and Nina were working when she next visited Capri. If he liked it he would send it to his literary agent in London who would find her a publisher.

****

Nell wanted to tell her parents that she was engaged in order to prevent them learning from any other source she was living with Nikolai. She wanted to talk to them by phone and counter any objections they might have to her choice of marriage partner rather than write a letter.

In the 1920s, booking a telephone call from Paris to Australia could take several hours. Australians with money often made calls home from the Ritz, enjoying a drink or a meal while they waited for the call placed by the hotel's operator to come through. They took the call in one of the marble-lined phone booths in the lobby. Nell chose this method to break the news of her engagement, carefully withholding certain information about Nikolai.

She told her parents she was engaged to be married to the son of a White Russian general. She did not tell them her future father-in-law drove a taxi and her bridegroom worked as a café singer. She hoped her parents would come to London for the wedding. They were getting married in the Russian Orthodox Church to please General Nadejine to whom the Orthodox faith was important.

Nell had already attended a couple of services at the Russian Orthodox Church whose liturgy and music she found uplifting and beautiful. She wanted to please Nikolai but did not want to upset her parents. She assured them that she was not going to convert to the Orthodox faith.

Nell's father, a staunch member of his local Anglican church, did not want to attend an Orthodox wedding in London in a language he could not understand with a service full of incense and bell ringing. Nell's parents had envisaged their daughter having a white wedding in their local church in Clayfield or at the Anglican Church in Paris. They asked Nell if she could change her wedding arrangements.

Nell tried to change the plans but General Nadejine was adamant. His deceased wife would have wanted her only son to marry in an Orthodox wedding ceremony.

Nell's parents were represented by Nell's married sister and her architect husband who took a passenger liner from Sydney to London for her big white wedding. As a wedding present her parents gave the newly-weds two return tickets on an ocean liner from Marseilles to Sydney. They would meet Nell's husband when the P&O Liner *Mooltan* arrived in Sydney.

At the Orthodox ceremony on the 11 December 1928, Nell wore an elegant white gown and, following the Russian custom, the couple wore small jewel encrusted crowns on their heads. After the white wedding with its beautiful music, Nell's elder sister acted as hostess and Matron of Honour at a reception paid for by Nell's parents at Claridges, one of London's most elegant hotels.

The wedding and the champagne reception were attended by leading Russian Orthodox dignitaries and Countess Yevgenia, resplendent in a magnificent hat. Several of the bridegroom's former army colleagues acted as ushers.

The *Brisbane Courier* ran a front page story headlined *London Society Wedding, Miss Nell Tritton bride of a Russian aristocrat.* They outlined the success of Tritton's department store and the bride's career as the first female journalist in Brisbane, and made the marriage sound like a Hollywood romance.

CHAPTER ELEVEN

Surviving a Difficult Marriage

Nell had married Nikolai blinded by love and sympathy for the fact he had lost his mother and everything he owned in the Russian Revolution and needed her help to create a new life.

Nikolai's father, General Nadejine, was ageing. Nell realised his failing eyesight meant he could not continue working as a taxi driver so she would use her own money to support him while they were in Australia. Nell had always been generous to a fault and felt guilty about her family's wealth when Nikolai and his father had nothing.

The honeymoon voyage her parents had given them as a wedding present had to be postponed as Nikolai had problems getting a passport. But this problem was finally resolved and the newly-weds spent several months staying with Nell's parents at *Elderslie*.

Miss Constance Harker and Miss Marjorie Jarrett, joint principals of Somerville House School, gave a tea party for their former pupil to meet her class-mates and the French teacher who had encouraged her to go to Paris and perfect her French.

On 6 May 1930, *The Brisbane Courier* wrote up the party for Nell at Somerville House describing Madame Nadejine wearing 'a stylish black dress with a white collar and cuffs by Coco Chanel, her favourite designer'. The journalist did not know Nell's husband was living on his wife's income when he claimed Nikolai was a successful opera singer or that Nikolai had failed to gain a contract as a result of any of the auditions Nell had worked so hard to secure for him.

Nell had based her ideas about a career as an opera singer on the success of Marie Bakshirtskeff when she had tried to become a singer. She failed to realise that this did not mean her husband would have the same success. Nikolai was one of many singers trying to enter the magic world of opera where a talent for acting as well as singing was required. Nell continued to believe her husband had talent and with her help would succeed.

By now Frederick Tritton had realised his new son-in-law was being supported financially by his daughter. Worried by the situation he organised a Brisbane recital for Nikolai and paid a large sum for the hire of His Majesty's Theatre for the night.

But tickets to a recital by an unknown singer proved hard to sell. Most were given away to friends and the 500 or so employees of Tritton's Department Store and their furniture factory. This ensured the recital was well attended. Nikolai received resounding applause when he sang his star piece *The Song of The Volga Boatmen,* a song with which many of his audience were familiar. After the recital, Nikolai was in a good mood, feeling it had been well advertised and well attended.

His mood changed when he discovered most of his audience were there on free tickets. Nikolai's pride suffered and he felt humiliated. At the reception following the recital he drank far too much. This was embarrassing for Nell and her parents. Later, when she tried to explain the situation Nikolai flew into a rage and refused to discuss it.

Nell's parents invited Captain Maximoff, a White Russian émigré to dinner. He arrived with his daughter who was supporting her elderly father by teaching German and Russian. Captain Maximoff approved of Nell and her interest in everything Russian and they talked at length. Later Captain Maximoff told his daughter he feared Nikolai lacked talent. He had come to the conclusion that Nikolai was a fortune hunter, playing on his bad experiences in the *gulag* to gain Nell's sympathy. It was ironic that Nell's father, Fred Tritton, had warned her about fortune hunters before she left for Paris.

The combination of Countess Yevgenia's devotion to Nikolai and his romantic past in St Petersburg had blinded Nell to the way Nikolai's character had been changed by the gruesome realities of the *gulag* where only the fittest survived.[26]

****

For the next three years the couple lived in Paris on money from Nell's family trust. Nikolai, who had been used to respect as a cavalry officer in Imperial Russia, had believed marriage to an Australian heiress would give him status as well as money. Accustomed to commanding soldiers, Nikolai wanted to be in charge of the household. He resented the fact his wife had money and he had to ask her to fund all major purchases.

Nell, who was trying to act as her husband's manager and publicist had little time to continue writing her spy novel with Nina.

Nell was convinced there must be an opera company who would

recognise Nikolai's talent. She took her husband to auditions with the managers of opera companies in Milan and Rome. She enjoyed entering the world of opera which she had read so much about in the journal of Marie Bakshirtskeff. She also enjoyed the excitement of attending first nights and learning about the works of various composers. But although learning a lot about opera, Nikolai was still not gaining any contracts from opera companies.[27]

Nell's generosity meant she paid all the housekeeping expenses and Nikolai's tuition fees to singing teachers. She bought her husband silk shirts and hand-tailored suits and paid for summer holidays on the Isle of Capri. Compton and Faith McKenzie were worried about the situation and they felt Nell was wasting her talent and putting her career on hold for a husband who seemed to be going nowhere.

Constant disappointments for Nikolai resulted in black rages interspersed with bouts of depression. In one of these he told Nell that being married to her was the only thing that prevented him from killing himself. His emotional blackmail had the desired effect of making Nell feel guilty. She felt she could never leave Nikolai no matter how difficult their marriage became.

When they returned to Paris from a summer holiday in Capri, Nell told Nina that at times she felt Nikolai was more like a problem child than a husband with his behaviour becoming increasingly challenging. But Nell had married for love and was determined to make a difficult marriage work. Nikolai did have a talent for singing Russian folk songs displaying a great deal of emotion and would probably have had success in Russia. Unfortunately French and Italian audiences did not want to listen to Russian songs. They wanted to hear Italian operas sung by Italians.

Nikolai's heavy drinking was taking its toll on Nell. She enjoyed a glass of wine with meals but had never drunk to excess. Many years later in her memoirs, *The Italics are Mine,* Nina was worried fearing as she had predicted, Nikolai had become 'far too fond of Nell's money and was taking advantage of her friend's generous nature'.

Nell's hopes for Nikolai's success were dashed on a short holiday in Milan when he failed to obtain a contract with one of the three important opera companies in that city.

Nell was missing home and family badly so she paid for another cruise to Australia. She was happy to see her family again and tried to hide the fact that her marriage was facing severe problems. Well-meaning relatives and school friends asked Nell if she was upset by not having children. Nell, aware that neither she nor Idie were likely to fall pregnant, told them that being childless was sad. However long ago doctors had warned her parents that she and her elder sister might have problems conceiving as a result of the lead poisoning. So she was resigned to the fact she could be childless. Her deceased brother Charles had given her parents grandchildren. Her younger brothers would no doubt marry and have children. The Tritton name would continue so she did not feel she had failed her parents by not providing them with grandchildren.

Elderslie and its wide verandahs photographed in 2016 by Jake de Vries.

On their return to Paris, bored and at a loose end, Nikolai once again drowned his sorrows drinking with fellow members of the ROVS and plotting how they could assassinate Stalin.

Nikolai loathed Stalin and called him an evil dictator. Nell, still interested in all things Russian learned from Nikolai that as a child Stalin had been savagely beaten by his father, a drunken cobbler. As a clever boy, his mother had gained Stalin a free education in a seminary and from the monks he acquired an appreciation of Russian poetry and literature Unfortunately his father's influence prevailed and in his twenties Stalin became a gang leader in Baku, the oil producing city and capital of Azerbaijan.

Stalin's gang ran protection rackets and robbed the safes of oil tankers, sending the money to the equally ruthless revolutionary, Vladimir Lenin, who was living in exile in Switzerland. The much younger Stalin believed in Lenin as a great leader who would eventually return to Russia, overturn the government and take control by force.[28]

Stalin finally came to power in 1924 after Lenin suffered a stroke, weakened by Fanny Kaplan's attempted assassination which had left him with bullets embedded in his neck and shoulders that could not be removed.

Upon the death of Lenin, Stalin expelled his former colleague and now rival Trotsky from Russia and took control. Trotsky and his wife fearing Stalin's vengeance sought refuge on a small island off the coast of Istanbul before continuing to Norway. In both countries they were initially welcomed but eventually expelled for plotting Marxist style revolution by organising general strikes by workers through their trade unions.

Trotsky eventually arrived in Paris where he lived under an assumed name. In Paris Stalin's secret police made several more attempts to assassinate or poison him but without success.

Nikolai and his friends at ROVS (the headquarters and social club for former Tsarist officers) detested both Stalin and Trotsky. They also loathed the former Russian Prime Minister, Alexander Kerensky and blamed all three of them for the loss of everything they had owned in Tsarist Russia.

Meanwhile unknown to the workers, Stalin and his cronies were living like Tsars in luxurious summer holiday villas in the warmth of the Crimea. When in Moscow, Stalin shut himself away in the safety of the Kremlin. He had a huge propaganda department devoted to praising everything he did complete with flattering photo opportunities. Stalin blackened the names of his political opponents, Trotsky and Kerensky with false allegations of cowardice and bribery.

The man-made famine in Ukraine known as the Holodomor was caused by Stalin's decision to confiscate the entire grain harvest of 1932. Stalin used the money from selling Ukrainian grain to fund a Russian arms industry and modernise Russia with factories built by slave labour from the *gulags*. Meanwhile over a million Ukrainians starved to death after their crops, their seed corn and their livestock were confiscated by Russian soldiers. The wheat that would have saved many Ukrainians from dying was held in gigantic silos in the Ukraine before being sent to Russia.

Stalin believed in assassination as a way of removing troublesome enemies in foreign countries. On his orders, a unit of the Russian secret police (the former Cheka now renamed the NKDV), had kidnapped the elderly General Kutepov on a Paris street. He was a friend of Nikolai's father. and died of a heart attack as he was dragged into a car by Russian secret agents.

His successor as head of ROVS, General Yevgeny Miller, was also targeted by Stalin's secret police, kidnapped, drugged, and smuggled aboard a Russian cargo ship in the French harbour of Le Havre. Nothing more was heard of General Miller for many years. Eventually news leaked out through Kerensky's Russian language newspaper, *The Days (DNI)*, that General Yevgeny Miller had been kidnapped, taken to Moscow, tortured by the Russian secret police and shot without trial.[29]

So many kidnappings of White Russians in the heart of the French capital prompted revenge killings of Soviet agents, masterminded by ROVS. As the street violence from Stalin's secret agents increased in Paris, Nikolai spent even more time at ROVS. To Nell's distress, Nikolai neglected work on his singing and spent his time drinking and plotting revenge with fellow officers.

In 1932 four years after Nell had married Nikolai, events came to a head. France's President Paul Doumer was assassinated by a Russian veteran named Captain Pavel Gorguloff, who had received a head injury in the Russian Civil War. Living outside Paris he was an occasional drinking companion of Nikolai and his army friends.

After his arrest, Captain Gorguloff publicly claimed he had killed the French President because he had done nothing for White Russian war veterans who had fought bravely with the French in World War One. There was great sympathy for Gorguloff among Nikolai's friends who organised a petition to save him from the guillotine, explaining that Captain Gorguloff had received a debilitating head injury in the war. Psychiatry was in its infancy, PTSD was unknown and he received no treatment. However his army colleagues' pleas were not enough to save Captain Gorguloff. He was tried, found guilty and executed. His final words reported in the French press were: 'Goodbye Russia, my beloved country'.

Nikolai was distraught on the day his former drinking companion died by the guillotine. He claimed the trial had been mishandled and reacted by drinking even more. Nell was so worried she arranged an appointment with a doctor who specialised in alcohol addiction but Nikolai refused to see him refusing to believe he had a problem.

The assassination of the French President led to demands for the expulsion of all Russian exiles in France. Anti-Russian slogans were daubed on the walls of the headquarters of ROVS where Nikolai and his army colleagues were drowning their sorrows with vodka.

When Nikolai returned to their apartment, Nell rebuked him for being drunk. Nikolai, his rage fuelled by alcohol, hit her hard across the face. Nell fled to her bedroom, locked the door and realised her marriage was in serious trouble.

The next day she issued an ultimatum, should Nikolai hit her again, it would be grounds for divorce. She visited a lawyer and was horrified to discover that in a male-dominated society, wives could not sue their husbands for divorce on grounds of cruelty. In the 1930s, the only grounds on which a wife could sue for divorce were those of adultery.

Nell, raised in a happy family, had not realised the complexities of ending a marriage by divorce. When Nikolai sobbed and begged Nell to forgive him, blaming his behaviour on the fact his friend had been guillotined, she relented and took him back hoping the situation would change. In an attempt to save her marriage, Nell's doctor suggested she take Nikolai on a holiday.

In the early summer of 1932 Nell chose to go to the place she loved, the Isle of Capri hoping that Nikolai would dry out on the island.[30] Nell did not want her friends Compton and Faith Mackenzie to see her problems with Nikolai, so instead of staying with them at the *Villa Solitaria* she rented another villa overlooking the sea.

Nell was fond of Faith Mackenzie who was almost like a second mother to her. She admired Compton as a novelist and historian, brilliant mimic, raconteur and a talented jazz piano player. The Mackenzies gave impromptu parties at the *Villa Solitaria* where they came to relax when Compton had finished work on his latest book. Compton Mackenzie had used Nell as a source when he wanted background information about Paris for his novels and the Mackenzies always visited Nell when passing through the French capital.

Nell knew that Compton had worked for MI6 in World War One, where he had been based in Athens. He was clearly the ideal person to look at her completed spy novel, *To Moscow With Love* as he was the author of several successful novels of espionage. He had previously told her he would read her novel, explain if anything needed changing and once she had done that, send the manuscript to his literary agent in London.

At a party at Compton and Faith's villa to celebrate the success of Compton's new book *Greek Memories* Nell left the completed typescript of the novel in a binder on Compton's desk, not wanting to discuss it at the party. *To Moscow with Love* had taken Nell years to write as Nina had little time to help her, busy working on her own biography of Tolstoy, and a book of short stories about Russian émigrés in Paris and nursing her poet husband, whose tuberculosis was getting worse.

For a week Nell did not see the Mackenzies at the beach or any of their favourite haunts. Desperate to know what Compton thought about her novel as there was no telephone in her rented villa Nell walked up the steep road to the *Villa Solitaria.* She brought a good bottle of a wine with her that she knew the Mackenzies would enjoy.

The door of the villa was opened by the local girl who cleaned for the Mackenzies. There was no sign of Faith. The maid showed Nell into Compton's office whereas usual he was at his desk. Instead of being relaxed and happy he was clearly stressed.

He welcomed Nell, apologising he had not contacted her sooner but there was a crisis – legal problems with *Greek Memories* – and he was leaving for London that afternoon to consult a barrister as he was about to be sued by the British Attorney General.

Nell was stunned by this news and asked what had happened. Compton said *Greek Memories* was now a banned book. All copies had to be withdrawn from sale or they would be destroyed by the police. He was being sued for contravening the Official Secrets Act and he could go to jail for as long as ten years or be fined up to a million pounds.

He said he had enjoyed Nell's spy novel, but it was too dangerous for a reputable publisher to handle. It would be clear to political journalists that Campbell-Boyd, Nell's fictitious Scottish hero was really Robert Bruce Lockhart. She had revealed details about the British Lockhart Plot that involved the proposed kidnapping and killing of Lenin. Exposure of the British Government's financial backing of this plot and the loss of so much money could lose them the next election.

Exposure of the rivalry between the MI6 and the Foreign Office had cost British taxpayers millions of pounds. The British Government would ensure that Nell's novel *To Moscow with Love* would never be published. The government would invoke the Official Secrets Act for which the punishment was imprisonment as they were doing to him with his spy novel *Greek Memories* which they felt revealed far too much about the ineptitude of MI6 and their government contacts. He had now realised that the legal cost of fighting his summons under the Official Secrets Act could bankrupt him unless he sold his beloved villa in Capri to retain a leading barrister and his team of solicitors.

Compton handed Nell the binder containing her typescript. He advised her to put it in a safe or burn it or it would get her into serious trouble. He showed her a letter from Cassells, his publishers. They had been notified by the Attorney-General, Sir Thomas Inskip, that he was to be prosecuted at the Old Bailey Criminal Court under the Official Secrets Act for revealing prohibited information.

In shock at Compton's disclosures Nell realised the novel she and Nina had been working on for many years would also be liable for prosecution under the Official Secrets Act so could not be published.

Nell knew Compton had headed an MI6 unit in Athens during the recent war against the Kaiser's Germany. King Constantine, married to a German princess, supported his German in-laws by refusing to let the British and French use Greek ports for shelter and refuel their warships. His novel *Greek Memories* had revealed the joint British and French plot to scare King Constantine of Greece so that he would help the British and French and give shelter to their warships as this was a war mainly waged at sea.

In *Greek Memories* Compton had unwisely named the real head of MI6, Captain Sir Mansfield Cumming (known as 'M'). Mansfield Cumming was furious and had invoked the Official Secrets Act, determined Compton would be jailed or fined so much money he would be bankrupted.

Nell's book was equally as serious as it exposed British Government incompetence in handing a bribe of a million pounds in gold bullion to the Soviets. She would also be tried at the Old Bailey in for contravening the Official Secrets Act, convicted and jailed without the possibility of an appeal. They could lock her up and throw away the key.

Compton was retaining a top barrister and a junior to defend him in court because the Attorney-General would be prosecuting him in person. Faith had been so distressed by the situation that she had been unable to sleep and was in bed with a migraine and regretted she would not be able to see Nell as they were departing on the night boat for the mainland and taking a train to London.

Nell remembered Faith telling her with pride how Compton, when serving as an army officer, had received medals from Britain, France, Greece and Serbia. He would be humiliated at being tried at the Old Bailey along with crooks and murderers and jailed. She felt enormously sorry for him and Faith and was scared at what could happen to her through her ignorance of the legal position regarding government secrets. Nina being a Russian citizen living in France was safe from persecution under The British Official Secrets Act.

Compton looked at his watch, and apologised he could not spend more time with Nell as he had to start packing to catch the night boat. Nell, horrified by what he had told her, was at a loss for what to say. She picked up her typescript, and assured them she would be thinking of them and hoped things would go well. She would see them in Paris in happier times.

The maid who had let her in had disappeared so Nell showed herself out, walked back to her rented villa and wrote a letter to Nina explaining why their spy novel could never be published.

When she was back in Paris, Nell consulted her lawyers. They made enquiries and learned that *Greek Memories* had been withdrawn from sale and removed by the police from British book shops and lending libraries. They offered the same advice as Compton Mackenzie. She should hide or burn the manuscript so that no one could find it. [31]

****

In August 1934 Nell returned to Australia to see her family. Once again Nikolai had told her that he felt suicidal and she made another attempt to kick-start her husband's operatic career in Sydney and Melbourne.

On 23 August, soon after their arrival in Sydney, Nell arranged interviews for herself and Nikolai with *The Sydney Morning Herald* and *The Canberra Times*, in which Nell praised her husband's voice. Nell hired a Sydney concert hall for Nikolai's recital, but once again, ticket sales were poor and Nikolai's performance disappointed the critics.

Nikolai felt humiliated and drank too much. This led to a bitter row, after which he sulked and refused to speak to Nell for days.

From Sydney they travelled by train to Melbourne, where Nell had rented an apartment at the Paris end of Collins Street. She hoped that her husband would be more successful there than he had been in Sydney. At a press conference, acting as Nikolai's publicity manager, Nell told the press if her husband received a contract they would consider moving to Melbourne. But unfortunately there was no interest and no contract.

During a visit to Nell's parents at *Elderslie,* they gave a party to celebrate their arrival in Australia. At the party, feeling he had been a failure at his recitals in Melbourne and Sydney, Nikolai boosted his damaged ego by flirting with other women. Nell could see her parents were worried that Nikolai was drinking heavily but by now she was tired of defending him. She finally admitted the truth to her parents that her love match was failing.

After a long discussion about her options Nell decided it would be wiser to move to London rather than Paris for two reasons. Nikolai had been turned down by the opera houses in France and Italy and the only major opera house he had not tried so far was London's Covent Garden Opera Company.

There was also the fact that if she decided to brave the scandal of a divorce, obtaining one would be much easier in England than in a Catholic country like France.

CHAPTER TWELVE

Divorce & Helping Jewish Victims of Hitler

My soul is Jewish, my heart Russian, my passport British.
Flora Benenson Solomon, OBE, Russian-Jewish philanthropist

In spite of reservations about her marriage, Nell made one last effort to help her husband by obtaining him an audition at London's Covent Garden one of the world's greatest opera companies. She believed Nikolai had been badly treated by the Russians and still wanted to help him. But his heavy drinking and wild rages were becoming intolerable.

Covent Garden was the only big opera company Nell had not yet contacted. So in spite of the additional expense they moved to London where Nell rented a serviced apartment in Mayfair so that Nikolai sounded successful. In order to get a good night's sleep because Nikolai snored heavily, Nell insisted he slept in the spare room which he resented.

Using a letter of introduction to a titled friend of the late Nellie Melba (which Nell had obtained years earlier), Nell wrote to Melba's friend who was a member of the powerful Covent Garden Opera Board. Nell explained that her husband had suffered badly in Communist Russia and was recovering. He had a beautiful baritone voice and she hoped he might be given an audition for a part in a future Covent Garden production. Could she help?

Melba's friend replied a few days later that she was recently widowed and had spare complementary tickets for several first night performances. She suggested Nikolai act as her escort to the opera and post-performance parties and she would introduce him to producers who might agree to audition him.

Nell wrote back expressing her thanks.

Handsome in evening dress and a gleaming white evening shirt Nikolai was collected by Melba's widowed friend in a taxi. He stayed out all night, did not phone and did not re-appear until mid-morning with a hangover. Nell's angry questions as to where he had spent the night sparked another row.

The next time her husband escorted the titled lady to the first night of a new opera at Covent Garden he stayed away for two days and nights and did not contact Nell.

By now she had had enough. It was obvious Nikolai was having an affair with Melba's friend. She consulted lawyers who warned her that in Britain divorce laws were weighted against wives. To gain a divorce she would need to prove cruelty as well as adultery and they advised it was easier to obtain a divorce in England than in Catholic France. If she were to divorce her husband it would be expensive. She would need witness statements and photos to confirm he had committed adultery. These complex divorce laws were unfair to wives seeking a divorce and were under review but it would take a long time for the review committee to publish their findings.

Nell remembered reading *Bleak House* in which Dickens observed 'the one great business of law is to make business for itself'. She realised reform of divorce laws would be slow. All she could do was fulfill the complex requirements and obtain a witness report and photos to prove that her husband had committed adultery. She must appear in person at the hearing and not be seen in public with any eligible men or her husband could counter-sue. She might have to pay him damages and share the money remaining in her family trust with her unfaithful husband. As a feminist Nell was angry at how the law treated women and felt powerless as the law was weighted against wives.[32]

Fortunately Nell still had the two halves of a pearl necklace Nikolai had torn off her neck in a drunken rage as evidence. Her lawyers agreed to hire a private detective to follow her husband and produce evidence of adultery. They also advised that should her husband turn violent she should photograph any bruises or damage to property that resulted.

A few weeks later the detective reported he had followed Nikolai and the titled lady to the Dorchester Hotel on Park Lane where they went to a room on the fourth floor. He paid a chambermaid to open their bedroom door with her pass key and quickly snapped photographs of Nikolai and the titled lady in bed together.

The chambermaid and the detective signed the required witness statements and the detective obtained a photograph of the relevant page of the hotel register in which Nikolai and his lady friend were booked in under false names. It had cost money but Nell now had sufficient evidence for any judge to grant a divorce.

From the photographs Nell saw Melba's friend was years older than Nikolai. Nell didn't know whether to laugh or cry. She remembered their traditional Russian wedding when she had felt she was marrying a prince. And now the prince was the toy-boy of an elderly woman in exchange for the promise of a part in an opera.

Five years ago the press ran a story about her wedding under the headline *A Fairytale Russian Wedding for an Australian Heiress.* Unfortunately the fairytale had turned into a nightmare.

Nell had mistakenly believed that love could change Nikolai's attitude to life and undue the psychological damage he suffered in the *gulag*. Psychologists told her to face reality. Their marriage had become untenable, causing misery and costing her a lot of money. The lawyers were right. Divorce really was the only solution.

Nell was told her petition for divorce would be heard by a judge at the Old Bailey Criminal Court on Fleet Street which dealt with cases in central London. Divorce was still viewed as a crime in the early 1930s when there were no such things as family law courts.

The Old Bailey, London's main criminal court in which Nell dreaded having to face cross examination about intimate aspects of her marriage to obtain her divorce. (Photograph David Castor)

Nell had heard about the Old Bailey, where, a century earlier, convicts were sentenced to transportation to Australia. She had avoided appearing there by not publishing her spy novel but if she wanted to divorce her husband she would have to appear in the witness box to answer probing questions about her sex life. She hated the thought of doing this in open court and any subsequent newspaper publicity in the gutter press. But it was time to end this marriage no matter the cost.

She was told waiting time for a hearing at the Old Bailey Criminal Court varied between a year and eighteen months. She had to present her divorce petition in person and answer any questions the judge put to her no matter how embarrassing. Self-pity was no good, Nell told herself. She had got herself into this mess: she had to get herself out of it.

There was no word from Nikolai but she presumed he was living with the widowed friend of the late Dame Nellie Melba. Nell packed the clothes and personal belongings she had bought him into suitcases and did as her lawyers advised, adding a note giving the lawyer's address saying all queries should be addressed to them.

She entrusted the suitcases to the concierge and employed a locksmith to change the lock on her front door. Her lawyer suggested she move as in other cases he had dealt with where the husband was losing a comfortable way of life, wives had faced threats of renewed violence or even murder. Leaving no forwarding address and staying with friends or relatives was the wisest solution.

Fortunately at this juncture Nell received an offer of hospitality from a Russian friend. Ruth Shapiro, the widow of a Jewish banker, was a fellow member of a small group of enthusiasts who attended first nights at Sadler's Wells ballet, supporting the former prima ballerina, Ninette de Valois in her efforts to establish London's first ballet company.

On learning that Nell had initiated divorce proceedings and had no relatives in London to support her, Ruth was sympathetic and invited Nell to stay in her beautiful home on Abingdon Road just off Kensington High Street.

Ruth Schapiro had a security system and a resident housekeeper so Nell would be safe. Ruth's only son was away for a year working for an American bank. Ruth said she would be delighted to have Nell's company as a guest as she was lonely and she might like to assist with some of her work on behalf of Jewish charities.

Nell gave up the lease on the Mayfair apartment and moved to Abingdon Road, known locally as Millionaire's Row. Ruth was kindness itself, took Nell under her wing and treated her like the daughter she had never had.

Nell received a letter from Faith Mackenzie telling her that Nikolai was living on the Isle of Capri and acting as caretaker at his lady friend's holiday villa. Nell prayed he would remain there and never come back.

At a dinner party given by Ruth, Nell found herself at the opposite end of the table to her hostess, in the place Ruth's son used to occupy. She was seated between a balding man with a small Van Dyck beard and a Russian accent named Chaim Weizmann and a large Jewish lady with flaming red hair who also spoke with a Russian accent.

Chaim Weizmann had twinkling eyes and an avuncular manner which made him look more like a kindly Father Christmas rather than one of the world's leading scientists and the President of Britain's Zionist Association.

As a journalist Nell had been fascinated by Chaim's rags-to-riches story, told her by Ruth, his neighbour. Chaim, who lived only a few doors away on Abingdon Road was happy to answer Nell's questions. He had been the eldest in a family of fourteen children, their father a wood-cutter, living in a poverty-stricken Jewish settlement in Belarus in the 1870s, a period of intense persecution of Jews after Tsar Alexander II, the Tsar who had freed the serfs, was assassinated after false rumours had circulated that his assassin was Jewish.

In retribution, the Tsar's heir, who later ruled as Tsar Alexander III instituted even harsher laws against Jews. They were herded like cattle into special settlements or *shtetls* from which the penalty for escaping was death. Ruth explained to Nell how from the 1870s to the start of World War One almost a million Russian Jews managed to bribe their way out of Yiddish speaking *shtetls* (Jewish villages) and escape to New York or London.

Chaim's father remained in the poverty-stricken *shtetl* in Belarus with a lack of basic amenities such as proper roads or sanitation. Chaim had been fortunate to attend a *yeshiva* or Jewish school run by a *rabbi* who nurtured his passion for science. Attendance at university was denied to Russians because the Romanovs believed the Jews had killed Christ, so their descendants deserved to be punished. Supported by this *rabbi,* the young Chaim Weizmann won a scholarship to the University of Geneva and studied chemistry to post graduate level.

By the onset of World War One Chaim was working in a university laboratory in Britain, developing a new method of manufacturing cordite, the replacement for gunpowder in armaments. In wartime cordite was scarce but vital for the British army to defeat the armies of the Kaiser.

Due to Chaim Weizmann's invention of a new method of manufacturing cordite, War Minister Winston Churchill became his friend and supporter. Chaim eventually established his own chain of laboratories all over Britain making more important discoveries. He donated large sums of money to educate the children of Jewish refugees and vowed once the Jews had their own homeland, he would endow a university there.

Nell now understood why Ruth Schapiro and her Zionist friend believed Chaim Weizmann should be Israel's first Prime Minister when they were finally able to establish their own homeland.

Seated on Nell's other side was tall, plump red-headed Flora Benenson Solomon, another leading Zionist, daughter of a wealthy Russian Jewish banker and property developer in New York. Ruth had told her Flora was widowed with a young son and was doing wonderful work helping Jewish families who had been persecuted in Nazi Germany, lost everything and fled to England.

Nell would have liked to have asked Flora Solomon about this but the older woman ignored Nell's attempts to open a conversation, doubtless thinking Nell was a colonial nonentity. For the rest of the meal she ignored Nell and concentrated on talking to her other neighbour. Chaim Weizmann explained he was an Israeli Cabinet Minister and Flora Solomon was using this as an opportunity to put the case for the government providing these fugitives from Nazi Germany with some financial support.

Nell spent an enjoyable evening talking and laughing with Chaim and Vera, his French wife, who invited her to lunch at their home the following week. Nell was delighted to accept.

A few days later, to her surprise, Nell received an invitation to a party at the home of Flora Solomon in nearby Hornton Street. Nell, put off by Flora's previous rudeness, hesitated before accepting.

Ruth persuaded Nell to accompany her to Flora's party, claiming that under her brusque manner she was a very generous woman. Flora was doing wonderful work financing Jewish families who had fled from persecution in Nazi Germany.

At the party in her Kensington home, Flora talked about wealthy German Jews forced to flee from persecution under Hitler's National Socialist government, known as Nazis. Hitler hated Jewish bankers, and placed Jewish companies under German control. Jewish children were forbidden to attend school or university. Hitler robbed Jews of their possessions and their livelihoods and then charged them an exorbitant sum for exit visas so that once prosperous families left Germany almost destitute. Flora believed Hitler was using the money he had stolen to build armaments factories as he was preparing for another war.

The British Government had refused to help Jewish families who had lost everything they owned so they were reduced to living in the East End slums as the docks were London's cheapest area. Entire families lived in rented rooms in squalid tenements blocks with a shared lavatory and one cold tap to each floor.

Thanks to Flora and her Jewish charity, many Jewish families were able to move from the London docks to more comfortable areas like Golders Green or Hampstead where their children would receive a far better education in government schools. These children were clever and hard-working and knew their best hope lay in a good education. They would go on to benefit Britain by becoming leading doctors, lawyers, architects and musicians.

Flora made a short speech and explained how more funds were needed as Hitler was stepping up his campaign against Jews. Nell was moved by her eloquence. She remembered what her parents had done at the Brisbane children's home and how well some of the children had done. At the end of Flora's talk Nell put up her hand to show she would sponsor a Jewish family, pay for their move from London's East End to better accommodation and obtain school uniforms and text books for their children.

Flora thanked Nell for her generous donation. As Ruth had told Flora Nell was a journalist, she asked if she could spare some time to help with the work of raising funds to help more Jewish refugees who were arriving in London from Nazi Germany.

Nell was taken aback by Flora's request. She saw her as a complex opinionated woman and was wary of her. But living in Ruth's house with no household duties she had plenty of free time. To please Ruth, Nell found herself agreeing to help Flora. She realised Ruth must have told Flora she had a private income which explained why she had been invited to this fund-raising party.

Over the next few months, Nell and Flora were thrown together as Nell worked at Flora's home in attractive Hornton Street in Kensington. Flora always provided an excellent free lunch for those who volunteered to work for her charity. Nell often sat at the same table as Flora and they talked about their respective childhoods. Flora, who had spent her first six years in a *shtetl* or Jewish village in Belarus, was interested in Nell's Australian childhood. Flora was interested in Australia because she said it was a country that valued personal freedom unlike Russia.

Nell believed Flora to be much older and was surprised to find the difference in their ages to be only four years. While Nell dressed stylishly, Flora wore matronly clothes. Considering Flora was wealthy and highly intelligent, Nell was surprised she was not more stylishly dressed but knew that someone with Flora's domineering personality would never accept fashion advice.

Flora appreciated Nell as a hard and reliable worker. When other volunteers dropped out, Flora came to depend on her Australian protégé. From shared conversations over lunch at Flora's home it was clear to Nell that Flora's personality was the result of a loveless childhood and adolescence.

Over many months Nell pieced together Flora's story She had been born in a Jewish *shtetl* or isolated village in Belarus. She had spent her early years in wooden huts with inadequate sanitation and the threat of night time attacks by Russian thugs. They beat up the unarmed Jewish owners, robbed their homes and often set fire to them, often encouraged by rogue members of the Tsarist police who took a share of whatever the thugs had plundered.

Grigori Benenson, Flora's father had started work chopping down trees in the vast forests of Belarus. But Flora's father was clever and ambitious and determined to leave the poverty-stricken *shtetl*. As a hard worker, he made money from the huge trees he felled, arranging to raft them down the Dnieper River, and sell them at a good profit to shipyards. Grigori Benenson used his money to bribe the Tsar's secret police to allow him to leave the *shtetl* to which by law the Jews were confined.

At the age of six, Flora and her parents escaped illegally from the *shtetl* and travelled third class in an uncomfortable, crowded train to Baku, in far distant Azerbaijan, a journey which took three days. Their train lacked washing facilities or a restaurant car. Flora described peasants they saw at each station with baskets of baked goods selling them to passengers at inflated prices.

The oil-rich sub-tropical capital of Baku was unlike most parts of the vast Russian empire in not persecuting Jews. Instead Baku welcomed Jews as hard workers and potential investors in the oil fields. Flora's father used what remained of his savings to buy a small plot of land at a government auction, praying it would contain oil. He employed local labour and helped them build a wooden tower to house a drilling rig.

At Baku tall wooden towers like these were built by Grigori Benenson to house his oil rigs and drills. They struck oil and made him very wealthy. (inset) Flora's father after his angry mistress threw acid in his face.

The Benenson building in the centre of New York, 1920. Flora had crossed the Atlantic to celebrate her father's purchase of this building when she first heard Kerensky speak before a large audience. Flora invited Kerensky to the Plaza Hotel and became his benefactor and (unknown to Nell) his secret lover.

Widowed Flora Benenson Solomon, daughter of Grigori Benenson, a wealthy Russian American businessman, used family money to help fellow Jews. Peter Benenson Flora's only child would grow up to become a lawyer and the founder of Amnesty International.

Grigori Berenson's prayers were answered when his drilling rig gushed oil. He sold the oil and re-invested the money in more oil-bearing land. Within two years, he was no longer a poor migrant but an enormously wealthy oil tycoon like the Rothschilds, the Gulbenkians and the Nobel brothers, who had made their fortunes in Baku, the Russian equivalent of Texas.

Flora's father bought his family a luxurious penthouse overlooking the Caspian Sea and employed a butler, several maids and a French governess for Flora. Her mother gave birth to two more daughters and enjoyed her social life among the wives of Baku's oil-rich barons. Sonia Benenson, Flora's mother doted on Flora's younger sisters who were petite, dark haired and pretty but had little time for gawky, red-headed Flora. She said that her height and heavy build, would make it hard to find a suitable husband when the time came.

When Flora turned thirteen, Grigori Benenson sold his Baku oil wells for a huge profit and moved his family to an elegant riverside apartment in St Petersburg, capital of Tsarist Russia. Flora's father invested in Siberian gold mines and founded Benenson's Bank, banking being the only profession open to Jews in Tsarist Russia other than money-lending.

Flora, virtually ignored by her socialite mother, rarely saw her workaholic father and was raised by a French governess. At sixteen, Flora spoke fluent French as her first language, at a time when all educated Russians conversed in French and only spoke Russian to their house servants, gardeners and the farm labourers on their estates.

At seventeen Flora was sent to a finishing school in Leipzig where she learned to speak fluent German and the social skills necessary to marry a wealthy man and entertain for him.

Flora was shocked to learn from the press the sensational story of an acid attack that blinded her father. It had been carried out not by an anarchist but by her father's mistress, a former prima ballerina of St Petersburg State ballet, of whose existence Flora and the rest of his family, including his wife, were ignorant.

The ballerina had been given an elegant apartment in St Petersburg when she bore Grigori Benenson a much wanted son. Aware he was now one of Russia's wealthiest businessmen the mistress had hoped that he would divorce his wife, marry her and legalise their child. When it became clear Grigori Benenson had no intention of doing this. the mistress, seething with rage that her career as a prima ballerina was over, plotted revenge.

For her lover's fiftieth birthday, she sent him a note saying she wanted to celebrate his birthday with him and give him his present. He invited her to join him on a train journey to Moscow with an entire First Class compartment reserved for them. She presented Grigori Benenson with a box of his favourite chocolates. As he bent down to select a chocolate, she withdrew a small bottle of sulphuric acid from her ermine muff and threw the disfiguring acid into his face.

Grigori Benenson's agonised screams were heard by the occupants of the neighbouring compartment who called for a doctor. The train was halted, an ambulance summoned and the mistress removed by the police. In spite of his horrific injuries, Flora's father did not pursue the matter as a court case as it would have meant bad publicity for

Benenson's Bank. The vengeful mistress escaped charges.

To avoid the scandal of divorce, Sonia Benenson, Flora's mother, had lawyers negotiate an enormous financial settlement and left Russia for California with their two youngest daughters. Flora, the daughter her mother disliked was still at finishing school in Germany and she never saw her mother again.

In the last letter Flora received from her mother, Sophie Benenson without a hint of regret told her eighteen year-old daughter she was expected to take care of her father, now blind in both eyes and with a badly scarred face as the result of the acid attack.

Flora duly returned to St Petersburg, engaged a team of nurses to care for her father, ran the household and fended off invasive journalists. Once her father was well enough to travel, Flora took him to Germany where facial surgery was more advanced than in Russia. A leading eye surgeon partially restored her father's sight while a cosmetic surgeon removed many of the scars. However, one of his eyelids still obscured part of his eye and this damage could not be repaired.

A decade later, Flora's entrepreneurial father went to New York to establish and run an American branch of Benenson's Bank while Flora remained in Germany to complete her studies.

In 1914, the Kaiser's armies invaded Belgium hoping to capture Paris, an aim they did not achieve. Studying in Germany, Russian-born Flora found herself classified as an enemy alien. Fearing she would be sent to an internment camp. Flora sewed all the money she had into the lining of her skirt, caught the last train for France and boarded the channel ferry for England, a country where she knew no one and did not speak the language.

Alone in London, lacking family or friends, Flora confronted life bravely and learned to speak English but with a strong Russian accent she never lost. With little contact from her father who was now establishing himself in New York as a property developer, she became an unpaid nursing aide and lived in a hostel for trainee nurses. Lonely Flora was befriended by a Jewish nurse and invited to her home for Sunday lunch.

Mrs Solomon, her friend's mother, knew Flora was the daughter of the multi-millionaire owner of Benenson's Bank. Flora was living on very little money but Mrs Solomon knew that her dowry and future inheritance made her an attractive match for her only son, a confirmed bachelor many years older than Flora and devoted to his army career.

The scheming Mrs Solomon organised tickets for the popular musical *Chu Chin Chow,* and told her son to take Flora out for a romantic dinner.

When Nell was working for Flora in London, Flora confided to Nell how she had been dazzled when Brigadier Harold Solomon arrived at the nurse's hostel resplendent in army uniform and medals. After the show, rather than a romantic restaurant, he had taken Flora to dine at his favourite haunt, the Naval and Military Club. There, surrounded by intimidating portraits of generals and admirals, he regaled Flora with stories of his war exploits and tedious details of campaign strategies she found incomprehensible.

This was Flora's first date and sent to an all-female finishing school and with no brothers, she had no experience of men or what they might want. Told by her mother that with her red hair and frumpy frame she would be lucky to find a husband, she was flattered at being courted by a much older man whom she saw as a war hero.

The disparate pair exchanged letters and met whenever Brigadier Solomon came home on leave. These evening outings were often chaperoned by the scheming Mrs Solomon. Flora became a frequent visitor to the Solomon's home at weekends where it was taken for granted the couple would marry once the war ended although they scarcely knew each other and were rarely alone.

Before the war Brigadier Solomon's father had been a successful London stockbroker. During the war, few clients invested in stocks and shares so stockbrokers' incomes were greatly reduced. Mrs Solomon saw her son's marriage to the daughter of a billionaire as the family's salvation. From Grigori Benenson, the Solomons demanded a huge dowry in addition to paying for an expensive wedding. Grigori was shocked. However, he was pleased that a man of means from a respectable Jewish family wanted to marry the plainest of his daughters so paid the enormous dowry the Solomons were asking.

Flora finally admitted to her Australian protégé she had been so thrilled by the idea of getting married she failed to see that her father's money had been the reason for the marriage.

Her first year of married life was spent in Palestine. Her husband, promoted to Brigadier-General Solomon, was serving as a senior member of the British High Commission to Palestine.

In contrast Flora, the dedicated Zionist, was an outspoken supporter of the plan to establish a Jewish homeland in Palestine. This caused conflict in Flora's marriage when her husband discovered his young bride was not as submissive as he had expected. Their sex life was a disappointment to Flora and even the birth of Peter, their only child who Flora adored, could not heal the couple's differences.

After the Balfour Declaration encouraged Jews to regard Palestine as their homeland, there was anguish among Zionists when several shiploads of Jewish refugees were refused permission by the Palestinians and the British to land in Palestine. This became a running topic of contention between Flora and her husband who was heading the British administration of Palestine.

On their return to London, Flora's husband rejoined his family's stockbroking firm. Without consulting her, he used Flora's dowry to buy a large house in Hornton Street, Kensington near his parents when she wanted to live among her Russian-Jewish friends in Hampstead.

Living in Kensington, Flora became friends with fellow Zionist, Ruth Shapiro. The fraught relationship between Flora and her husband led to talk of divorce. However, this became impossible when Harold Solomon injured his spine in a riding accident and was left semi-paralysed.

Flora installed a lift in their home and engaged nurses to care for him round the clock, but from then on they lived separate lives. Her husband consoled himself by spending a great deal of time with Peter, their young son, and by falling in love and developing a romantic relationship with his young nurse.

Flora's life revolved around Peter and the Jewish charities to which she devoted her time and her money.

In February 1929, Harold died from a heart attack. Flora inherited his assets including what remained of her dowry. By now she was a dedicated feminist and declared she had no intention of marrying again as she did not want another husband controlling her money.

At one of their lunches, she told Nell the brutal truth. It was a good thing Nell was divorcing Nikolai after wasting five years and so much of her money on supporting a self-centred violent alcoholic who had repaid none of her kindness.

Nell realised that Flora was speaking the truth. She had been through a harrowing experience in the witness box but had gained a divorce at the end of 1935. Nell knew that stories about her divorce in the Australian press had caused scandal. As Australia was more conservative than Britain it would be very difficult for Nell to return to Brisbane as a divorcee so she resolved to remain in Europe.

Nell's divorce brought a sense of relief tinged with sadness as she had expected so much happiness from her marriage. With her unhappy experience of marriage Flora had a very different approach to divorce and held a lunch to celebrate Nell's newly-won freedom. She gave Nell a copy of Virginia Wolfe's recently published A *Room of One's Own,* in which the ultra-feminist author argued that women would never gain control over their lives until they controlled their own money. Nell read Virginia Woolf's book and took it to heart.

Nell, at first despised by Flora as an Australian social butterfly became Flora's right-hand person. She helped Flora organise fund-raising lunches and dinners in expensive hotels like the Savoy, Grosvenor House and the Dorchester. Together they raised large sums to help destitute Jewish families in the East End of London from whom Hitler's government had confiscated every valuable asset, then charged them exorbitant sums to buy exit visas to leave Nazi Germany.

Having visited the East End with Flora and seen the squalid tenements which was all the destitute Jews could afford, Nell was glad she had been able to help them create better lives for their families.

Flora told Nell they must prepare for a larger influx of Jewish refugees as Hitler was building a series of concentration camps and it was important to get as many Jews out of Germany as soon as possible. Due to the 1929 stock market crash and the subsequent recession, America had reduced the number of Jews it would accept. As a result, many more Ashkenazi and German Jews were coming to Britain and France.

Nell had mentioned to Flora that once her divorce was finalised, she planned to return to Paris where she had been happy before her disastrous marriage and would seek work helping those in trouble. The money was not important but she wanted to continue making a difference to those in need.

Flora said that she knew of a job in Paris for which Nell would be ideally suited. She told Nell she was one of several financial supporters of Alexander Kerensky, Russia's first democratic Prime Minister, now in exile in Paris after being deposed by Lenin. Kerensky believed in the importance of freedom and hoped that the tyrannical Stalin would be deposed and Russia would be able to hold elections and become a democracy.

Flora explained that Kerensky was launching a new anti-Communist newspaper in Paris called *Novaia Rossiia, (The New Russia),* Kerensky's fortnightly publication would have a literary section as well as a large section on current affairs. The first issue was due out in the first week in March 1936 before Kerensky made an American tour to promote his book, *The Crucifixion of Liberty.* He spoke fluent French and German but very little English and needed an English translator who could act as his driver if required.

Nell said driving was no problem. Her family was car mad and she and her older brother used to enter car rallies together winning several prizes.

Flora had loaned Nell a copy of the English translation and Nell thought Kerensky wrote well. He described how Lenin had convinced the masses to rebel against Kerensky's Provisional Government with false promises he could never keep. It also related Kerensky's harrowing escape from Russia after Lenin put a price on his head.

Nell thought a job assisting Kerensky sounded interesting. Flora had warned that Kerensky was impractical but brilliant, an idealist devoted to the idea of freedom for people worldwide. Nell agreed to be interviewed by Kerensky in Paris the following week as the need for a translator was urgent.

Kerensky cleverly evaded Stalin's strict censorship of foreign news by arranging with the Scandinavian merchant seamen who had brought him from Russia to England to smuggle reports from his supporters inside Russia for his new publication. He wanted to keep alive the spirit of Russia and fight for freedom and democracy, the struggle to which he had devoted much of his eventful life.

Flora briefly introduced Nell to Kerensky at a party she gave for Russian expatriates to meet Russia's Prime Minister in exile.

Nell shook Kerensky's hand and noticed that although not regularly handsome by Hollywood standards, he had magnetic blue eyes and a strong stage presence derived from his acting days. Kerensky, at Flora's request, gave a short speech in which it was obvious his whole life was dedicated to the pursuit of freedom. He denounced Russia and Germany where he claimed dictators like Stalin and Hitler were destroying the lives of innocent people. Kerensky talked about his dream for his beloved Motherland when Russia would become a democracy with elections and candidates from various parties rather than hand-picked by a dictator. Kerensky's dream was for *Noviaii Rossia,* a new Russia with no secret police, no slave labour camps for political dissidents and writers who wrote the truth. He also wanted Stalin to abolish the death penalty, the enormous secret police and execution without trial.

Nell had no chance to speak to Kerensky as he was surrounded by excited Russians wanting his attention and had to return to Paris the following morning. She felt she would be able to ask questions when Kerensky interviewed her in Paris the following week.

Flora had assumed that when working for Kerensky her young Australian protégé and former assistant would mix with friends of her own age. She believed that an attractive vivacious young woman like Nell would soon find a lover or a second husband among her literary and ballet loving friends. It never occurred to Flora that Nell and Kerensky would be attracted to each other.

Flora was one of Kerensky's main financial backers for New Russia, his newspaper, but no one guessed that for years they had been secret lovers. They met only when their work schedules coincided or had an occasional holiday boating and fishing in a remote village on the French side of Lake Annecy where no one recognised them.

On his various speaking tours in America when Kerensky was promoting his books and his hopes for a new and free Russia, some women, carried away by his eloquence were determined to spend the night with him, the kind of treatment pop stars receive today. Kerensky who was separated from his wife in a marriage that had no hope of repair was famous for his success with women, something he refused to discuss with the press.

Three decades later in a frank memoir, *From Baku to Baker Street,* published the year before she died, Flora admitted she and Kerensky had been lovers on and off since they met in New York's Plaza Hotel in 1927. This loose relationship suited Flora who had made an arranged marriage with a husband who controlled her fortune and she had no wish to repeat the experience.

Years later Flora would tell her adult son, Peter Benenson, she had been naïve to believe Nell and Kerensky would have very little in common or she would never have recommended Nell to work for him.

In her memoir published when Flora was in her eighties she admitted the truth and said that before Kerensky met Nell they had shared a deep intellectual bond. She saw herself as 'Kerensky's kindred spirit and spiritual wife' and in old age admitted Kerensky had been a wonderful lover who had made up for the mediocre sex life she had experienced with her husband.

Nell, like many expat Russians was totally unaware of Flora's hidden relationship with Kerensky when she was interviewed by him in Paris in the first week in January 1936.

Flora had warned that Kerensky and Trotsky now headed a long hit list of Stalin's enemies. She was surprised that, married to a Russian for five years Nell knew so little about the history of the Russian revolution and Kerensky's role in it. She said she would get a historian friend to write a brief history or dossier on Kerensky's life and Flora's secretary would type it. Nell should read it on the train before she met Kerensky as she would need some background to understand the complex world of Russian and French politics she would be entering.

She warned that Kerensky had received several death threats from Stalin's secret police who had attempted to poison and shoot him in Paris. Living in danger of assassination Kerensky would only employ staff recommended by close friends. But Nell must not worry, she and his other backers had ensured the security provisions were good. Kerensky's combined office and living accommodation in Passy had barred windows and double locks on the doors. A 24-hour rota of armed guards from a security company cost them a lot of money but was worthwhile.

Nell realised that the fact she had family money and was willing to work for less than the going rate for a bi-lingual journalist might be one reason Kerensky was interested in employing her. The fact she had been so wrong about Nikolai had made Nell extremely cautious.

She wrote to Nina asking for information about Kerensky, aware Nina had known Kerensky in Berlin in 1922 when he ran an anti-Communist newspaper just as the Bolsheviks had changed their name to Communists.

Nina's reply to Nell's letter was prompt. She described Kerensky as a man of integrity, occupied with writing his books and making speaking tours to promote them. The Americans loved him as he promoted freedom and democracy, their core values. He was a hard worker, rose early, rarely took time off and expected the same commitment from members of his staff.

Nina warned that, as a former Prime Minister and Minister for War, Kerensky was used to ordering staff around and barking commands at them. He would not be easy to work for. He was volatile but inspired enormous loyalty among his supporters. He loved literature and classical music, knew many world leaders personally and Nell would learn a great deal about world politics if she took the job.

He could be very charming and enjoyed the company of intelligent women but Nell should be careful. In Berlin when Nina knew him he was separated from his Russian wife but was never alone for long and many of his girlfriends had been intelligent and attractive and tried to get him to divorce his wife and marry them but never succeeded. His charm was legendary so Nell should avoid staying late at work unless another woman was in the office or it could lead to disaster.

Nina said Nell needed a stable marriage in which her talents for writing and languages could flourish. For herself she hoped to become a literary writer and when she had published enough papers, obtain a tenured post at an American university lecturing on Russian literature.

Nina was delighted Nell was returning to Paris but would not be in Paris for long as she had plans to move to rural France. They would talk about future plans when they met. She said they had had their differences when she worked for Kerensky in Berlin, but admired him for taking up the cause of Jews persecuted in Russia when he did not have a drop of Jewish blood in his veins.

Nell read Nina's letter several times. The idea of working for liberty was heart warming but clearly Kerensky was not an easy man to work for. Nell reassured herself that she was now a bi-lingual journalist and she could always find work as Paris correspondent for an English, American, Australian or Canadian newspaper, should Kerensky prove a difficult employer.

The day before Nell left for Paris, she ate a farewell lunch with Flora. She brought a bottle of French champagne and was pleased Flora had gone to the trouble of commissioning a dossier on Kerensky of which she was to receive a typed copy.

Flora sat next to Nell at lunch and told her she and Kerensky's other backers had bought a new printing press so *The New Russia* would have a more modern typeface than *Dni,* his previous Russian language publication. The new and very expensive machine was now installed in the basement of the apartment in the rue Vineuse where Kerensky lived as well as ran the newspaper with the aid of a Russian secretary and free lance correspondents.

Flora warned Nell she would have to pass a security guard to enter Kerensky's office for her interview. She must take her passport so the security guard at the door could identify her and Flora told her of Stalin's most recent attempt to kill Kerensky. A Mercedes had pulled alongside Kerensky's Citroen at the traffic lights. His security guard who acted as his chauffeur on the rare occasions he left his office had seen a machine gun protruding from the window waiting to pump bullets into Kerensky. Fortunately the French police had also seen the machine gun and arrested the Russian gunman.

After several glasses of champagne Flora became expansive telling Nell of her first meeting with Kerensky who was on a visit to New York in 1927 to see her father.

Grigori Benenson, as the managing director of Benenson's Bank had just bought a New York skyscraper on Broadway, previously known as the City Investment Building.

Separated from Flora's mother who he never divorced, claiming being married prevented him making an expensive second marriage like so many Hollywood producers and stars, Flora's father lived in a penthouse in the Plaza Hotel with a changing series of young mistresses. But as a banker he was careful of his reputation and did not think a showgirl or a night club dancer, his current mistresses, would be suitable hostesses for events to which he invited senior political figures and on occasions, the Vice-President.

Normally one of Flora's two married younger sisters, Manya Benenson Harari, the well-known publisher or Fira, Countess Ilinska, wife of the Polish Ambassador to Washington acted as hostess for their father when he had important engagements. If they were unavailable Flora took on the role of hostess. She agreed to do so for a celebration luncheon in the skyscraper on Broadway when Grigori Benenson had bought and renamed the Benenson Building. This luncheon marked the culmination of her father's stellar career in America and would be attended by the press, several members of Congress and the Vice-President.

Flora's father had paid for her to cross the Atlantic in a luxury suite on a trans-Atlantic liner to act as his hostess. Flora's father's secretary had made the arrangements and regretted the Plaza had no vacant suites available so she had booked a double room overlooking Central Park for Mrs Solomon.

Her father, a great admirer of Kerensky after his brilliant defence of the Lena River miners, had obtained tickets to hear Kerensky that afternoon. He would be talking to a Russian audience in the largest stadium in New York, followed by a private reception given by Democrat friends and well-wishers.

The lunch went well. As Flora and her father were dropped by the chauffeur at the enormous auditorium, the police told her father they were expecting trouble as tickets had been sold to supporters of Kerensky but also to his sworn enemies. Some were supporters of the late Tsar Nicholas II, while others were Communists and supported

Stalin. As the Tsarists believed the Communists were responsible for murdering the Tsar there could be trouble.

Flora and her father had front row seats with her father's Democrat friends. Kerensky's supporters cheered and clapped as he mounted the rostrum. The supporters of Stalin brandished hammer and sickle flags in the gallery and brawled with the supporters of the late Tsar. Some had to be ejected by security guards.

Kerensky's speech ranged over several topics but concentrated on freedom and democracy for Russia should Stalin fall and what a superb future the country could have if this came about.

Amid huge applause for Kerensky, a young woman appeared on the platform with a big bouquet of flowers. As Kerensky leaned over to accept them she whipped out a knife and slashed him across the cheek, shouting, 'This is for those Russians who died in the Civil War'.

Security guards and police swarmed onto the platform and dragged her away. With blood trickling down his cheek, Kerensky assured his audience it was only a minor injury. The young woman had clearly suffered the loss of someone dear to her in the Civil War, which, as Prime Minister, he had done everything to prevent. He forgave her and would not be pressing charges.

His audience rose to their feet and applauded Kerensky's humanitarian gesture. Flora admired his composure and how well he had handled a very difficult situation.

Arriving at the reception given by a Democrat Senator, Flora bought two of Kerensky's books, *The Prelude to Bolshevism* and *The Crucifixion of Liberty.* When Flora reached the head of the queue to have her books signed she realised Kerensky was having difficulty dealing with readers due to his limited knowledge of English. She immediately offered to translate and Kerensky gratefully accepted.

Once the long queue of book buyers had dispersed, Flora told Kerensky she admired the way he had dealt with his attacker. She thought an anti-Communist magazine was overdue and would like to provide financial support. So Kerensky would know she was serious she told him she was the daughter of Grigori Benenson, the owner and managing director of Benenson's Bank and her father wanted to meet him.

Kerensky recognised the name 'Benenson' but said he was too tired to meet any more people. He suggested they go somewhere quiet and talk. Flora said they could go back to her room in the Plaza Hotel on 5th Avenue and apologised that on this visit she did not have a penthouse. But as her father rented a penthouse and was one of the hotel's best clients she did not think the hotel could object.

Inside Flora's bedroom it was quiet, and Kerensky relaxed and settled into the only arm chair. Flora sat on the bed and turned the bedside radio to a station playing Russian music. She offered her guest a brandy from a bottle she had brought with her as rigid prohibition laws governed America.

Kerensky explained his newspaper was banned by Stalin but was an important source of information for expatriate Russians in France and America. It was important to counter the lies about Russia sent to the West by Stalin's propaganda machine and pursue the course of freedom and social justice.

Kerensky told Flora how Soviet film director, Serge Einstein, had been paid by Lenin to make a film about the fictional storming of the Winter Palace showing Kerensky fleeing disguised as a nurse. He responded by sending Einstein a photo of him leaving the Winter Palace in army uniform taking the salute from sentries posted outside the Winter Palace.

Most of the readers of his previous publication were Russian *émigrés*, educated but with little money. He found out the hard way that advertisers did not buy space in newspapers whose readers lacked spending power.

Flora asked how much money was needed to bring out this new publication for a year, aware that *émigré* Russians were mainly poor and needed a publication which was subsidised. When Kerensky named the sum he needed, Flora did a quick calculation and offered to pay half the required sum which could be transferred immediately through Benenson's Bank.

Kerensky was overcome. He took Flora's hand in his, thanked her for her generosity which would help *Novaia Rossiia,* promote democracy and hopefully would lead to Stalin's downfall. They toasted the success of their joint venture and discovered they had both spent their youth in St Petersburg, a magical river city where in summer the golden twilight continued till dawn. Kerensky told Flora that having lost a kidney to cancer he rarely drank alcohol, but this was such a special evening, they should celebrate with more brandy.

Kerensky as a young and idealistic barrister defending free of charge, victims of injustice and Jews tortured and harassed by the Tsar's secret police.

Alexander Kerensky photographed on his American speaking tour when he met Flora Solomon. Now a successful author and a popular public speaker, he had acquired a large following of devoted admirers.

Flora had no intention of telling Nell the whole story. She had in fact found Kerensky very attractive and sensing this he had moved to sit beside her on the bed. Soon they were kissing but they heard a knock on the door. Kerensky gestured that he would hide in the bathroom. Flora adjusted her clothes and waited a few minutes before opening the door to an embarrassed night manager. He informed her that gentlemen were not allowed in ladies' bedrooms. Mr Kerensky had been seen entering the lift and journalists were waiting in the lobby to interview him.

Flora stared down the night manager and told him in an icy voice that for the past five years her father had been a permanent resident at his hotel. No one had ever complained when her father invited young ladies to his penthouse suite. Perhaps he would like to explain why he was complaining when she was merely having a business discussion with Alexander Kerensky, the former Prime Minister of Russia?

The night manager grovelled, offered his apologies and retreated.

Kerensky emerged from the bathroom roaring with laughter. He told Flora he admired the way she had dealt with the situation. He added it was not the first time he had had to retreat to a hotel bathroom on a speaking tour. They both laughed. Flora knew many women found Kerensky irresistible and some had hoped to become his second wife. She was not looking for another husband and was happy with a casual relationship. This set the pattern for their future. Flora knew Kerensky had other women in Paris and made many conquests on his author tours but chose to ignore this.

They spent the rest of the night together. She found he was an imaginative lover and realised what had been missing in her marriage.

Early the next morning Flora smuggled Kerensky down the staff staircase in case journalists were waiting in the lobby. For the next ten years they remained close friends and occasional lovers.

Unaware of the exact nature of the relationship between Kerensky and Flora, in the first week of January 1936 Nell set off for Paris and the interview with Kerensky which would change her life.

In her dossier Flora included a photograph of the Winter Palace where Kerensky lived in the suite of Tsar Alexander I as Prime Minister of Russia. In government he had hoped to hold democratic elections which, had he succeeded, would have changed the course of history. (Private Collection)

CHAPTER THIRTEEN

Flora's Dossier & Kerensky as the Defender of Russian Liberty

He who does not defend liberty everywhere, defends it not at all.
Alexander Kerensky.

Nell had reserved a seat on the Golden Arrow express train which took passengers from London to Dover in the days before regular air services. In her bag she carried the dossier on Alexander Kerensky typed out by Flora's secretary that she wanted to read. She remembered Nikolai and his White Russian friends had hated Kerensky, calling him 'the man who had lost Russia to Lenin and his murderous Bolsheviks.'

Nell with a journalist's scepticism was prepared to believe they were wrong. Unable to continue reading the account of Kerensky's life on the choppy crossing of the English Channel, Nell put the papers away in her bag.

She did not resume reading it again until she boarded the train from Calais to Gare du Nord train station in the centre of Paris. She was fascinated by the story of the brilliant young barrister turned politician who had hoped to turn a vast reactionary empire run by the pleasant but incompetent Tsar Nicholas II into a democratic society. His tragedy was to have been caught up in a bloodthirsty revolution and a civil war.

Flora's assistant had set out Kerensky's story in chronological order:

Born in May 1881 in a provincial town on the Volga River Kerensky was almost twenty years older than Nell, one of four clever children of a provincial schoolteacher. His grandfather had been a priest and his father had at one time taught his son's worst enemy, the sly revolutionary Vladimir Lenin. It would be Lenin, who Tsar Nicholas II had banished to Siberia, and Kerensky had threatened to jail years earlier who would oust Kerensky and his government at gunpoint in October 1917.

Back in 1899, Kerensky's father had been promoted to Head Inspector of Schools in Tashkent. This important post included a handsome official residence which is now Tashkent's British Embassy. All four Kerensky children attended university and entered professions. Alexander and his younger brother Fyodor read Russian history and law at St Petersburg's Imperial University. Tall and strong with a beautiful speaking voice, Alexander Kerensky enjoyed acting in student productions and considered becoming an actor. But this idea horrified his parents who wanted their clever eldest son to become a lawyer.

Commonsense prevailed. Alexander Kerensky studied law and graduated with honours. In 1904, just before the November 1905 revolution against the autocratic rule of Tsar Nicholas II, thousands of peasants were starving. This was when Kerensky gained his post-graduate qualifications in law and, as an idealist and a firm believer in freedom was admitted to the bar.

Kerensky had defended free of charge or *pro bono* Jews persecuted by the Tsar's secret police for the crime of being Jewish. The Romanov Tsars were devout but bigoted. Urged on by church elders they had sought to punish the Jews in their vast empire for the crime of murdering Jesus Christ. For years Kerensky fought in court to defend Jews who had been prosecuted on trumped up charges by the Tsar's secret police and he had won many of them their freedom.

Kerensky had shocked his religious parents by falling in love with his rebellious but attractive cousin, Olga Baranovskaya who shocked her family with her left-wing ideas. Kerensky, raised in a religious household, had his first sexual experience with Olga and became besotted by her.

Olga, the beautiful attention-seeking daughter of a general in the Tsar's army defied the conventions for upper-class girls by working for the Socialist Revolutionary Party and introducing her studious cousin Alexander Kerensky to her SRP political friends, some of whom talked wildly of assassinating Tsar Nicholas II. Their passionate affair in the era before birth control resulted in Olga falling pregnant. In 1904, against his parents wishes, they married. Kerensky's parents refused to attend their wedding or have Olga as a guest in their home.

In 1905, Olga gave birth to baby Oleg, their first son on what became known as Bloody Sunday. On this day the Tsar's troops and the police fired on a peaceful demonstration of workers outside the Winter Palace in St Petersburg, killing and injuring over 1,000 people, spurring several revolutionary groups to demand the abdication of Tsar Nicholas II or his assassination.

After the disaster of Bloody Sunday, Nicholas II sought to make amends by establishing a rudimentary Parliament called the Duma. But he soon disbanded the Duma fearing it would result in too many contentious reforms, aware that his grandfather, Tsar Alexander II, had been assassinated for this reason.

Tsar Nicholas II was a poor leader of men but a loving father to four beautiful daughters and a haemophiliac son. He and his wife lived in fear of his little son dying. His wife, a German princess had fallen under the spell of Rasputin, the mad monk who convinced the Tsarina he was the only person who could save little Prince Alexei from bleeding to death.

The Tsar obstinately refused to bring about much needed reforms and relied instead on his brutal secret police to keep order in the vast empire of conquered nations. The Bolsheviks hated the Tsar's German wife. They put up street posters showing her having sex with Rasputin.

Revolutionary groups were formed and Vladimir Lenin, leader of one of them was arrested by the Okhrana, the Tsar's brutal secret police and exiled to Siberia. He would later flee to Europe and organise the Russian Revolution from there aided by the young Stalin.

Kerensky's devout parents had hoped he would marry Olga Baranovskaya's equally beautiful but more stable and studious cousin, Lilya Baranovskaya, a student at Petersburg's medical school.

Lilya's parents were socially ambitious. They wanted an advantageous marriage for Olga, their beautiful talented daughter. In this era of arranged marriages a high-ranking army officer from a wealthy family was considered a catch and he received permission from Lilya's father to marry her.

Far too late Kerensky realised that apart from sex he had little in common with Olga. He should have married Lilya as his parents had wanted. But it was too late. Lilya married her army officer who was promoted to a general in the Tsar's army but the marriage was not happy.

Under Olga's influence, Kerensky had joined the Socialist Revolutionary Party and abandoned the Russian Orthodox Church. Admitted to the bar Kerensky defended victims of the Okhrana, the Tsar's brutal secret police, *pro bono*. He had a revolutionary wife who spent much of her time attending protest marches and demonstrating. Olga neglected her son and her husband, now, a young barrister with a gift for public speaking. Kerensky would soon become famous throughout Russia for his brilliant defence of the widows of 200 miners murdered by soldiers on the remote Lena River gold fields in Siberia.

In a strange coincidence, Flora's father, after selling his oil wells had bought shares in the Lena gold mines. The Lena mines were two days journey on the Trans-Siberian Railway from St Petersburg to remote Irkutsk followed by a day's journey by horse and cart into the wilderness. Flora's father never visited the mines in which he owned a large block of shares so had no idea how terrible the working conditions were for the miners.

The Lena River in the extreme west of Siberia was so cold and arid no crops would grow there. All food for the miners had to be imported and was sold through the company's stores. A dishonest mine manager made money by buying poor quality food including rotting meat, and charging the miners exorbitant prices, which led to a general strike of the underpaid Lena River miners in April, 1912.

The manager called soldiers to force the miners back to work. When they refused, the soldiers opened fire leaving 200 miners dead, 180 badly wounded and grieving widows and children who no one wanted to compensate.[33]

An inquest was held in St Petersburg. Gregori Benenson and other major shareholders had to appear in court. When Flora's father, now one of Russia's wealthiest businessmen, encountered the brilliant young Alexander Kerensky, representing the widows of the Lena River free of charge, he admired the report Kerensky had written about the appalling conditions at the Lena Mines.

Kerensky's spirited defence of the miners won their widows and children compensation from the company and secured the jailing of the mine manager. Kerensky became a national hero as a humanitarian barrister who took on cases *pro bono* and won justice for the underprivileged. Flora's father was so impressed he told the young Flora that if he ever needed a barrister he would engage Kerensky.

Kerensky with his humanitarian ideals also defended Jews who had been victims of racial persecution and won several landmark cases which made him popular with Russian Jews. They had been persecuted under the Tsars for centuries, made to live in isolated settlements or *shtetls* and denied education. Many Jews escaped and migrated to America and would become ardent supporters of Kerensky in exile.

Kerensky was now leading a group of moderate Socialists, known as Trudoviks, who called for the abdication of Tsar Nicholas II, as did the revolutionary Bolsheviks who wanted the Tsar assassinated for refusing all demands for reform. This prolonged war with Germany, now in its third year, was a disaster for Russia as the Treasury had been depleted by the high-spending Romanovs which left little money for guns or winter uniforms for the soldiers. The Imperial Russian army were poorly fed and poorly armed as the Romanov Tsars had depleted the Russian Treasury by building enormous palaces filled with expensive art.

In World War One St Petersburg had been renamed Petrograd to make it sound more Russian and less German. Meanwhile Russian workers and their families were half-starved and angry.

Kerensky was at the height of his popularity with the workers and the army, the only Duma member who was also a member of the revolutionary Petersburg Soviet (Workers) Group. Kerensky was appointed Justice Minister in the Fourth Duma, the watered-down form of Parliament the Tsar eventually disbanded.

On 8 March 1917 (by the Western calendar thirteen days in advance of the Russian Julian calendar) hungry striking workers took to the streets. Soldiers on the front line mutinied and went home or many went to Petersburg to support the striking workers.

On 15 March 1917 the generals serving the ineffective Tsar Nicholas II realised that with the Tsar in charge they would lose the war and persuaded him to abdicate. A Provisional (caretaker) Government was formed with elderly Prince Lvov as leader and Kerensky as Justice Minister. Kerensky's first task was to abolish the Tsar's brutal secret police, grant religious freedom and halt the brutal persecution of Russia's large Jewish population.

In April the revolutionary leader, Vladimir Lenin, was sent back to Russia by the Germans, to destabilize the country by instigating a revolution.

In June 1917 Kerensky was made War Minister despite having no military experience, because he was the cleverest and most hard-working member of the Provisional Government. Kerensky, seen as the champion of soldiers was carried shoulder high when made War Minister, although as a barrister he had no campaign experience and his appointment would be a disaster.

Kerensky launched a troop offensive against German and Austrian forces in Galicia which failed. After bitter arguments he left his wife, Olga, and as Prime Minister and Minister for War, moved into the Winter Palace with Lilya. They lived in great splendour in the suite of the murdered Tsar Alexander II.

In July 1917 due to more unrest in Petrograd the ageing and ineffectual Prince Lvov resigned and was replaced by the 36 year-old Kerensky as Russia's Prime Minister. Kerensky ended the persecution of those involved in street demonstrations and granted Russian women the right to vote. He ordered the arrest of Lenin who went into hiding and Lenin's Bolsheviks staged more demonstrations.

Unknown to the public and many of his colleagues, the stoic Kerensky was recovering from a major operation to remove a cancerous kidney. He was often in pain and took morphine tablets, the only pain killer known at that time, but continued working long hours under severe stress. By now, the German army was dangerously close to St Petersburg and Kerensky knew he needed to rally the nation to defend the capital.

General Kornilov who Kerensky had made commander of the Russian army, ordered his troops to advance on Petrograd to counter the threat of the Bolsheviks. Kerensky was alarmed. He saw this as a dangerous right-wing coup so armed the striking workers of Petrograd. They disappointed him by joining Lenin's Bolsheviks who promised soldiers who had mutinied and striking workers 'Bread, Land and Peace' although the workers never received the land or the bread.

Lenin hoped to establish enormous collective farms, by taking away land from the peasants. Small farmers or kulaks who owned their land and refused to join the collectives were sent to Siberian *gulags* or shot. However Lenin's gigantic collective farms were run so badly that combined with a drought, the result was a two year famine that killed hundreds of thousands of people.

On 14 September 1917 Prime Minister Kerensky officially declared Russia a Republic. Lenin realised that the Bolsheviks would never win the elections which Kerensky was trying to set up, and aided by the cunning Trotsky he decided to seize power by force.

On 7 November 1917 (26 October in the old Julian calendar) the Bolsheviks took control of the Telephone Exchange and other important buildings in Petrograd. Kerensky tried to phone the frontier post of Pskov asking for more reinforcements to guard the Winter Palace against the Bolsheviks but as they had already taken over the Telephone Exchange his message did not get through. He realised with alarm only the Women's Brigade and a few inexperienced military cadets were now guarding the Winter Palace where the Provisional Government were deliberating how to run the forthcoming elections in the magnificent surroundings of the Malachite Chamber.

On 8 November at 9am the Russian Revolution began, heralded by a cannon fired at the Winter Palace and known as 'the shot that echoed around the world'. But by the time the shot was fired, Kerensky and his aide Lieutenant Vinner had already left for the Winter Palace. Kerensky had been due for a final sitting for his portrait by the famous artist Ilya Repin and for the sitting he wore a simple brown woollen army tunic.

In order to create maximum chaos, in the midst of the war, Germany, Russia's sworn enemy, sent back the banished Lenin from exile to St Petersburg in a sealed train, 'like the plague bacillus', said Winston Churchill, Britain's War Minister when he heard what had happened. Lenin's second-in-command Leon Trotsky had instructed the Bolsheviks to disable the car pool available to the Provisional Government.

When Kerensky's aide Lieutenant Vinner and an assistant were unable to start any of the government cars, in desperation they commandeered a red sports car with a sunroof from a startled American diplomat, telling him this was an emergency.

Just as the Red Guard arrived to arrest him or kill him if he resisted, Kerensky left the Winter Palace with the sunroof open in a car flying a small American flag wearing the military uniform in which Repin had painted his portrait earlier that morning. Kerensky stood erect in the open car to take the salute from sentries outside the Winter Palace. Disregarding the truth, Lenin's propaganda department claimed the improbable story that Kerensky had fled in terror from the Red Guard disguised as a nurse with the gold from the Russian Treasury hidden beneath his long skirts.

The rest of Kerensky's Provisional Government were arrested at gunpoint in the Malachite Chamber by the Red Guard. Lilya and her children escaped by a back staircase. The Provisional Government were jailed inside the Peter and Paul Fortress and from the windows they saw minor members of the Romanov family being shot in the courtyard which was scarcely consoling. But the man Lenin was desperate to face a firing squad was Kerensky as he feared his oratory and his popularity with the workers.

The storming of the Winter Palace against armed defenders is a heroic legend propagated by the Bolsheviks in reconstructed photos to create an event that never happened to inspire the workers.

Portrait of the young Kerensky as Prime Minister and War Minister by the famous artist Ilya Repin (Courtesy of the Harry Ransom Center, The University of Texas at Austin)

Marble staircase of the Winter Palace (today's Hermitage Museum) which the Red Guard climbed to arrest the Kerensky Government. (Private collection)

The impressive Malachite Chamber with its green marble columns where Kerensky's Provisional Government were arrested at gunpoint by Lenin's Red Guard. Kerensky had already managed to escape. (Private collection)

The reality was very different to Bolshevik and Communist propaganda. Resistance to the Red Guard was minimal as there were so few soldiers guarding the Winter Palace. Kerensky had phoned military headquarters at Pskov on the front line to ask for additional soldier to guard the Winter Palace. But as the Post Office and the Telephone Exchange were in Bolshevik hands his messages never reached the front line headquarters at Pskov. The Red Guard walked into the Winter Palace unopposed. It was only guarded by a small inexperienced Women's Brigade and a group of young military cadets who surrendered without a fight to the much larger Bolshevik force so could not be called 'a storming' of the Palace.

The Red Guard in their hob-nailed boots with their guns at the ready clambered up the marble staircase of the Winter Palace. At gunpoint in the magnificent Malachite Chamber the Red Guard arrested unarmed members of the Provisional Government. It has been alleged that as some of the Red Guard were illiterate they had to ask members of the Provisional Guard to write their own arrest warrants but this may be another legend.

Trotsky's skilful propaganda turned the unopposed entry of the Red Guard into the unguarded Winter Palace into a truly heroic event which in fact never happened. The Soviet government put on a magnificent 'reconstruction' employing extras and photographers to act out what was called the 'Storming of the Winter Palace" and photograph it in an attempt to create evidence when no storming ever took place. There was little resistance from the inexperienced guards and the few female staff left inside the Winter Palace.[34]

The famous film director Sergei Einstein reinforced the legend and made a film in which Kerensky is seen fleeing the Winter Palace disguised as a nurse. This was an attempt by the Lenin and Trotsky to make Kerensky out to be a coward and a laughable figure. They also called him a thief for allegedly stealing all the gold from the Russian Treasury which was laughable bearing in mind how much even one gold ingot weighs. But by spreading propaganda based on lies, Kerensky had his reputation destroyed by Lenin and Stalin who claimed that he was a coward and a thief.

***

So that Nell understood what had led to the Russian Revolution, Flora's friend the historian recapped events leading to the rescue of

Kerensky by the dashing young diplomat Robert Bruce Lockhart. Bruce Lockhart had been left in charge of the British Embassy in St Petersburg after the British Ambassador, Sir George Buchanan, had been recalled to England. The British Government and broken off diplomat relations as they disliked the idea of making a formal recognition of Lenin as the leader of Russia, fearing this would lead to a Russian style revolution at home.

Lockhart described attending a public meeting in St Petersburg addressed by Kerensky. After Kerensky had finished speaking, the huge crowd rose to greet him, feeling that Kerensky was the only man who could save Russia from ruin. Aware that his government was desperately short of money to send arms to the troops, women took off their jewellery and presented it to Kerensky.

Against doctor's orders, still convalescing and in constant pain, Kerensky had visited the front at Pskov, to rally Russian troops who had been fighting the better-equipped German army for years and were totally exhausted.

The Russian Treasury was almost empty ensuring the Russian army would be poorly fed and lack boots or winter uniforms in what a bitterly cold winter. Morale was low and many soldiers mutinied. They demanded peace with Germany so they could return home, sow crops and bring in the autumn harvest, something Kerensky could not promise.

Kerensky, as a lawyer, believed in the moral right of legal documents and felt it was ethically wrong to break a signed treaty to assist France which had been attacked by the Kaiser's Germany.

Believing the promises of money and equipment to Russia made by Britain and France would be honoured, (although they never were) Kerensky as Prime Minister, and Minister for War and Justice refused to make a separate peace with Germany seeing doing this as dishonourable as he had signed a treaty to attack Germany with France and England. However the continuation of the war led to immense suffering in Russia.

By autumn 1917, desertions by Russian soldiers at the front line had reached 2,000,000 men with hunger strikes by half-starved workers as the price of bread and food essentials had risen enormously.

Lenin came to power on the slogan of 'Peace, Land and Bread', well aware it was impossible to achieve all three aims. These false promises won support for Lenin but he knew they were not enough for him to win the elections that Kerensky was setting up. Desperate to seize power Lenin planned a worker's revolution and issued orders to kill Kerensky to prevent any serious opposition.

After leaving the Winter Palace Kerensky and his aide Captain Nikolai Vinner drove the commandeered American car to the front at Pskov where the Russian army was fighting the Germans.

In a rousing speech Kerensky asked troops to return to defend Petrograd against the Bolsheviks who had illegally arrested the Provisional Government to prevent it from holding elections.

Kerensky's emotive speech rallied troops including a detachment of Cossacks from the Don River. Aware of the value of a rider on a white horse symbolising a force for good, Kerensky rode a white horse into the village of Tsarskoe Selo. He was repeating what Napoleon had done to inspire his troops on several of his campaigns. But this ploy failed as Kerensky's troops were totally outnumbered by armed Bolsheviks and striking workers and Kerensky was forced to seek refuge in the now vacant Gatchina Palace, another of the many Romanov residences.

Alexander Kerensky convalescing after an operation to remove a cancerous kidney, shortly before he was appointed Prime Minister of Russia.

During prolonged negotiations between the opposing sides which lasted several days, the first of many attempts were made on Kerensky's life although this one was not by Lenin but by a deranged Tsarist. Kerensky's life was saved by Count Valentin Zubov, who was in charge of restoring the Gatchina Palace and he knocked the pistol out of the assassin's hand.[35]

By 31 October Kerensky and his staff were still prisoners in the deserted Gatchina Palace. At 11am Kerensky was warned that the Cossacks from the Don River, meant to be guarding him, were debating whether to switch their loyalty to Lenin. They offered to escort Kerensky to Petersburg so he could meet Lenin and discuss plans for Russia's future.

Kerensky knew the proposed meeting would be a death trap. Lenin had hated and feared him for years and would have him shot. Kerensky preferred suicide and discussed this possibility with his aide and friend, Lieutenant Vinner.[36]

A supporter was able to telephone Kerensky's friend, Bruce Lockhart at the British Embassy and Lockhart agreed to send an Embassy car to collect Kerensky and help him escape. A palace servant provided the uniform of a sailor and a pair of aviator's goggles to hide Kerensky's face. Corporal Belenky calmly led the Prime Minister through a crowd of angry workers and striking soldiers and sailors in this bizarre disguise as a sailor in goggles without being stopped.

As Kerensky walked through the main gate another of his supporters feigned a collapse in order to distract the Bolshevik sentries who would have arrested or killed Kerensky had they recognised him.

A car sent by Lockhart from the British Embassy was waiting at the Chinese Gate of Gatchina village. Crouching on the floor so no one could see him, Kerensky was driven away and hidden by loyal supporters in a series of mountain huts in the hills near Pskov where he remained in hiding for the next six months.

The British Ambassador Sir George Buchanan had been recalled to London so that the British Government could avoid having to open diplomatic negotiations with Lenin, who they considered a terrorist. The fact that Lockhart had the title of Special Envoy to negotiate with Lenin gave the British Government time to decide if they would send troops to help Kerensky regain control of Russia or accept Lenin as head of the new Communist Union of Soviet Socialist Republics.

The Winter Palace sacked by the mob during the October Revolution of 1917.
(Private collection)

Lenin had offered a large reward for the capture of Kerensky but unable to kill his political opponent, Lenin took revenge on his family and staff. Kerensky's younger brother Fyodor, a lawyer in Tashkent was executed by a firing squad as was Kerensky's former private secretary, Boris Flekkel.

Tsar Nicholas II and his family were still missing after Kerensky had sent them to Siberia to ensure their own safety where they were captured and imprisoned by the Bolsheviks. Nothing had been heard from them so the Imperial family were presumed dead but no trace of their bodies had been found by the time Kerensky escaped from Russia aided by Bruce Lockhart. The young diplomat collected Kerensky who he regarded as a friend by car from a hut in the hills near Pskov. Lockhart gave Kerensky the uniform of a Swedish sailor as his disguise and wearing this managed with bribes of money to place him on a ship bound for London via Sweden.

Arriving as a penniless exile in London, Kerensky hoped that the British and French Governments, his former allies against Germany, would provide troops to help him recapture St Petersburg from Lenin's Bolshevik or Red Army.

The young Winston Churchill, Britain's War Minister, felt a barrister-turned-politician like Kerensky was not the right person to deal with the murderous Bolsheviks. Churchill had taken advice from a conniving Russian armaments dealer employed by MI6. George Relinsky, a man of many aliases, had volunteered, for a large fee, to organise the assassination of Lenin in Moscow. Relinsky advised Churchill that if the assassination succeeded, the brutal Boris Savinkov (Prime Minister Kerensky's former Assistant War Minister) would be the right person to succeed Lenin.

Relinsky was given a false passport by the British Secret Service in the assumed name of Sidney Reilly and travelled to Moscow where he groomed the vulnerable Fanny Kaplan to attempt the assassination of Lenin. The attempt failed but Kaplan was arrested and tortured by Lenin's secret police She refused to betray Reilly and was executed by firing squad.

The British Embassy was raided by the Russian secret police who believed the British had a hand in Fanny Kaplan's assassination attempt. Bruce Lockhart, who was involved in a separate plot to assassinate Lenin, was also arrested along with his accomplice Countess Moira Budberg. He was due to be shot by firing squad but thanks to Moira's seduction of his captor, at the last minute was exchanged for a Russian diplomat who had been caught spying in Britain..

Eventually Kerensky and Lockhart met up in London. Lockhart told Kerensky about the two plots to assassinate Lenin and how he had become the scapegoat for the failed plot by the Foreign Office and had been forced to resign.

Kerensky, as Russia's Prime Minister in exile, was granted an interview with Prime Minister Lloyd George. But the British Prime Minister offered no help to his former ally to regain control of Russia. Kerensky encountered the same lack of official help from France's President Clemenceau and was angry and disillusioned with both politicians.

Finally Lenin negotiated a separate peace with Germany on 3 March, 1918. A victorious Germany negotiated harsh terms with Bolshevik Russia at the treaty of Brest-Litovsk under which Soviet Russia lost one-third of the former Russian empire and nine-tenths of Russia's supplies of coal and iron ore.

In London as a penniless refugee, Kerensky had been given hospitality and support by Dr Jacob Gavronsky, who had worked in the Russian Embassy in London when Kerensky was Prime Minister. Kerensky was also helped by the wealthy Jewish scientist Chaim Weizmann. Both of them provided financial assistance in gratitude for Kerensky's efforts to protect Russia's large Jewish community against brutal persecution by the Tsar's secret police.

When the assassination plan by Sidney Reilly and the Lockhart plot failed, with reluctance the British Government had to open diplomatic negotiations with Lenin as head of the newly formed Union of Soviet Socialist Republics. For this reason they found the presence of Russia's former Prime Minister an embarrassment.

Kerensky never forgave the British Government for their lack of support. He left London for Berlin. There, on a shoestring he ran *Dni,* an anti-Communist newspaper aided by Jewish and Armenian money. The publication failed financially because its Russian readers were so impoverished it could not attract advertisers.

Germany's liberal-minded but weak Weimar Government failed and was eventually replaced by Hitler as head of the National Socialist or Nazi Party which Kerensky later denounced in his newspaper for its harsh treatment of Jews.

The fear of Hitler's Nazis meant many *émigré* Russian Jews who spoke French as their second language fled Germany for Paris and Kerensky did the same. His loyal Russian Jewish supporters raised enough money for him to lease an apartment in Passy from where he established a new and larger publication *Novaia Rossiia (The New Russia).*

Kerensky's second anti-Communist publication had copies smuggled into Stalin's' Soviet Russia on merchant ships in order to educate his readers on the evils of Communism and the growing menace of Hitler and the Nazis.

The dossier Flora gave Nell contained an extract from the American *Liberator Magazine* by American journalist John Reed, who had been in Russia during the October 1917 revolution.

Reed recorded his admiration for Kerensky's stoicism in continuing to work while recovering from an operation to remove a cancerous kidney. At the same time Kerensky had been endeavouring to run an almost bankrupt Russia and attempting to set up democratic elections.

At the opening of the Council of the Russian Republics, Kerensky had collapsed exhausted after working most of the night on a speech highlighting the importance of democratic elections for Russia's future.

Reed observed *'Kerensky is alone amid a class-struggle, which deepens and grows more bitter day by day, as his rule becomes more and more precarious. Things are moving swiftly to a crisis between the bourgeoisie [the middle class] and the proletariat [the workers], in a civil war which Kerensky is trying to avert and on him is concentrated the hatred of both sides.'*

After waiting several days, Reed and his journalist wife, Louise Bryant were finally able to interview Kerensky in the library of the murdered Tsar Alexander II in the Winter Palace.

The dossier Nell was given included an extract from Reed's article stating, *We entered a room, lined with heavy Gothic book-cases. This was the Tsar's private library and reception-room. As Kerensky shook our hands he looked into our faces searchingly for a second, and then led the way to a big table and chairs. His whole attitude was quizzically friendly, as if receiving reporters was an amusing relaxation from politics.*

"What do you consider your job?" (Reed) asked.

"To free Russia and prevent civil war," Kerensky replied.

CHAPTER FOURTEEN

An Interview with Kerensky

In the first week in January 1936 Nell arrived in Paris to be interviewed by Kerensky at his combined home and office in the tree-lined rue Vineuse in the riverside suburb of Passy. Here, affluent members of the Russian community lived, unlike Montparnasse, the area Nell had loved which housed the poorer Russian *émigrés*.

Nell pushed the bell which admitted her to the lobby of a modern apartment block. It was modern and utilitarian rather than luxurious. As instructed by Flora she walked up the three flights of concrete stairs so the uniformed security guard could check her identity. Warned by Flora, Nell had brought her passport with her as identification. She had applied for a passport soon after the end of the Great War when the fledgling Australian Commonwealth Government did not issue its own passports and all Australians carried British passports.

Kerensky's bodyguard had a strong Slavonic accent and was built like a champion wrestler. He kept Nell's passport saying they had to be careful as there had been several attempts by Stalin to assassinate Kerensky. A different secret password was issued each week as further protection. Nell, raised in Australia, unaffected by war or terrorism, felt that as an Australian with a British passport she would not be targeted by the Russian secret police. Assassins sent by Stalin wanted to kill Kerensky rather than Australians. She liked the idea that there was an element of danger about this job.

Nell saw that the windows of Kerensky's apartment were fitted with heavy steel bars. After the latest attempt to assassinate Kerensky with a letter bomb, all parcels were opened in the basement by a staff member wearing protective clothing.

She was shown into Kerensky's book-lined office by Olga Vasilieva, his middle-aged personal assistant who Flora told her had been with him for many years. Facing her behind a large desk was Kerensky.

Aware that Kerensky was in his mid-fifties Nell saw a very attractive man who looked younger with his thick iron-grey hair, cut very short and piercing blue eyes. As a former journalist used to interviewing celebrities, the fact Kerensky had been the Prime Minister of one of the largest countries in the world did not worry her. Nell took the chair opposite and prepared to be interviewed in French, aware Kerensky spoke very little English.

Kerensky addressed her as 'Madame Nadejine' and used the formal French 'vous' rather than the informal 'tu'.

Looking at the letter in front of him he said that Mrs Solomon's recommendations had been most complimentary. He asked a few questions and remarked that her spoken French was excellent. He added that he was sure as an experienced journalist she could easily do the work he needed and her contribution would be invaluable.

He explained that he needed a translator who could act as his press secretary. He wanted someone to source materials for his editorials from English and American newspapers and, if necessary, source additional material in libraries or from embassy staff in Paris.

The leading American and British papers were delivered to his office by air but as the air services were irregular, the newspapers often arrived late. However the telex machine he had recently installed was proving invaluable as a means of communication.

Kerensky explained that the readers of his *Novaia Rossiia* newspaper were expatriate Russians in Europe and America. He added that Soviet Russia had strict censorship so most Russians knew nothing of the outside world. Stalin's propaganda department only allowed favourable stories to be published in Russia and ignored the two year famine, Stalin's slave labour camps and the torture chambers of the secret police. Kerensky's newspaper told them the truth.

He wrote his articles and books in French and Nell would be asked to translate any articles he had written into English to send to the American press. In America his book on the Russian Revolution, translated by his son, Oleg who was now an engineering student in England, was selling well. He was scheduled to make another speaking tour of America very soon.

Nell found Kerensky fascinating. He had that indefinable thing that actors called 'presence' and she understood why Flora had claimed so many people were drawn to him and offered money to help him in his quest for freedom in Russia.

Kerensky apologised for not being able to pay Nell the salary her experience as a journalist deserved and added she would have the satisfaction of serving the cause of freedom and fighting dictators.

He explained how in the basement of this building his backers had just paid to install a new printing press. This would make a big difference to the look of his Russian language newspaper and its sales. At present sales of his books and financial help from his backers were funding the newspaper which was currently running at a loss.

He was leaving for New York in March and if Madame Nadejine took the job, he would need her to start work as soon as possible. It would be necessary for her to stay late occasionally to get enough material edited before he left for America. As if he had read her mind, he assured her that Olga Vasilieva, his personal assistant with whom she would share an office, would also be staying late, and would work with her.

Nell remembered Nina warning her about Kerensky but she detected no hint of flirtation in his very formal and correct manner. She could see why Nina told her so many women had fallen for him as his appeal was powerful. She started daydreaming about working for Kerensky and having a chance to understand this complex man.

She came back to earth aware that Kerensky was offering her the job of his translator and press secretary and was waiting for her reply. She thanked Kerensky and accepted.

Kerensky remained businesslike and formal, said he hoped she would find the work interesting and repeated that he regretted he could not pay her more.

Nell replied that money was not as important as feeling she was doing valuable work. She would start next week after finding suitable accommodation nearby.

Kerensky gave her the name of the real estate agent who managed his building and said he had found him trustworthy should she want to rent somewhere in Passy. This was a very safe area which due to the high amount of unemployment after the stock-market crash was not true about many other areas of Paris. He told her he owned a Citroen saloon car that was rarely used, because always having been supplied with chauffeurs, he had never learned to drive. If at any time she needed a car she would be welcome to use it.

The former Prime Minister rose to his feet to indicate their interview was over. He escorted her to the door telling her the password for the next two weeks was 'Battle of Waterloo'. This amused Nell as it revealed Kerensky's love of history.

They shook hands formally in the French manner when they parted and he said he looked forward to working with Madame Nadejine.

As she walked down the stairs Nell was glad she had accepted the position even though the salary Kerensky offered was ridiculously low. But thanks to the Tritton family trust she could afford to take this interesting job, rent a pleasant apartment and hope to have an enjoyable life again in Paris.

Nell spent the rest of the afternoon with the rental agent Kerensky had recommended, looking at rental apartments. She chose a light airy modern apartment only a few streets away with a balcony overlooking the River Seine. Nell still had her French bank account and wrote a cheque, signed a three year contract with an option to renew and felt she was making a promising start to a new life as a free woman.

On her return to London, as most of her furniture was still in Paris, she packed up the few belongings she had accumulated in London along with her clothes. Ruth said how sorry she was to see Nell leave and organised a farewell dinner, attended by good friends including Chaim Weizmann and his wife, and Flora.

In thanks to Ruth Shapiro for her hospitality, Nell gave Ruth a large and beautifully illustrated book on the Russian ballet. She felt she had been lucky to meet Ruth and Vera Weizmann and to have made such interesting friends in London.

She was not so certain about Flora as they had had a few differences during the time they had worked together. But at least Flora had given her a good reference which had secured her what promised to be an interesting job with Kerensky.

It did not enter Nell's mind that there could be any kind of intimate relationship between the matronly Flora and the charismatic Kerensky.

A quai along the Seine. In the distance is a Citroen saloon car similar to the model in which Nell drove Kerensky. (Private collection)

CHAPTER FIFTEEN

In Passy: Countess Moura a Russian Spy?

In 1936 Nell found elegant riverside Passy inhabited by wealthy Russian aristocrats and foreign ambassadors very different to the vibrant area of Montparnasse with its many students and artists' studios where she had lived on arrival in Paris years earlier.

A visit to Montparnasse to catch up with Nina for lunch at the Closerie de Lilas made her realise the area had become a tourist hotspot. It swarmed with American tourists wanting to see where Hemingway, now a famous author, had lived when he wrote *The Sun Also Rises*. The studio Stella and Ford Maddox Ford had rented had been repainted and was looking much smarter. Hemingway's dusty studio over a saw mill had been demolished and replaced by a large school. She was thankful that her former home in the rue du Regard was untouched.

Nell had no way of knowing it, but as she started working in Paris she would see the rise of new enemies of liberty for Kerensky to fight. Hitler, Mussolini and General Franco came to the fore this year. Hitler was about to stage the 1936 Olympic Games in Berlin, keen to impress the rest of the world with the power and might of Nazi Germany.

Hitler hid from the world that he was funding new armaments factories by confiscating valuable art and businesses from wealthy Jews. Nazi dealers sold the art profitably in Switzerland then charged terrified Jews an exorbitant price for exit visas to leave Nazi Germany.

Nell, a keen swimmer, wanted to apply for leave from her new job to visit Berlin to watch her fellow Australians, Evelyn de Lacey and Sally Foster compete in swimming events, hoping they would bring home Olympic Gold.

When Nell moved into her new apartment in a quiet tree-lined street in Passy she was relieved to find that the furniture and paintings she had left behind in a storage facility in Montparnasse fitted well. She bought whatever else she needed from the elegant shops in Passy, a *quartier* which extended from the quais along the Seine to the Eiffel Tower and the Champs Elysées. Now she was no longer a student Nell, was determined to wear designer clothes to work. She would dress as elegantly as any Parisian and as she spoke faultless French with no trace of an Australian accent many foreigners were convinced she was French.

Nell discovered that Passy had plenty of good French and Russian restaurants, *patisseries* and fruit and vegetable shops. Through a domestic agency she engaged a cleaner to give her a few hours help once a week. She had read in her *Baedeker's Guide to Paris* that the famous composers Claude Debussy and Gabriel Fauré were buried in Passy as were the Impressionist artists Edouard Manet, Berthe Morisot and the young Russian artist Marie Bakshirtskeff. She was pleased to learn that Marie, who had been her role model was now deemed famous enough to be included in guide books to Paris and she decided to visit Marie's grave.

She walked to the nearby Passy Cemetery and found the grave was much larger than expected. In fact it was more like a small church framed by chestnut trees. Marie's birth date of 1858 and her death in 1884 were engraved on the stone walls of the memorial with its Byzantine domes that resembled a miniature cathedral erected by Marie's grief-stricken mother. As it was January, too early for spring flowers, Nell took a bunch of winter flowering chrysanthemums to leave in memoriam. It had been Marie's journal that had made her so determined to spend a couple of years in Paris.

In an enjoyable reunion with Nina at their usual meeting place, in Montparnasse in the garden of the Closerie de Lilas café restaurant Nell learned that Nina's marriage to the ailing poet Khodasevich had ended amicably. This was a merciful release for Nina who had supported him valiantly as his consumption became worse. Khodasevich, now terminally ill, had fallen in love with a fellow poet, who was now nursing him so Nina felt free to leave. Nina had started a love affair with a young French artist and decided to leave Paris for the country. They had started work on renovating an old house just outside the rural village of Longchêne, some 200 kilometres to the south-west of Paris.

New love had done wonders for Nina who was glowing with happiness. She told Nell she was writing a novel set in Montparnasse and a literary publisher in Paris liked her work enough to publish it. Nina felt at last she was getting somewhere with a literary career.

Nell and Nina lunched together in the tranquil garden of the Closerie de Lilas and discussed the tangled love affairs of their friends. By chance Nina had bumped into Countess Moura in a café in the Boulevard de Raspail. Moura had told her that the wealthy Maxim

Gorky, in whose writers' commune Nina and her husband had lived when Gorky had been besotted with Moura, was no longer fashionable. As a result sales of his books had dropped sharply but Stalin still loved them.

The Russian dictator had lured Gorky back to Soviet Russia with the promise of a free apartment in Moscow, a seaside *dacha* (villa) in the Crimea, Russia's answer to the French Riviera and a well-paid appointment as Director of the Soviet Russian Writers Union.

Nina had kept in touch with Gorky's second wife who disliked Countess Moura, who had superseded her as Gorky's mistress. The second wife was angry and claimed Moura had taken a great deal of money from the besotted Gorky when he was wealthy. Moura had used it to make an arranged marriage to the cash-strapped Baron Budberg, an Estonian aristocrat. She did this in order to qualify for an Estonian passport so she could visit her children in Estonia; a country that refused to recognise Russian passports. Young Baron Budberg had huge gambling debts and needed money quickly so the marriage-for-cash in return for his title and an Estonian passport had been arranged by his lawyer.

The former Countess Moura Benckendorff, now promoted by her second marriage to Baroness Moura Budberg used her new, grander title to good effect to impress people. She added the romantic detail that she was a descendant of the Romanovs, the Russian royal family, which Nina soon discovered was yet another of her many tall tales.

Baron Budberg with his gambling debts had been threatened with knee-capping by gambling syndicate thugs and was desperate to leave the country for South America. So the newly weds parted a few hours after the ceremony and Moura returned to live with Gorky.

Gorky, having lost his money, was lured back to Soviet Russia by Stalin. Moura refused to accompany him to Moscow fearing the Soviet secret police would use her to entrap prominent Russians who had sought Gorky's aid to escape from Soviet Russia at the time of Stalin's purges. Gorky had left a suitcase full of letters from these desperate Russians in Moura's safekeeping when he left for Moscow.

Later, Moura, who to save Lockhart's life had become a double agent, was blackmailed by Russian threats to her children into handing over the suitcase of letters written to Gorky. Eventually she had handed over the letters to her controller in the Russian Secret Service. This had led to the torture and execution of prominent Russians who had contacted Gorky, trusted him and requested his help to escape.

Moura, who Nina regarded as having blood on her hands had moved to London and become the mistress and Russian translator for the wealthy science fiction writer H.G. Wells.

Moura's former lover, Robert Bruce Lockhart, the dashing young British diplomat, had been made to resign from the Foreign Office and was now a journalist, writing a book about his years as a diplomat and the plot to assassinate Stalin.

Nina told Nell that Moura had acquired a second 'sugar daddy' in the wealthy writer H.G. Wells. This was how she had the money to make a shopping trip to Paris to buy designer clothes, where Nina had bumped into her by chance. They had spent a few hours chatting in a café about their time together in Berlin.

Moura became angry when Nina mentioned that she and an Australian journalist friend had used the plot to kill Lenin as the basis for a spy novel. Nina added that the novel had a love story with a character called Countess Nathalie, based on Moura and another based on Lockhart and their affair, thinking she would be flattered. Instead Moura was furious. She threatened to use H.G. Wells' lawyers to sue Nina and Nell unless the character based on her was removed from the novel.

Nina, scared at the thought she might be involved in an expensive lawsuit was certain there must be secrets in the life of Countess von Benckendorff-Budberg she did not want exposed. Nina immediately consulted the respected reference source on European aristocracy, the *Almanach de Gotha*. It proved Moura was lying when she claimed to be Countess von Benckendorff. Her husband, Djon von Benckendorff had never had a title and was only a distant cousin of the titleholder. Neither Moura's father nor her first husband had a title so in fact she was a bogus Countess with an equally bogus degree in English Literature from Cambridge. Her only genuine title came from the gambling addict she had married to obtain the Budberg title using Gorky's money.

Nell laughed and said Moura had also picked the wrong university for claiming a fake degree. Cambridge had withheld degrees from women for almost a century, did not grant them before World War One and even now in the 1930s did not grant women degrees.[37]. Her false claims had won her a job in Gorky's publishing company and she was now using the same tall tales to impress H. G. Wells. In short Moura was a very successful con woman. Nell hoped that one day Moura would overdo her lies and tall tales and be exposed.

Nina vowed that if she outlived Moura, she would write the truth in a biography titled *The Wicked Life of Baroness Budberg* as the dead cannot sue.

When they hugged and said goodbye, Nina cautioned Nell once again about becoming too fond of the charming, charismatic Kerensky who had broken many hearts.

CHAPTER SIXTEEN

Working for an Exceptional Man

'I hope to meet an exceptional man, fall in love and get married'
– Nell Tritton, 1926

Nell wanted to create a good impression by being elegant and efficient. For her first day working for Kerensky she chose a navy Chanel suit with a braided jacket, teaming it with a red silk blouse and navy high heels. She studied her appearance in the mirror, changed her lipstick to a richer shade and added a spray of Chanel No 5.

Nell was stopped by Boris, the gigantic Russian security guard at the door to Kerensky's combined home and apartment. She gave the secret password 'Battle of Waterloo' and showed him her passport as identification.

Inside the door she was met by Kerensky's personal assistant Olga Vasilieva who took her to the office they were to share. Olga told her that Kerensky's combined office and bedroom were further down the passage. He had asked Olga to collect whatever work needed translating by Nell and take it to her. Boris would bring her the British and American newspapers as soon as they arrived so she could make a translated précis of important news items Kerensky needed to know.

The large combined dining and reception room overlooking the street had become a reference library with an antique oak table used for conferences in the middle of the room.

The third and smallest bedroom was known as the Correspondents' Room where the Russian freelance journalists who supplied articles and news items for Kerensky's newspaper worked whenever they visited. It was also used by Kerensky's wealthy friend and backer Mikhael Ter-Pogossian, who worked for free as he enjoyed the excitement of publishing. He told Nell working for Kerensky made a change from his profitable but boring business of importing dried fruit from Greece and Turkey. Thanks to this kind backer there was always a box full of dried figs or apricots in the small kitchen for the staff to nibble on and which Nell enjoyed.

Olga Vasilieva had worked with Kerensky since 1922, when he

started publishing *Dni,* his first newspaper in Berlin. She was utterly devoted to Kerensky. When the German currency crashed and inflation soared, Olga moved with him to Paris. She had never married and lived with her cat and a canary in a small apartment in the suburbs. She prepared simple healthy lunches for Kerensky as he ate the diet his doctors told him was suitable for someone who had lost a kidney. Nell learned he never ate meat and rarely drank alcohol but was fond of the delicious cakes Olga bought him from a Russian shop at the end of the rue de Vineuse.

Nell enjoyed her work but wondered why she had so little contact with her employer.

Each morning after Kerensky had called Olga into his office and dictated letters to her, Olga would bring Nell whatever work had to be translated. Meanwhile Nell looked through the latest editions of *The New York Times, New York Herald Tribune, Times, The Guardian* and the *Daily Telegrap*h to see if there were items of interest for Kerensky that needed translating.

She gave her completed work to Olga Vasilieva who took it to Kerensky's office along with typed letters for Kerensky to sign. Nell thought this was a crazy arrangement. It wasted precious time as they were all working hard to a publishing deadline. It would be much quicker if she collected whatever Kerensky needed translating herself and returned it to him so anything that needed clarifying could be dealt with straight away.

Tactfully Nell asked Olga what she thought of her idea.

Olga shrugged and said she didn't make the rules she just did what 'A.K.' wanted. She found it wisest to humour him.

On the rare occasions Nell met Kerensky in the passage, she smiled at him, hoping he might exchange a few words with her but he never did. He was always very polite and greeted her formally with '*Bonjour Madame Nadejine*'. She was tempted to remind him she was divorced and no longer Madame Nadejine.

Nell soon decided it was time to return to her maiden name of Tritton at work and see if that made any difference to Kerensky.

Some things puzzled her. If Kerensky was a constant womaniser as Nina had implied, what was wrong with her because he never even talked to her?

On newspapers where Nell worked she was used to men giving her attention and paying her compliments. In Kerensky's office the younger freelance correspondents, who shared an office with the telex machine would flirt with her as well. So why did Kerensky ignore her?

Nell wondered if there was something about her that Kerensky did not like. Was her Chanel perfume too heavy and it annoyed him? She switched to a lighter more flowery fragrance but he still did not talk to her. She had to do everything through the middle-aged prim Olga Vasilieva who was certainly not one of Kerensky's lady friends.

Initially Olga said very little to Nell as the newcomer to the office when they had morning coffee together. Olga finally thawed when she realised that Nell was helpful, competent and no threat to her job as secretary to Kerensky and sub-editor of his Russian language newspaper.

Soon Olga trusted Nell sufficiently to chat to her over their morning coffee. She explained she was a cousin of Kerensky's wife, Olga Baranovskaya, from whom he had been separated for over 20 years. He was unable to obtain a divorce as they had married in Tsarist Russia. His wife and his sons had been imprisoned by Lenin and when they were freed, had fled to London where they were now living.

Olga admitted she had never liked her cousin. She had always thought her slightly crazy and totally wrong for Kerensky. Kerensky's parents also thought she was crazy spending her time in revolutionary meetings and street marches. When Olga fell pregnant they refused to attend the wedding. They saw his new wife as narcissistic and unstable and had always hoped their clever son would marry another cousin, Lilya Baranovskaya who, like Kerensky's elder sister Elena, studied medicine. Elena Kerensky had urged young Lilya to do post-graduate study and become a paediatrician hoping she would marry her favourite brother, a plan that failed.

The rebellious Olga Baranovskaya who now had a young baby and a toddler, continued to march in processions carrying banners and attended meetings where there was talk of assassinating Tsar Nicholas II. Kerensky under Olga's influence joined her group of militant Socialists, another thing which horrified his parents.

Olga continued to spend her time at political meetings rather than supporting her husband who was just starting out as a human rights barrister. She dressed like a worker and was an embarrassment to her family. Gradually the married couple drifted apart as Kerensky found they had little in common other than their two young sons.

Meanwhile Lilya's parents had arranged her marriage to an ambitious senior officer promoted to the rank of general in the Tsar's army. This arranged marriage proved to be as unhappy as the marriage of Olga and Alexander Kerensky as both couples were incompatible.

With her three year-old daughter, Olga had left her husband and wanted a legal separation, something considered scandalous. At the same time the unhappy marriage of Kerensky and his wife also broke up. Kerensky realised that he was in love with Lilya, the woman he realised he should have married just as his parents had hoped.

Nell was fascinated as Olga continued her story.

Deeply in love with Lilya, Kerensky defied convention and left his wife and young sons. As Russia's Prime Minister he lived with Lilya and her little girl in the magnificent surroundings of a royal suite in the Winter Palace. Soon it became obvious Lilya was pregnant with what everyone presumed was Kerensky's child. This was considered even more scandalous by some of Kerensky's conventional political associates.

After the Red Guard had arrested his government and Kerensky, hunted by Lenin spent a year in exile in England, before starting his Russian newspaper in Berlin. Lilya, now legally separated from her husband joined him there with two young children, one fathered by her husband and one by Kerensky.

But Kerensky was no longer a world leader, short of money and under pressure to bring out an anti-Communist newspaper, he was often not easy to live with and in pain caused by the loss of one kidney. Their relationship broke down amid tears and recriminations. Lilya left Kerensky and refused to see him again or let him visit his young daughter.

Meanwhile in Moscow, the malevolent Lenin had taken his revenge by having Olga and their young sons arrested and imprisoned in the Lubianka jail. They were surrounded by prisoners who were being tortured or shot and feared they might suffer the same fate.

A powerful friend secured the release of Kerensky's wife and sons and they were helped to flee to London where Kerensky was able to visit them but any reconciliation with his wife was out of the question. The acrimonious break up with Lilya who he regarded as the love of his life had scarred him badly. From now on Kerensky's relationships with women were numerous but never long lasting.

Although Nina had implied that Kerensky chased women, Nell was piqued that they had never even had a proper conversation although he often sent messages via Olga congratulating her on doing good work.

Nell looked in the files and read the published speeches Kerensky had given on his America-wide tours. She admired his courage in confronting Stalin at a time when few Western journalists or editors criticised the powerful Russian leader. Only Kerensky and a British journalist named Malcolm Muggeridge, writing anonymously in *The Guardian,* had dared to expose Stalin's imprisonment of his political enemies in the *gulags.* Stalin's huge press office had successfully hidden the fact that Stalin had caused the famine in the Ukraine which had killed over a million people.

A brave young Welsh journalist named Gareth Jones had dared to write the truth that Stalin had sent soldiers to confiscate the harvest and livestock of Ukrainian peasant farmers but Stalin had banned his entry to Russia. On a fact-finding mission in China Gareth Jones was found murdered. Reading an article in *The Guardia,* Nell learned Gareth Jones' guide in China had been a member of the Russian Secret Service. The story of Gareth Jones' murder increased Nell's admiration for Kerensky as one of the few leaders who dared to criticise the murderous Stalin. She remembered Flora telling her how Stalin had ordered several unsuccessful attempts to assassinate Kerensky.

Kerensky's headlines for his anti-Communist editorials were forceful. One of them was headed *How the Bolshevik Dictatorship is impoverishing and killing Russia's peasants,* referring to the Ukrainian famine that had killed over a million people. Kerensky was the leader who had dared to point out that Stalin, while claiming to be the 'father of his people,' was ordering the deaths of thousands of people each year.

Stalin used terror tactics and forced labour in *gulags* to stay in power. [38] Olga told her an attempt had been made to poison Kerensky with a box containing his favourite sweet cakes delivered by hand which made her suspicious as she had not ordered them. Laboratory tests revealed they were laced with poison but the courier was never identified.

Olga said Russian history was riddled with poisonings. It was the way Russia's leaders usually disposed of their enemies. From that time on, all gifts of food or wine that arrived by post or by special delivery were rejected or disposed of in case they were poisoned.

Letter bombs were also addressed to Kerensky. This explained why all the mail was carefully screened by the security guards in the safety of the basement.

Whilst working as a journalist in Brisbane and Sydney, Nell had been annoyed that as a female she had never been given political assignments. She was enjoying her translating work for Kerensky as it concerned major political events in Europe. She felt involved and as Olga had a wide knowledge of politics she enjoyed in depth discussions with her as she was clearly far more than just a secretary.

The year 1936 was a critical one in Europe and the telex machine hummed with the latest news from Nazi Germany and Hitler's Olympics.

In Spain a new Socialist Republican Government had just been elected to the dismay of the Fascist party and the Catholic Church.

The Fascist Colonel Franco soon returned to Spain with a battalion of Moroccan mercenaries to overthrow the new government appointing himself Generalissimo Francisco Franco in support of Spain's Fascist party backed by Hitler.

****

Five weeks after starting work in the rue Vineuse, Nell was alone in her office as Olga was taking dictation from Kerensky in his office. Nell was sitting at her desk with her back to the door when two strong arms enveloped her from behind. Twisting round to see if this was a of practical joke by one of the freelance correspondents, Nell was horrified to discover the arms belonged to her ex-husband.

As she struggled to free herself from Nikolai's embrace she smelt the alcohol on his breath. She yelled at him to leave her alone but he continued to hold her, pleading with her to take him back as he had changed. As Nell struggled to free herself, Nikolai tightened his hold, and she fought back. In their struggle a chair was overturned, a vase of flowers smashed and papers and dictionaries strewn all over the floor.

Hearing raised voices and the crash of broken glass, Kerensky appeared followed by two bodyguards. The three men grappled with Nikolai and pulled him off Nell. She identified the intruder as her former husband as Nikolai shouted insults in Russian. He continued shouting as the two guards dragged him downstairs and threw him into the street.

Kerensky saw Nell was shaking and on the verge of tears. He invited her into his combined office and bedroom, sat her on his big sofa bed, went to his filing cabinet and poured them two glasses of brandy. He handed her a glass and a clean white handkerchief and waited.

Once Nell had stopped shaking he asked if she would like his driver to take her home. Nell was very embarrassed that Nikolai had broken through the security arrangements. She feared that Kerensky might think she had given her ex-husband the secret password and he would ask her to leave a job she enjoyed.

In answer to his question as to whether she would like to be taken home, she shook her head and thanked him.

Kerensky's bodyguards returned and told their employer that they had let the stranger into the apartment because he claimed to be Madame Nadejine's husband. He had shown them legal documents and insisted that they needed to be signed immediately by Madame Nadejine.

Kerensky told the security guards that they had been foolish and had broken the rules. Captain Nadejine should not have been allowed inside. Stalin's secret police had tried tricks like this to get inside the apartment and would never stop until he and Trotsky were dead. Sternly he told them to go back to their posts and he would deal with them later.

Kerensky's tone softened as he addressed Nell. As an experienced barrister he made a few tactful but probing questions about Nell's marital situation. She was relieved at least he wasn't going to fire her as she had feared.

In answer to his questions she told him about her failed love match to Nikolai, the alcoholic cavalry officer whose career as a singer she had tried so hard to establish. She explained how difficult it had been to get a divorce and emphasised she wanted no more contact with her ex-husband. As far as she was concerned Nikolai was now the 'toy boy' lover of Melba's friend, care taking her villa on the isle of Capri. She was surprised he had returned to Paris. She did not hate Nikolai but never wanted to see him again. She had wasted four years of her life and a large amount of her money, trying to give Nikolai a new life. She had done her best and now she was free.

Kerensky listened and nodded sympathetically. To Nell's surprise he opened up about his own disastrous marriage. He and his wife had separated twenty years ago but obtaining a divorce had been complicated because they had married under the Tsarist regime in Russia.

His marriage had been a dreadful mistake, he should have married Lilya, his wife's cousin who he had known since childhood. He confessed he had been intrigued when Nell arrived for an interview because she looked so much like Lilya which was why he had been avoiding her. The feelings she aroused in him were very strong, but he knew from past experience workplace love affairs often ended badly.

Seeing Nell distressed by her ex-husband's unwanted arrival had broken the barriers he had built around his emotions.

Nell was stunned he was revealing feelings for her, of which she was totally unaware. She said nothing as Kerensky told her about his love for Lilya which had gone so wrong and resulted in disaster for them and their daughter.

As Prime Minister, Lilya had been his unofficial First Lady and lived with him amid the splendour of the Winter Palace, waited on by servants in the suite of former Tsar Alexander II. They had been surrounded by loyal servants and had a nanny for their little girl. The fact Lilya had left her husband, General Biriukova, had shocked many of his supporters but they were in love and ignored all disapproval.

Had Kerensky remained as Prime Minister things might have been different but as he was also the Justice Minister he could have made the rules on divorce more flexible. He had hoped to divorce his wife, have a second chance at happiness and marry Lilya.

However the invasion of the Winter Palace by the Red Guard and the arrest of his government, meant Kerensky had to go into hiding with a price on his head. This had changed everything and he was now powerless and penniless.

Kerensky explained how he and Lilya were separated for almost a year and her husband the general was shot by the Bolsheviks. Kerensky had left Britain for Berlin and on money supplied by his Jewish supporters, had started his anti-Communist newspaper. Lilya had joined him in Berlin with a toddler fathered by her late husband and a baby fathered by Kerensky. They lived in a cramped apartment on very little money. His mother had often cited the proverb 'When Poverty knocks on the door, Love flies out of the window' and in their case this was true. Lilya had found life difficult with two babies, living in relative poverty, which was very different to being surrounded by servants in the Winter Palace.

Kerensky had been stressed by starting a new publication, the teething baby had been screaming constantly and Lenin had sent assassins to kill him. He had to work long hours to establish his newspaper and one evening returned home late to discover Lilya had left him.

He felt her departure was the tragedy of his life and blamed himself. No other woman had come close to what he felt for Lilya.

When he met Nell he had been stunned by her physical resemblance to Lilya and part of him longed to get to know her much better. But this likeness had opened an old wound and he had dealt with it by choosing to avoid his beautiful new employee.

Their conversation was interrupted by a knock on the door. It was Olga who told Kerensky the Czechoslovakian Ambassador was waiting to see him in the Conference Room. With her emotions in a whirl Nell left Kerensky's office and went home to think about the changed situation. She passed a sleepless night wondering what the future could hold for them.

The following morning Kerensky followed his usual routine of opening the post and dictating letters to Olga Vasilieva and asked Olga to send Nell into his office. Nell knocked on the door and he told her to enter and pull up a chair so she could sit next to him to discuss the articles he wanted her to translate. He then asked her to come back at midday and share his frugal lunch.

When she returned Kerensky showed her a silver-framed photograph of an attractive young woman who did indeed resemble Nell but had shoulder-length dark hair unlike Nell's short bob.

Nell realised this was Lilya, the woman he could never forget. Kerensky explained how after they had broken up, Lilya, who had qualified as a doctor in Russia, could not get her qualifications recognised in France and could only work as a poorly paid nurse. However the death of her parents gave her money and independence. In spite of requests made through his lawyer she refused to see Kerensky again or let him see their daughter.

The fact Nell and Kerensky had experienced the pain of failed relationships drew them closer. He regretted he had to leave as he had an appointment that afternoon and another one for the evening. As Nell was about to leave, Kerensky leaned forward and touched her cheek softly. She turned to face him and they stood there, eyes locked together, both of them unwilling to break the spell.

At Olga's knock on the door, both of them stepped back and Nell returned to her desk her cheeks burning. She worked hard all afternoon but Kerensky was still closeted in the Conference Room so she did not see him that day.

At home Nell wrote in her diary how much she had wanted Kerensky to take her in his arms and kiss her.

She passed a restless night and decided to take the initiative in this unexpected turn of events. She wrote a note, enclosed it in an envelope and slipped it under his door, inviting him to her apartment for dinner so they could talk without fear of being interrupted.

Kerensky sent back a note saying he would be delighted to dine with her. His bodyguard would drive him to her apartment at eight o'clock. He knew the address as it was on her file.

Now Kerensky was to be her guest, Nell worried about a suitable menu. Olga had told her that after Kerensky's operation his doctors insisted he eat a strictly vegetarian diet.

As she knew he had a weakness for French pastries and cheese Nell went to a local delicatessen in her lunch hour and bought a selection of delicious cheeses and vegetarian dishes. From the *boulangerie* she bought a long *baguette* of crusty bread. Countess Yevgenia had taught her how to make Russian *borscht* with beetroot and sour cream and she bought the ingredients to make this for their meal.

The problem was what to wear. Something elegant but not too revealing would be the answer. An admirer of Chanel's designs, Nell had become a client of Maison Chanel on the Rue de Cambon where she had bought several fluid jersey dresses and exquisitely cut suits. For this important dinner Nell chose a flattering little black dress by Chanel and put Russian music on the radiogram.

The candlelight dinner broke the ice between them. She found Kerensky entertaining and easy to talk to, but neither of them were ready to make the first move towards greater intimacy, wanting to know each other better before taking such an important step.

Kerensky told her he had had far too many brief encounters in hotel bedrooms. Like Nell, he wanted a serious relationship as this was her first emotional encounter since her divorce from Nikolai.

Over their enjoyable meal they talked about their childhoods in Russia and Australia. Hearing about the wildness of Tashkent where Kerensky had spent his boyhood appealed to Nell who loved the Australian bush and they shared their experiences of discovering the fascination and beauty of Paris.

Nell told Kerensky how her love of all things Russian had begun by reading the journal of Marie Bakshirtskeff and her tutorials in Russian literature with Nina Berberova. It was a strange coincidence that Nina, her best friend in Paris, had been a book reviewer for Kerensky's newspaper in Berlin. They discussed books and discovered their favourite Russian authors were Tolstoy and Dostoyevsky.

Kerensky explained he wanted to take this relationship slowly and get to know Nell better before they made love. He laughed as he observed that this had been the reverse of most of his past relationships. But Nell was special, and he did not intend to make the same mistakes again.

Although Kerensky could not drink much alcohol he enjoyed the wine that Nell had chosen and was able to relax. He told her that from the moment she had walked into his office he had thought she was the most beautiful woman he'd met in years but was wary that the age difference between them was almost twenty years. He assumed that as an attractive divorcee she must have a lover so had kept her at a distance.

The evening went rapidly as they had so much to say to each other and they lost count of time. However the workaholic Kerensky, believing in early to bed early to rise had ordered his bodyguard to collect him at 11.00 pm. The bodyguard arrived on time, rung the bell and waited outside for his employer.

Kerensky held Nell's hand as he thanked her for a wonderful evening and said he was sorry he had to leave but had an early appointment the next morning. He hoped she would dine with him the following night at *Kalinka,* the best Russian restaurant in Paris.

She said she would love that. He kissed her lightly on both cheeks and left.

Their dinner the next night fulfilled all of Nell's hopes of a perfect romantic evening. Kerensky presented her with a single red rose. They ate Beluga caviar with *blinis* and sour cream and other delicious Russian dishes. The elderly waiters knew Kerensky well, bowed low when they spoke to him and called him *Monsieur le President.*

Kerensky toasted Nell with vintage Pol Roget champagne and said her presence had made an enormous difference to him. She made him laugh and feel young again; she was not only beautiful but highly intelligent and witty. Now he had found her he was sad he had to leave for America for five months on a speaking tour.

When their dinner ended his bodyguard dropped them at Nell's apartment. Kerensky sent him away and spent the night with Nell. She found him a sensitive and thoughtful lover.

Nell did not want to be seen as Kerensky's mistress by any of his office staff. In the two weeks that remained to them before he left for America, she never stayed overnight in his combined bedroom and study. They always stayed in her apartment. The only person who realised that the situation had changed was Olga Vasilieva. As she had disliked Kerensky's wife and some of his other women, she remained friendly with Nell.

One night as they lay in bed after lovemaking, Nell remembered the series of tapestries that she had seen in a museum in Paris showing a young woman in medieval dress embracing a white unicorn. In one of them, the white unicorn, a symbol of masculinity, rests his head on the lap of the beautiful lady he adores. As a gesture of affection Nell called Kerensky her 'beloved unicorn'. Nell who enjoyed playing with words told her lover that, *'like the unicorn, he was horny, handsome, unique and threatened by extinction'*. She was aware of Stalin's attempts to kill him and realised this was a fear she would have to live with.

The fact that he had to leave on his American speaking tour so soon meant Nell would miss her 'beloved unicorn' badly. Her consolation was that she was able to talk to him on the phone, although in the 1930s transatlantic phone calls were extremely expensive. Nell had access to the telex machine but as it lacked privacy all messages via the telex had to be very formal.

She waited eagerly for Kerensky's return from his speaking tour which had been successful and made him the money he needed to continue running his anti-Communist, anti-Fascist newspaper, which was his life's passion.

They kept their love affair secret and only a few friends knew about it. They were invited to delicious Armenian meals by Kerensky's friends and financial backers, the Ter-Pogossians or to the riverside apartment of the former French President Leon Blum on the Isle de St Louis in the middle of the Seine.

However he refused to accompany Nell to the Russian ballet and so she took Nina with her as she had season tickets.

Nell was worried that whenever Kerensky had to go out in the black Citroen, driven by one of his bodyguards, he was at risk. Aware of this he sat in the rear passenger seat with a hat pulled down low over his forehead to hide his face.

In Brisbane, Nell had enjoyed driving her father's large silver Buick and had loved the excitement of competing in motor rallies with her brother. Desperately worried about Kerensky's safety she acted as his chauffeur so that his bodyguard could sit in the passenger seat and concentrate on protecting Kerensky from any of Stalin's gunmen.

So Nell, the former champion rally driver became her lover's chauffeur. The bodyguard was now able to protect Kerensky with his loaded Browning pistol on his knee with Kerensky in the back seat. Nell greatly enjoyed the excitement of being at the wheel of a big, powerful car once again.

****

Nell's love affair with Kerensky was a very different experience to her married life with Nikolai. Kerensky worked from early morning until dinner time then, over a meal prepared by Nell or sent in from a nearby restaurant, they discussed recent political events. Nell relayed to him what she had read in the British and American press that day.

Occasionally they would have another romantic dinner at The Kalinka, Kerensky's favourite restaurant. After dinner, at Nell's apartment, they listened to music or read.

They walked on the *quais* that bordered the Seine and browsed bookstalls in front of the towers of Notre Dame. They worked hard for causes in which they both believed, lived quietly, and according to her diary Nell was very happy with her new life, until she received a shock.

A week before Christmas Nell was at her apartment when a letter arrived, marked Private and Confidential. Ruth Shapiro had written to warn her that Flora had learned of her affair with Kerensky and was furious. Flora had admitted to Ruth that Kerensky had been her secret lover although her friends had been told her lover was a foreign ambassador who could not be identified.

Nell was stunned by the news that Flora had been one of Kerensky's many lovers. The loyal Olga Vasilieva, not wanting to betray Kerensky, had hinted to Nell that Flora had shown a proprietorial interest in Kerensky when she had visited the office for meetings with his other financial backers.

On learning that the two of them had kept this important information from her, Nell felt betrayed and taken for a fool.

That night Nell could hardly sleep and decided she was not going to put up with this situation. She would make a stand. She left early the next morning for Kerensky's office in the rue Vineuse to ensure she arrived before his other staff. She found Kerensky seated at his desk and handed him Ruth's letter along with her letter of resignation. She turned on her high heels and walked out of the room without saying a word.

Kerensky took one look at Nell's face, read both letters and turned white. He asked Nell to come back into the office and tried to embrace her and offer an explanation. She stepped back to avoid all contact and refused to let him touch her. Kerensky pleaded with her to sit down, and asked her to listen while he told her the truth.

He admitted that ten years before, under unusual circumstances in a New York hotel, he had started a casual on-off relationship with Flora. The physical side to their relationship occurred on the night when a Tsarist female supporter had slashed his face with a knife in front of an audience of 5,000 people. She could see he had been shaken by the event and had invited him to her room to treat the wound. They talked about their shared past in St Petersburg and his new Russian language newspaper which was in desperate need of capital.

Flora then offered a generous gift of money to support his new publication with whose aims she agreed. Of course he had accepted and it had made all the difference to that first penniless year of production.

As a matronly older woman she was not his type but he found her very interesting. Of course he should never have made love to her but she had initiated it.

He vowed that after falling in love with Nell he had broken off the relationship with Flora; he had never been in love with her and had never pretended be. He was grateful for her financial backing and their on/off affair had continued out of habit because Flora wanted it.

The only breaks he took from work were trout fishing and boating on Lake Annecy on the borders of France and Switzerland and Flora had sometimes accompanied him.

He promised Nell that from now on his relationship with Flora would be purely platonic. He loved Nell and wanted to marry her as soon as he could obtain a divorce from Olga. This came as welcome news to Nell who was tired of hiding their affair from the press. It was the first time Kerensky had mentioned the word 'marriage'.

She accepted his explanation. But Flora's money was still invested in his newspaper and was helping to keep it going. Nell told Kerensky she would break off their relationship immediately if she had any reason to doubt his word.

In the summer of 1937, Kerensky's lawyers advised that his wife, Olga, now living in the London suburb of Putney, was refusing to divorce him unless he gave her half the money he received from the sale of his manuscripts and research notes from an American university library. She also wanted a share in royalties of future books. They advised him that his wife had no legal claim whatsoever to this money. She was obviously being advised by some very greedy lawyers. Arguing over this would be lengthy and expensive and cause his divorce to take much longer than Kerensky had envisaged.

Later that year, the fact they were not married would cause Nell embarrassment in America when she accompanied Kerensky on his next speaking tour as his press secretary and interpreter.

Wives of many senators and mayors in America's Bible belt were conservative in their thinking. They treated Nell, who had no wedding ring on her finger, as an outcast. They regarded her as Kerensky's 'kept woman'. In reality she was supporting herself. Her small salary was insignificant compared to the Tritton family trust which gave her access to more money than Kerensky would ever earn. Nell Tritton, as she now styled herself, using her maiden name again, was certainly not a 'kept woman'.

In America Nell was never seated at the same table as Kerensky at formal dinners. Seating plans placed her at the rear of the room on these occasions, and at a couple of events Kerensky was even asked not to bring her, which led to rows between them.

****

The only person other than Olga Vasilieva who knew about the previously hidden relationship between Kerensky and Flora Solomon was the dashing young diplomat, Bruce Lockhart, who had twice saved Kerensky from assassination by Lenin. The first time, he helped Kerensky escape from the Gatchina Palace and the second time he drove Kerensky from his mountain hide-away near Pskov, to the Russian port of Murmansk to escape Lenin's vengeance.

When Kerensky was staying with Flora Solomon in her house in Hornton Street she would sometimes ask Lockhart to join them for a dinner when they spoke Russian and reminisced about the romance of life in St Petersburg.

Nell was amazed to find that Lockhart and Countess Moura, the basis for a character in her banned spy novel set in Russia, were known to Flora. Even stranger was the fact Kerensky had told Nell that Lockhart, forced to resign from the Foreign Office, when desperate for money, had also written a spy novel based on the plot to kill Lenin. He had managed to get it past the Official Secrets Act by making the plot sound like a schoolboy prank. In Lockhart's novel Lenin was not going to be kidnapped and assassinated, but would be shamed by having his trousers removed then marched thought the streets of Moscow, his power broken.

Nell was amazed at how the paths of people from totally different worlds had crossed. It had made her aware of how spy networks operated. She wanted to marry Kerensky and hoped that one day he would return to Russia in triumph as Prime Minister.

CHAPTER SEVENTEEN

Saving Spanish Orphans

By 27 April 1937, Kerensky had returned to Paris from America. Nell opened an airmailed copy of *The Times,* and read an article by journalist George Steer describing the bombing of Guernica. This city was regarded as sacred to the Basque people who occupied the northern part of Spain and a part of south western France.

On the afternoon of Saturday, 26 April 1937, during the Spanish Civil War the picturesque market town of Guernica had been bombed; destroyed by planes from Hitler's Condor Legion. More than half the civilian population had been killed and the rest rendered homeless. In desperation many had fled to France.

Nell was certain Kerensky would want to see this story as he was monitoring Hitler's actions, worried by his harsh treatment of Jews. She translated *The Times* article into French for Kerensky which provided evidence of Hitler's duplicity. Hitler and Mussolini had signed a non-intervention pact with Britain promising not to send armaments or troops to the Spanish Civil War and had broken the pact.

Nell found homes for Spanish refugees whose homes had been destroyed by German bombs. The children's school fees were met with money raised by Nell who organised a combined charity dinner and fashion show for their aid.

Because Nell spoke a little Spanish and had visited Spain's Basque country, she had been following events in the Spanish Civil War. She made a précis of the article in *The Times* and showed it to Kerensky along with her translation of the destruction of Guernica. She explained to him how Hitler's Condor Legion of elite pilots had deliberately chosen a market day in Guernica, when it would be full of unarmed civilians. Hitler was clearly showing the Spanish nation that Franco and the Fascists aided by Nazi Germany and their planes were taking control of Spain. She pointed out to Kerensky there was a certain similarity in the fact that the Republican Government of Spain had been legally elected and was being overthrown by the brutal forces of General Franco with the overthrow of Kerensky's Republican Government by Lenin.

In April 1937 the men of Guernica were away fighting for the Republican cause leaving their wives and children in the undefended town. Farmers' wives had arrived in Guernica with their children to sell their produce and cattle in the Saturday market. George Steer's article pointed out there were no army camps or military installations in Guernica, or any reason at all for the merciless attack by German planes.

Hitler's Germany, like Britain, France, Italy and Stalin's Soviet Union, had signed a non-intervention pact that they would not intervene in the Spanish Civil War or send armaments to either side. Hitler, seeing this as an ideal opportunity to test out his planes and pilots for the war that he was planning to wage against France, sent his Condor Legion of elite pilots to help General Franco fight the elected Republican Government of Spain.

At precisely 4.30 in the afternoon, Hitler's pilots flew over the town on market day aiming to kill the maximum number of people. Heinkel and Junker planes with swastikas painted on the underside of their wings, unleashed a rain of firebombs on the town's attractive wooden chalet style houses. Observers recorded the pilots were laughing as they bombed and strafed the women, children and livestock in the market square.

This made history as the first ever air attack recorded on a civilian population. Terrified women and children ran into the fields to escape as the Heinkel fighter pilots swooped low like birds of prey hunting them down like rabbits. After two hours of bombing, Guernica was reduced to rubble and ashes. Over a thousand adults and children lay dead in the streets and hundreds more were buried under smoking rubble.

In sending his pilots to destroy the town, Hitler was demonstrating his ability to kill and intimidate civilian populations with the superiority of his air force known as the Luftwaffe in preparation for his attack on France.

In an editorial Kerensky denounced Franco and Hitler over the bombing of Guernica. He was already on Hitler's death list for denouncing his treatment of Jews and unknown to Nell, had been placed on Franco's secret Death List. This meant Kerensky was banned from entering Spain.

The destruction of Guernica and photographs of the town reduced to rubble featured in the Paris Exposition which opened in June 1937. Later Picasso's famous painting titled *Guernica* would go on tour around Europe and America.

Nell visited the exhibition and found the German and Soviet pavilions facing one another across a central plaza, the largest of the pavilions in the enormous exhibition. Nell saw an exhibition of photographs in the Spanish pavilion condemning the attack on Spanish towns and villages by Nazi planes and Franco's troops.

At the entrance of the exhibition, female refugees from the Spanish Civil War were handing out leaflets telling visitors of the massacre of defenceless women and children in Guernica highlighting the fact they were fighting for the survival of the elected Spanish Government.

Inside the auditorium, Nell watched a documentary about the civil war called *Spanish Earth,* scripted and produced by Joris Ivens and the young American author Ernest Hemingway. She remembered his name as Hemingway had been living in the next street to her in Montparnasse when she first went to live there. He had written his famous novel about Spain *The Sun Also Rises,* in the Clos des Lilas café where she and Nina used to meet for lunch. Hemingway had subsequently been sent to Madrid to cover the civil war as a journalist when the Spanish capital was besieged by Franco's troops. Hemingway had made the emotive documentary which reduced Nell to tears.

It showed the unfortunate women of many Basque towns including Santander where Nell and her cousin had stayed when she first came to Europe. Defenceless women had been left homeless and were raped by Franco's Moroccan troops as the men were away fighting. The film with its Spanish soundtrack was subtitled in English and had a powerful effect on Nell.

The Basque women had fled in terror to France believing that the French Government would help them. Unfortunately Kerensky's Socialist friend Leon Blum was no longer in power and the right wing Government of Edouard Daladier did not want to spend money on helping them. So these unfortunate women and their children were immediately imprisoned in barbed wire enclosures lacking sanitation or running water with only a few tents for shelter.

Nell was deeply moved to hear about living conditions from the haggard Spanish women begging outside the Spanish pavilion and gave them all the money she had with her. She remembered how Flora had raised money in London for Jewish refugees from Nazi Germany. She decided she must raise money to help the homeless who were flooding across the Spanish border into France but needed more money than the Tritton family trust could provide. She would give whatever she could then use her skills as a journalist to raise money to help the Spanish widows, their children and orphans. The children needed an education so Nell realised she must help the Spanish refugees as Flora Solomon had done for Jewish refugees.

Working with Flora, Nell saw how wealthy women would attend a charity function in an elegant hotel which gave them an excuse to dress up and wear jewellery normally kept in the bank. They would gain recognition for their generosity. Their husbands would pay big money for the privilege of having a named table to which they could invite friends or business associates and be seen to support a worthy cause.

Nell approached a titled Russian *émigré* friend who worked as a vendeuse, at the House of Chanel on the rue de Cambon. Nell asked her friend to intercede with Madame Chanel to allow some of her models to appear in a charity fashion show at The Ritz to raise money for Spanish refugees. Chanel, whose early life had not been easy, was not known for her generosity. But, as an astute business-woman, she realised that this fashion show would be excellent publicity for the House of Chanel.

Coco Chanel agreed to lend a few of her fashion models and part of her latest collection for a catwalk display and champagne dinner at The Ritz. In a written agreement the name of Chanel had to be displayed on the catwalk and appear on all publicity material for the event.

Nell wrote the press releases for the event at which she acted as *compère*. Although nervous at giving a speech in French in front of a room crowded with wealthy clients of Chanel the event was a great success.

Nell, looking elegant in an evening dress by Chanel, made an impassioned appeal for money to provide housing for the women and children from the towns of Guernica, Santander and Badajoz, whose homes had been destroyed. Nell explained to her wealthy audience how after suffering gang rape by Franco's Moroccan soldiers, many women and their children had hitched rides in farm carts or walked hundreds of miles to cross the French border in search of safety.

Instead of being welcomed, women and children were herded into barbed-wire enclosures lacking fresh water and sanitation. The Daladier government refused to provide any financial assistance. Donations to the Aide Espagne Charity, of which Nell was a committee member, enabled the Spanish woman and children to leave the barbed-wire enclosures and move to houses the charity had rented in villages near the Spanish border. The women could return home to Spain once peace returned to their country.

The guests at Nell's fashion show and dinner at The Ritz, having dined well and drunk plenty of champagne were in a generous mood. Large sums were raised from the sale of lottery tickets and an auction for which Nell had persuaded Paris department stores like La Samaritaine and Galeries Lafayette to donate prizes. The seafront Hotel Negresco in Nice offered a prize of a weekend for two in a suite overlooking the Bay of Angels.

The event was a huge success and some of the audience were so moved by Nell's speech they offered to house some of the Spanish women and children in empty cottages on their country estates. Others offered employment as domestic staff in their Paris residences. These offers were followed up by committee members of Aide Espagne.

Nell had already sent parcels of tinned food and soap to the family in Santander where she had stayed in 1926. She knew that sending money by post was far too risky. Many Spanish banks had closed as the Spanish civil war was now causing chaos with a huge death toll on both sides.

Nell received a letter of thanks which took months to arrive. The letter told her that in Santander, men and women with trade union cards or being merely suspected of supporting the Spanish Republic had been arrested. The Republican prisoners were handcuffed by the Moroccan mercenaries, forced into trucks provided by Mussolini and Hitler and driven to the high cliffs on the edge of Santander which bordered the Atlantic Ocean. Franco's Moroccan mercenaries, short of bullets, threw prisoners with pockets filled with stones off the cliffs to drown in the sea below.

Others who had been office holders in the local Republican Government were tied to stakes in the main square and garrotted to death with piano wire in front of friends and relatives. This most brutal war became the *cause célèbre* of the late 1930s.

The charity committee liaised with the socialist Dominican and Mexican embassies in Paris on behalf of the Spanish widows who hoped to travel to South America and start a new life. Nell and her hard-working volunteer committee raised or donated money for sea passages to Mexico, the Dominican Republic and the United States.[39]

Although Hitler had sent a large force to Spain, Kerensky's second issue of *Novaia Rossiia* published a warning to Stalin not to intervene in the Spanish Civil War. But it was too late. Stalin had already sent volunteers to Spain, known under the acronym the POUM or the Marxist Workers Party of Spanish Unification. Members were instructed to spread Marxist doctrines among the International Brigades rather than help the Republic.

Stalin was playing a devious role in Spain's Civil War. Nell would learn that Stalin sold ancient rifles for a good price to the cash-strapped Spanish Republican Government. The rifles were so inefficient they would often backfire and kill the Republicans who fired them rather than their Fascist enemies.[40]

With information translated by Nell from the British press Kerensky denounced Fascist atrocities carried out by the forces of General Franco. Franco and his bloodthirsty Moroccan mercenaries were exposed in issues of *The New Russia* and in articles printed in *The New York Times,* published on 16 October and 30 October 1936.

Franco's propaganda department had even fabricated the incredible story that Spanish Republicans had bombed and strafed their own people in Guernica. Fortunately no one with any sense believed them.[41]

CHAPTER EIGHTEEN

'Beloved Unicorn'

Back in 25 June 1934 Austria's political leader had been found dead on the floor of his office assassinated by Nazi thugs who left him to bleed to death. After Chancellor Dollfuss was assassinated, the weak-willed Kurt Schuschnigg took over as Austria's Chancellor. He agreed to a plebiscite being held in favour of an Austrian union with Germany which, thanks to Nazi infiltration, became a farce. Voting areas were hung with swastikas and filled with Nazi storm troopers. Each voter received a gift bag decorated with a portrait of Hitler with the slogan, *Ein Volk, Ein Reich, Eine Fuhrer,* (*One People, One Reich, One Fuhrer*). Austrian Jews were forbidden to vote and jailed if they attempted to record their opposition to Nazi Party Candidates.

Kerensky had pointed out this was a perversion of democracy by Hitler. Kerensky had now run his newspaper in Germany for two years. He spoke fluent German and had studied Hitler's book, *Mein Kampf (My Struggles*) in which Hitler outlined his philosophy and his plans for the future. Kerensky was therefore well aware of the threat Hitler posed with his Nazi ideologies and discussed these with Nell.

Kerensky's enemies had claimed he was Jewish but his spirited defence of the Jews in Russia, Nazi Germany and German occupied Austria in his newspaper had been done on purely on humanitarian grounds. He watched with alarm as the situation deteriorated.

Planning another speaking tour in America he took English lessons from Nell so he could give speeches in English to Americans as well as in Russian to his exiled countrymen and women.

In March 1938 Kerensky arrived in New York for his second prolonged speaking tour. In his speeches he warned of the danger to Austria's large Jewish population after the Nazis marched triumphantly into Vienna having murdered Dollfuss.

Wearing the same brown uniform as his storm troopers, Hitler gave the Nazi salute to cheering crowds as pretty girls in national dress threw flowers into his car to impress the Austrian public. The whole operation including the carefully choreographed photos that Hitler had masterminded in one of the most successful publicity campaigns of all time. By annexing Austria, Hitler gained some valuable mining resources which helped re-arm Germany illegally and recruited a vast new population of Austrians receptive to Nazi ideology.

****

Kerensky had promised Nell his physical relationship with Flora Solomon was over. Their relationship was now purely platonic. Flora remained a patron of *Novaia Rossiia* and outwardly, as their intimate relationship had always been kept secret, nothing had changed.

However, privately Flora was seething with rage that Nell, her little Australian protégé had won the affections of the man she regarded as her intellectual equal and 'spiritual husband'. Kerensky had been her ideal sexual partner at times when it suited her. She knew he had liaisons with other women in Paris and on his speaking tours; such a powerful speaker, would inevitably find women who offered to spend the night with him.

Flora's anger over Kerensky's changed relationship with Nell came to a head in November 1938 when Kerensky paid a visit to his sons in London. As usual, he came to visit Flora in her house in Hornton Street, Kensington where he had always stayed in Flora's spare room to save money on hotels. By now their relationship was platonic but he still needed somewhere to stay free of charge. He certainly couldn't stay in Putney with Olga, the wife he was trying to divorce.

Kerensky and Flora listened to the BBC commentary about the horrific events of Kristallnacht, known as the Night of Broken Glass, on 9 November 1938, when Nazi storm troopers smashed the windows of Jewish-owned shops in several German cities. Jews who defended their shops were arrested by the Gestapo and sent to concentration camps, often with their wives, leaving their children without parents.

Flora had been increasing her efforts to bring orphaned Jewish children to England in what became known as the *kinder transport* and was horrified to hear of Hitler's persecution of German Jews. She wanted Kerensky to write about this in his newspaper and was angry that he didn't share her anguish. He replied that this was nothing new, *pogroms* or persecutions had been happening for centuries in Jewish settlements in Russia. Unfortunately the world had paid no attention and persecutions were not big news to his Russian readers.

This coupled with his rejection of Flora in favour of Nell sparked a row between Flora and Kerensky and ended their relationship.[42] As a result, Flora's financial contributions to *New Russia* ceased which made it harder for Kerensky to pay his staff.

****

Hitler had now decided to recoup lands owned by Germany before World War One. He claimed a large proportion of the Czech Sudetenlands were filled with Germans, due to the fact he had urged Germans to move there so he could claim they were German.

Hitler blackmailed the leaders of Britain and France by threatening a second world war if they blocked his take-over of the Sudetenlands of Czechoslovakia to 'protect' its German population. These were people who Hitler had encouraged to go and live there.

Britain's Prime Minister Neville Chamberlain was terrified of a second war remembering the million men who died in World War One and made no protest when Hitler announced that the German occupation of the Sudetenland region of Czechoslovakia would begin on 1 October 1938. Kerensky's acid comments about Hitler's occupation meant he was likely to be listed as an enemy of Nazi Germany and would be on a death list if the Nazis ever invaded France.

Hitler now had a bitter enemy in Stalin who each year became more disturbed and murderous. The years 1937-1938 became known as the era of Stalin's Great Purges or Killings. Letters smuggled out to Kerensky aboard cargo ships told him of the many Russians shot by Stalin's secret police 'for crimes against the State'. Hundreds of thousands more Russians were sent to *gulags* as slave labour in mines and for road building.

Nell, worried about Kerensky's safety ignored the danger to herself now she was his wife. At that time Australians travelled under British passports and she regarded her passport with its dark blue and gold cover as a talisman that would protect her.

As Hitler's demands for more lebensraum or 'living space' in Eastern Europe and Austria for Germans increased, Kerensky arrived in New York for another of his very successful speaking tours. He spoke in Russian to fellow Russians and to Americans from notes translated by Nell. He warned America's Jewish population that Austria's large Jewish population was under threat as the Nazis were preparing to march in triumph into Vienna.

The publicity organised by Goebbels with carefully choreographed photos of Hitler striding past a phalanx of black banners ornamented with swastikas made Germans proud of him. In America, Kerensky saw the photographs of Hitler surrounded by an adoring public and feared that the two dictators, Hitler and Stalin might join forces and threaten Poland.

One evening while Nell was at the ballet with Nina and Kerensky was still in America, a cat burglar scaled the walls of Kerensky's apartment building in the rue Vineuse. The burglar swung from a rope, broke a window, entered Kerensky's office and stole important papers. Nell and Olga had to clear up the mess and assess what had been stolen. When he received the news Kerensky commented with relief that it could have been worse. The burglar could have planted a bomb on a time fuse to wreck the apartment and kill Olga and Nell. [43]

The police were called but could not trace the culprit. Olga was convinced the burglary had been arranged by Stalin's secret police, now called the NKDV. Nell wondered if the cat burglar had been sent by Hitler in revenge for Kerensky's criticism of the Fuhrer.

Kerensky, still in America, wrote to Nell worried about the burglary and the fact that Hitler had gained a large number of new supporters in Austria which was now under Nazi rule in an occupation known as the Anschluss. The vibrant Europe of the mid-1920s when Nell had arrived in Paris was rapidly being taken over by dangerous dictators.

Kerensky made withering comments about Hitler in his talks to Russian émigrés, aware that doing this would place him even higher on Hitler's list of those who should be exterminated if the German army managed to invade France. He was determined to avenge Germany's defeat in the previous World War.

By now the fear of Hitler had reached Australia and the government was talking of arming for war. Nell's father wrote to her revealing the Commonwealth Minister for Defence had announced plans for railway workshops to start manufacturing munitions in anticipation of this happening.

The British Cabinet realised with horror that they had mothballed too many battleships and greatly decreased the size of their armed forces. Belatedly they started to rebuild the army, navy and air force.

The forceful young Winston Churchill, anticipating danger, insisted that Hitler had stated in his book *Mein Kampf* that he planned to invade France and Britain. Lulled into a false sense of security few people believed Hitler's threats or took heed of Churchill's warnings. Some British aristocrats mistakenly believed Hitler would save them from the menace of Communism.

CHAPTER NINETEEN

Stalin Denounced and Nell Marries in America

Like Churchill, Kerensky had been warning his readers and audiences on his American tour of the inevitability of war but had no real idea of the huge numbers of atrocities being initiated by these dictators .

When, decades later, researchers were able to inspect Communist archives after the dissolution of the Soviet Union, they revealed that Stalin and his staff had approved of 799,544 executions. Stalin sent over a 1,000,000 Russians to die in *gulags,* with at least 390,000 more deaths caused by the forced resettlement of hard-working peasant farmers (*kulaks)* whose lands had been confiscated.[44]

Russians who had managed to escape from Soviet Russia arrived penniless at Kerensky's office and met Olga Vasilieva or Kerensky, telling them the grim truth about life in Communist Russia. They added that Stalin and his cronies lived like the Tsars they had replaced. Communist leaders now owned the handsome Romanov summer villas and enjoyed luxurious holidays in the warm weather of the Crimea while the workers shivered from cold and starved.

Nell felt sorry for those who had families, giving them money from her Tritton trust fund to help pay rent while looking for a job as Kerensky could not employ any more people.

Russia's working classes for whose benefit the revolution was supposed to have taken place were still queuing for hours to buy a single loaf of bread. Stalin had fulfilled his promise to industrialise Russia but, as would be discovered later, this came at the cost of almost 200,000,000 Russian lives.

In 1939 Kerensky once again defied Stalin and published an open letter from Fyodor Raskolnikov, a former Communist leader and Russian ambassador to Afghanistan, to the Russian people denouncing Stalin for betraying the revolution and its workers. A friend sent a copy of Raskolnikov's letter to Kerensky via a seaman on a Swedish merchant vessel.

Aware he did not have long to live as he was suffering from cancer, Raskolnikov didn't care if Stalin had him shot. He just wanted the truth about Stalin's Russia to be known. He had become increasingly worried about Stalin's state of mind as the number of arrests, imprisonment and deaths mounted.

In the past Raskolnikov had been a friend of the author Maxim Gorky, the one-time employer of Nina's husband'. In a letter to Gorky, Raskolnikov confided he was thinking of escaping to Western Europe and asked the famous author about the best way to escape to the West. He was unaware that Gorky was being wooed by Stalin with promises of honours, money and a lucrative job as Head of the Writers' Union to entice Gorky to return to Russia. [45]

Raskolnikov's open letter to the public dated 17 August 1939, described Stalin as *'the embodiment of evil, lacking in moral sense, signing death warrants for old friends and colleagues when drunk.'* His letter was lucid and detailed and Kerensky translated it from Russian into French. He asked Nell to translate it into English hoping to shock the Americans into realising the danger they faced. But Nell's translation was never published in America as the danger was labelled remote. Kerensky published the letter in Russian in his newspaper *The New Russia* at the end of 1939 in Paris. Kerensky quoted Raskolnikov word for word in his editorial:

I shall tell the truth about you Stalin. Under pressure from the Soviet people you granted them a democratic constitution in 1936 but what have you done with it? Fearing free elections that would threaten your power you have trampled on the constitution. You have transformed elections into a miserable farce of voting for a single candidate. You have filled the sessions of the Supreme Soviet with ovations in honour of yourself.

You have quietly annihilated deputies. You have done everything you could to discredit Soviet democracy. You will enter the history of our revolution as an époque of terror. Nobody in the Soviet Union feels safe. Nobody when they go to bed knows whether they will escape arrest during the night. There is no mercy for anyone. The righteous and the guilty, the hero of the October Revolution, the old Bolshevik, the non-party man, the collective farm worker, the ambassador, the manual worker, the intellectual and the Marshall of the Soviet Union are all subject to the blows of your whip. All are whirled about in your devil's roundabout.

Raskolnikov had written the truth. Lies and half-truths had been used by Stalin's propaganda department to create a benign public image of Stalin who as his paranoia grew became increasingly cruel and unpredictable. His letter explained how Stalin had enriched himself at the expense of the workers. Raskolnikov knew that in writing these words he had signed his own death warrant but he no longer cared, aware his cancer would soon kill him.

Raskolnikov paid the penalty for speaking the truth and met a mysterious death later that year. The Russian press recorded him 'falling out of a high window'; the usual way the Russian secret police disposed of their victims.

As a result of Kerensky publishing the Raskolnikov letter denouncing Stalin, members of Kerensky's immediate family became a target for Stalin's revenge. Stalin ordered the execution of Kerensky's much loved elder sister, Dr Elena Kerensky, a leading paediatrician in Moscow, having already ordered the death of his younger brother Fyodor, a prominent young lawyer in Tashkent. [46]

When Gorky returned to Russia he entrusted Raskolnikov's incriminating letters and those received from other high ranking Russians officials wanting to defect to his mistress, Baroness Moura Budberg who had refused to return to Communist Russia with Gorky.

Aware the Communist regime treated its critics with a bullet to the back of the head, Gorky warned Moura, who was later suspected of being a double agent, that should she receive word he was dying and wanted to see her, on no account should she bring the suitcase of letters he had entrusted to her for safe keeping to Moscow.

Gorky was prophetic.

In 1939, aware he was dying of a mysterious illness (possibly poisoned on the orders of Stalin to entice Moura back to Russia with the letters) and still in love with Moura, Gorky wrote to Moura, begging her to visit him in Russia as he was dying. Fearing the Communists might kill her children who were still in Estonia, Moura did what she had specifically been told not to do. She brought the suitcase of letters with her and on arriving in Moscow, handed them over to her Secret Service controller Jacov Peterss.

The writers, critical of Stalin and seeking a better life in the west were immediately tortured and shot by firing squads on Stalin's orders.

On several speaking tours of America Kerensky warned his audience that Stalin's jovial façade was a veneer. It covered the truth that smiling 'Uncle Joe Stalin' was a paranoid murderer who had ordered the arrest, torture and execution of many of his own colleagues who had once been his drinking companions.

****

In January 1939 Kerensky made another American speaking tour to help fund his newspaper.

In Paris, Nell was anxiously hoping that the last of the divorce papers from Olga Kerensky's lawyers would arrive in New York. She hoped to join Kerensky and marry in America having told him she would never return to play what Nell called in French *'la comédie de la fiancée.'* In fact wives of American politicians regarded the term *fiancée* as a euphemism for 'mistress' and those jealous of Nell's poise and good looks referred to her as little better than a whore

In Australia Nell's mother had become increasingly worried about her daughter being referred in the press as Kerensky's 'common-law wife' and wrote to Nell about this. Nell hated to worry her now elderly parents and wanted the situation settled. She wrote to Kerensky explaining how important it was to her church-going parents that she was married even if they married with a celebrant rather than a clergyman in church.

By now Nell had not seen her family for a long time and with Kerensky away in America and no progress on the divorce papers, she booked her passage to Australia on a cruise liner. Early in March 1939, Nell arrived back at *Elderslie,* the home she loved.[47] Staying with her parents, she tried to avoid the topic of the delay in her marriage plans aware her parents were upset she was 'living in sin' with a married man.

Three month later, early in July 1939, Nell received a telegram from Kerensky telling her how much he missed her and imploring her to join him in New York. He said his divorce papers from Olga were almost through. They could marry in New York as soon as she arrived.

Relieved and delighted that she could inform her parents of her impending marriage, Nell told them the happy news. She packed her trunk with her best outfits including several Chanel suits which she felt would be more suitable for a second wedding than a long white wedding dress and bridal veil. At a farewell party at *Elderslie* for family and friends she received wedding presents and good wishes for her new life as the wife of Russia's former Prime Minister in exile.

Nell was driven to Sydney in the Buick and at Circular Quay she boarded the transatlantic liner bound for New York. She found her cabin filled with flowers sent by family and friends, who had never approved of Nikolai and were delighted that at last she had found a husband worthy of her.

On her arrival at Kerensky's hotel in New York, expecting to learn the date fixed for their wedding, Nell was shocked and angry that although Kerensky's *decree nisi* had been granted, the final document, or *decree absolute,* still had not arrived.

Nell was embarrassed and angry, feeling she had been lured back to America by Kerensky under false pretences. The Australian press had reported her marriage to the former Russian Prime Minister would take place in New York soon after she arrived and journalists were contacting her wanting information. Nell knew how upset her parents would be at another delay happening in the public eye. She had no intention of being made to look foolish in the American press, hanging around week after week in New York waiting for Kerensky's divorce papers to arrive; the perpetual fiancée.

Nell wanted to make the point that she was a financially independent and in control of her own life. She left Kerensky's suite and as her shipping trunk had still to be brought up to their rooms, sitting at a desk in the lobby she wrote on hotel stationery, 'I am leaving as I am deeply upset that you made me leave my home and my family when you knew I would refuse to continue playing *'la comedie de la fiancée'.*

Nell phoned for a taxi which took her and her luggage to the Plaza, New York's most elegant hotel and reserved a room with a view over Central Park. From there she phoned a travel agent to book a passage on a cruise ship leaving New York for Sydney in two days' time.

She telephoned the reception desk at Kerensky's hotel and left a message giving the receptionist her date of departure and said she was not taking calls.

Kerensky rushed to the Plaza Hotel to reassure her that his *decree absolute* from Olga would soon be finalised. Nell said she had heard that story before. Aware of how persuasive Kerensky could be, she refused to allow him into her room and met him in the lobby, saying she had had enough of American politicians' wives despising her as a kept woman, refused to discuss the matter further and took the lift back to her room.

Nell refused to take Kerensky's anguished phone calls. She told the staff at reception if anyone asked for her they were to say she was tired, wanted to sleep and would not be talking to anyone.

When a massive bouquet of flowers arrived for her at reception Nell refused to accept it. She told the receptionist to send it back and refused to take calls from a Mr Kerensky, no matter how urgent he said it was.

Nell repacked her trunk and prepared to return to her parents' home. She only reconsidered when Kerensky's French lawyers sent her a telegram assuring her that Kerensky's *decree absolute* had been granted and they were airmailing it to New York.

Once she received the lawyer's letter Nell agreed to meet Kerensky. Their reunion, arranged on her terms, changed her position in this new relationship. She would no longer be just the paid translator of a powerful man. Nell had made her point. She would not be pushed around and due to her stance at a time when many wives were doormats, their relationship had undergone a transformation.

Kerensky, worried that the danger from Stalin's secret police could now affect Nell as well as himself felt it vital that the American press did not report the date and place of their wedding. Kerensky took it upon himself to arrange a private ceremony at the Pennsylvania home of a Justice of the Peace named Harry Stein.

However, although Kerensky's *decree absolute* had been granted on 29 July 1939 there was a postal hold up and the decree did not arrive for another week. Rather than hire strangers from a New York security company Kerensky arranged for them to be driven to Harry Stein's home by Victor Soskice, the son of Kerensky's best friend in London who had worked as an aide in Moscow. Victor Soskice was young and strong and could act as bodyguard and witness at their secret wedding in Pennsylvania. Stein had promised Kerensky he would remain silent about conducting this private ceremony and they believed him.

On 20 August 1939 the three of them arrived at the small town of St Martin's Creek, Pennsylvania, where Harry Stein conducted a dignified private wedding in the privacy of his home. At her second wedding Nell gave her age as 38 and Kerensky as 58 but both of them looked considerably younger. Nell wore an elegant navy suit by Coco Chanel with her long hair in the traditional Russian style that Kerensky so admired.

After a celebration lunch the newly-weds were driven back to New York but found the New York press had been tipped off by the perfidious Harry Stein, who wanted to see his name in print as the marriage celebrant of a celebrity couple.

As the secret had been leaked they agreed to give an exclusive interview to *The New York Times.* Their secret marriage would eventually be published in the Washington and London press and in American women's magazines. Brisbane's *Courier Mail* dated August 23, 1939 carried an article on their marriage in the same issue as the ominous news about the signing of a Hitler-Stalin pact. Kerensky realised the seriousness of this development, which would lead to the invasion of Poland and the start of World War Two.

A few days after their wedding, Kerensky gave a joint talk in a major New York auditorium with Nobel Prize-winning author Thomas Mann. Both of them pleaded for America to enter the war on the side of the Allies and resist dictators like Hitler and Stalin. Kerensky's speech had been translated by Nell into English and typed out with the phonetic equivalent of difficult words so he could pronounce them correctly. With some coaching from her on his pronunciation he spoke in English to a large audience. He became emotional as he urged the Americans to join the Allied cause and fight for the freedom and liberty of the democratic world when believers in democracy would turn their eyes toward the United States as an inspiration.[48]

Kerensky's important speech was broadcast on several American radio stations at the same time as Winston Churchill was using the fact his mother, Jennie Jerome and many of her high profile relatives supported America joining the war. Churchill hoped this would be an incentive for America to support the Allies.

In another interview with the *New York Times*, Kerensky warned Americans that Stalin's Great Purges (mass killings) had resulted in the show trials and murders of thousands of innocent people. Aware Stalin was trying to silence him, Kerensky accused Stalin of killing any colleagues the Russian dictator feared could become his rivals. Stalin had secret agents in New York who had recently murdered an American secret agent called Walter Krivitsky. So Kerensky retained the services of Victor Soskice as his bodyguard.

Consulted by several members of the American State Department as he was regarded as an expert on Russian affairs, Kerensky warned them that the secret Hitler-Stalin pact signed by Joachim von Ribbentrop, German Foreign Minister and his Russian equivalent, Vyacheslav Molotov was a 'betrayal of democracy'.

Kerensky realised that under the terms of this pact Stalin and Hitler would invade Poland and carve up the country which had rich resources of coal and other minerals.

In his speeches he warned that Stalin was likely to kill educated Poles fearing they would oppose Soviet rule. Kerensky was correct as Stalin ordered the mass killing of many thousands of Polish officers in the woods of Katyn, blaming the massacre on the Germans who had entered Poland at the same time as the Russians.

At a political dinner given by the Democrats a few days later, Kerensky was accompanied by his wife, elegant in a long dress by Chanel. Now Nell was officially Mme Kerensky the organisers seated her at the top table beside her husband instead of relegating her to the back of the room.

In his speech at the Democrat dinner Kerensky urged America and Britain to recognise the danger Stalin posed and to 'fight for the overthrow of Stalin's dictatorial regime in Russia'.

****

The news of Nell's wedding took several weeks to appear in the Australian press. Not until September 1939, did the *Australian Women's Weekly* publish a account of Nell's marriage to the former Prime Minister of Russia as did several of the quality Sunday papers in Australia and in Britain.

The Women's Weekly article ran a long, illustrated article headlined 'AUSTRALIAN GIRL WEDS FAMOUS RUSSIAN EXILE'. They published a photograph of Nell, explaining her hair was styled with the traditional Russian plait around her head in the way her husband loved (See photo).

Interviewed by the *Australian Women's Weekly*, Nell's mother carefully avoided the embarrassing topic that Nell and Kerensky had been living together for almost three years before their marriage. Mrs Leila Tritton told the journalist,

When Nell arrived in Brisbane to visit us last February she wore a magnificent ring given her by Alexander Kerensky. She had met the former Prime Minister of Russia in France some years ago and done some translations for him. Having retained her interest in international politics she enjoyed long discussions with Kerensky. She told us that she liked him because he was a highly intelligent man of the world. We suspected that their mutual interest might develop into a romance.

The French press had always been aware of the relationship between Nell and Kerensky but were more tolerant than the British or Australian press when it came to matters of the heart and took it for granted the couple had been living together.

On 27 August 1939, the sensationalist Australian tabloid *Truth* featured on the front page a photograph of Nell with the bizarre headline, *BRISBANE WOMAN'S ROMANCE NOW WIFE OF EX-DICTATOR?'* across the front page. Presumably the ex-dictator was Kerensky or they thought Nell had married Stalin. The article was full of mistakes and referred to Nell's ex-husband Captain Nadejine as a 'world-famous baritone' which was far from the truth.

The tabloid also revealed Kerensky had been married to Olga Baranovskaya, his Russian wife for 30 years. However they altered the sequence of events to make it look as if Nell had broken up Olga's marriage to Kerensky. The journalist clearly had no knowledge of the chronology or would have realised that at the time when Kerensky was married to Olga, Nell was a teenager living thousands of miles away in Brisbane. The article omitted to mention that Kerensky and his first wife had lived apart and in different countries for over two decades.

****

Kerensky now had dangerous enemies including Hitler who he had frequently denounced in his newspaper editorials for the way the Nazis treated Jews.

In January 1939 as the leader of Germany, Hitler made a speech in the Reichstag blaming Jewish financiers for the steep devaluation of the German currency and subsequent financial problems caused by heavy reparations to France for damage by the German army in World War One.

Hitler was now sending Jews to concentration camps which had originally been set up for political prisoners. Nazis in charge of running the programs to imprison Jews now instituted a programme under which Jewish businesses could be taken over by Germans and Jewish homes and possessions confiscated.

Hitler, the dictator who had wanted to become an artist, was aware that wealthy cultured Jews had valuable collection of art which could be confiscated and sold profitably through selected Nazi art dealers to dealers in Switzerland who would ask no questions about provenance. The money obtained from looted art would be used to fund Germany's war preparations.

Kerensky had written about Hitler's persecution of the Jews in *The New Russia* which ensured he was on Hitler's death list.

In March 1939 Nell, monitoring the British press, translated into French an article in *The Manchester Guardian* headed *'Mussolini and Hitler rejoice.'* It related how pleased Hitler had been to hear the news that General Franco and his Fascist troops and Moroccan mercenaries had won the Spanish Civil War. Nell was horrified by the news remembering her happy Spanish holiday and the people she met when she first arrived in Europe.

Kerensky ran an article in *The New Russia* recording the fact that the victorious Fascists who had taken over the government of Spain had killed thousands of Republicans. Stalin was becoming increasingly paranoid as he aged and after several unsuccessful attempts to have Trotsky and Kerensky assassinated, told his secret police to renew their efforts.

Kerensky would learn from underground Russian sources that a psychopathic Spanish Communist named Juan Ramon Mercader had been sent from Mexico to Russia for special training to kill Trotsky. In 1938 Mercader was in Paris when the headless body of Trotsky's former secretary, Rudolf Klement was found floating in the Seine. In the same year Trotsky's young son, Lev, was murdered in Russia by Stalin's secret agents and no one was prosecuted for either murder.

In 1940 Trotsky and his wife, the subjects of further assassination attempts, fled to Mexico as guests of Communist artist Diego Rivera, who was in New York painting a mural for Rockefeller. The Trotskys stayed with Diego's wife, the fascinating artist Frida Kahlo in their Mexico City home, *La Casa Azul* (the Blue House). When Diego discovered Trotsky was having an adulterous affair with his wife, although he had frequently been unfaithful to her himself, he insisted the Trotskys leave the safety of his home and move to a rented house on the outskirts of Mexico City.

On the night of 24 May 1940 Trotsky and his wife were woken by the sound of breaking glass and realised intruders had entered the house. The curtains were drawn and their bedroom in darkness so they quickly arranged the pillows to resemble two figures under blankets. The assassins fired several rounds of ammunition into both pillows and fled just as the police arrived. Unsuccessful once again, Stalin still did not give up.

On 20 August 1940, pretending to be a Belgian journalist named Jacques Mornard, Juan Ramon Mercader introduced himself to Trotsky as a journalist interested in Trotsky's writings. Trotsky, flattered by the young journalist's admiration, invited the disguised Mercader into his combined office and library, where they discussed Trotsky's writings and his promotion of world-wide revolution through the trade unions of various nations.

Trotsky went to his bookshelves to take down a book he wanted to show the alleged journalist. While Trotsky's back was turned, the assassin took out a small lethally sharp ice-pick he had hidden under a raincoat carried over his arm. Lunging forward, Mercader buried the ice pick deep into Trotsky's skull. Trotsky fought him off but fainted and was still alive when rushed to the nearest hospital. It took him twenty-four hours to die in agony.

Nell and Kerensky were appalled to hear of the horrific death of Trotsky. Kerensky realised that as an enemy of Stalin he could be next. The Mexican police arrested the phoney journalist and investigations revealed his real identity. Juan Ramon Mercader was a dedicated Communist paid by the Russian secret police. Mercader was brought to trial, found guilty and received a twenty year jail sentence.[49]

On his release the assassin received an official welcome to Cuba from Fidel Castro. In 1961 Mercader was invited to Soviet Russia and awarded the country's highest decoration, created a 'Hero of the Soviet Union and given a pension.

CHAPTER TWENTY

Escaping from the Nazis to New York

In September 1939 when Nell and Kerensky were in America, Germany invaded Poland. To guarantee Poland's safety, Britain and France declared war on Nazi Germany and hoped that America would join them. Churchill did his best to persuade Roosevelt to enter the war on the side of the Allies but was opposed by a strong anti-war lobby as many Americans felt they had lost far too many young men in World War One. This was a European war and America should stay well clear of it.

In February 1940 the French press reported Alexander Kerensky and his new wife had returned to France in a honeymoon suite aboard the transatlantic liner *SS Normandie*. As events turned out, they would have been wiser to have remained in America but with Kerensky's anti-Communist newspaper in Paris, they decided to ignore the danger from Nazi Germany and return.

In Paris they heard that Hitler might invade and Churchill had sent British soldiers to help repel a German attack. Kerensky still feared that Stalin would now target Nell and send more assassins so whenever the new Madame Kerensky went shopping, visited her hairdresser or went with Nina to the ballet she was accompanied by one or other of Kerensky's bodyguards.

French right-wing President Edouard Daladier had hoped to keep the stock market stable by reassuring French voters there was no real danger of a German invasion although this was bluff and he knew an invasion of France by the German army was a strong possibility.

Kerensky disliked Daladier who had not invested nearly enough in armaments while Hitler had been building a superbly equipped German army with radio-controlled tanks and well-trained soldiers. Hitler was also ready to deploy his Condor Legion of modern fighter planes and capable pilots.

But the months that followed became known at the 'Phoney War' as nothing happened to disturb the peace. The newly married Kerenskys continued working together aided by Olga Vasilieva and freelance Russian-Jewish journalists working in shifts in the

Correspondents' Room. Nell and Kerensky continued working hard on the newspaper, eating out at their favourite restaurant in Passy, where the waiters continued to flatter Kerensky by addressing him as 'Monsieur le President'.

Nell's cleaner, promoted to the role of housekeeper, as Nell now worked long hours in the office, prepared them a meal and left it ready to be cooked in Nell's apartment. On some evenings they ate with Olga Vasilieva, worried that with Kerensky's marriage she might feel neglected.

Nell received a letter from Ruth Shapiro who told her Flora Solomon had become one of the organisers of the *kinder transport* of Jewish children out of Germany to Britain whose parents had been sent to concentration camps. Flora and her co-workers had found foster homes for all the children and she was now trying to find British families to adopt orphaned children whose parents had been killed by the Nazis.

Upset when she had read in the European edition of *The New York Herald Tribune* that Kerensky and Nell were married, Flora sought to denigrate her former protégé by referring to her as Kerensky's 'Australian typist' when Nell was doing much more vital work. She was Kerensky's press secretary, entrusted with producing a précis of important events from British and American newspapers and she helped Olga organise her husband's personal affairs and schedules in which he had little interest. She helped the Russians who had managed to escape from Soviet Russia to Paris seeking Kerensky's help and from them learned a great deal about life in Soviet Russia.

Nina Berberova, now divorced from her poet husband, was living with her young French artist partner in a converted farmhouse to the south-west of Paris and only came to Paris to accompany Nell to the ballet. Nell and Kerensky enjoyed escaping for weekends to the attractive farmhouse Nina and her partner were renovating.

Decades later in her memoirs Nina described how Nell, who had spent her childhood in a house with a big garden, loved staying with Nina in her converted farmhouse near the tiny hamlet of Longchêne. In *The Italics are Mine,* Nina recorded happy weekends with Nell helping her prepare meals and picking lettuce, dill and onions from the kitchen garden before an early dinner. Nell loved sitting and chatting with Nina on a terrace overlooking the rose garden where almond trees blossomed in spring.

In her memoir, Nina described Nell as *'beautiful, calm, intelligent.*

She had shoulders and a bosom like Anna Karenna, her eyes were always alive, and disobedient locks of hair curled around her ears. I did not at that time speak English so all our conversations were carried on in French, which she spoke perfectly. In a photograph she and I are lying in tall grass, in similar cotton dresses, happily smiling at one another.'[50]

Years later Nina recalled Nell as being witty and entertaining and telling fascinating stories about countries she had visited and people she had met. After dinner the four of them sat on the terrace under the stars and Nell told them about her Australian childhood at *Elderslie* and Kerensky and Nina talked about St Petersburg.

Once, when they were alone, Nell asked Nina if Stalin were eventually overthrown and Kerensky recalled to Russia as President or Prime Minister, would he be able to enter Moscow in triumph on a white horse as he had done all those years ago at Tsarskoe Selo after the capture of the Winter Palace?

Nina felt she must shatter Nell's daydream that Kerensky would return in triumph to Russia. She told her Stalin was unlikely to fall, his reign of terror surrounded by secret police who executed anyone who criticised the regime, meant Stalin and his successors would never lose their iron control over Soviet Russia.

Nell refused to believe her best friend, wanting to believe in the dream that inspired Kerensky and continue his crusade for freedom for all Russians from the dictatorship of Stalin.

Kerensky's fears about a German invasion of France soon came true. They both knew Kerensky must be on Hitler's death list for accusing the Fuhrer in print of being a dictator. It was time to leave.

In May 1940 the German army invaded the north of France and the French Government fled to Tours and then south to Biarritz. Churchill had sent British forces to northern France to protect Paris but they were outnumbered and had to retreat to the port of Dunkirk amid fears the German army would soon be marching on Paris.

Nell was worried about her husband, whose one remaining kidney was causing him pain. She wanted him to rest as she knew they had a long tiring car journey ahead to escape before the Germans captured Paris. She realised she had to act quickly to save her husband's Russian-Jewish correspondents who would be arrested by the Nazis and sent to concentration camps. Most had very little money but had been of an enormous help to Kerensky and had wives and young children.

Nell had loyal Spanish friends as a result of her financial help for

Spanish widows and children from Guernica and Santander. These friends warned Nell that acquiring entry visas to Spain was lengthy and complex with enormous queues at the Spanish Consulate of frightened people desperate to escape to America from the Spanish ports of Bilbao and Malaga. They advised bribing a corrupt consular individual would be her best hope but it would be expensive. Nell decided to use money from the Tritton family trust for this.

Much of northern France was now under German control. Roads and trains going south were crowded with British holiday makers caught in France by the German invasion. Escape to Britain by sea was dangerous as the English Channel was heavily mined and dangerous for shipping.

In addition to helping their Russian employees, Nell needed a Spanish entry visa for Kerensky, plus one for herself and another for Olga Vasilieva. It could take an entire day of queuing to obtain the necessary visa forms and if it was fiesta time the Consulate would be closed.

There was so little time to save the Russian-Jewish free-lancers and their families. Spanish friends confirmed they know of a corrupt official in the Spanish Consulate who in return for money would provide blank visa forms with official stamps which would pass an inspection at the Spanish frontier. All that was needed was to fill them in and add passport photos.

Nell withdrew some family trust money to pay the corrupt Spanish consular official the obscene amount of money he had requested. She needed to obtain visas for herself, for Kerensky, Olga Vasilieva and the Jewish members of Kerensky's staff. Unless she helped them they would be arrested by the Nazis and sent to concentration camps.

Her Spanish female friends, grateful for her help rallied to her aid. They arranged a meeting with the consular official and she was told to bring the money he required in cash or gold bullion as both were untraceable. She met the consular official in a seedy Spanish nightclub with a lone gypsy guitarist strumming away before the flamenco dancers and musicians arrived.

Nell handed over the cash and checked he had provided the right number of blank visa forms stamped with the official seal of the Spanish Consulate. All that was needed was to fill in the names and addresses of the users and attach small identity photos. Nell brought the blank forms back to the office. She filled in visa forms for Kerensky and gave one to Olga Vasilieva. She did her best to copy the entry visa she had been given on her visit to Spain in 1926.

She had told Kerensky's freelance staff to bring their families to the office with one suitcase per person plus identification photos for the visas. The consular official had told her that trains for the border between France and Spain were so crowded that passengers were crushed together in the corridors and no reserved seats were available.

When Kerensky's helpers arrived Nell filled out the forms and saw their photographs were glued into the correct space. With tears in their eyes they hugged her for saving them from the Nazis and said a sad goodbye to Kerensky. Nell drove Olga Vasilieva and the freelancers in relays to the Gare du Lyons railway station. Olga was going to take a ship from Spain to relatives in Buenos Aires who had promised her a job.

Nell reminded them to change trains at the Spanish border as train tracks were a different gauge in Spain from France. As Franco would not give permanent residence to Jews, they should head for Bilbao or go south to Malaga and with the money she had given them, obtain a passage by ship to North or South America. She saw them aboard a crowded train whose corridors were filled with people sitting on their suitcases.

In a long and emotional phone conversation with Nell, Nina refused to leave her partner, claiming that during the German occupation they would be safe in the depths of the country. It was Paris which would be dangerous but as in the last war there would probably be a universal shortage of food and heating fuel.

It was vital Kerensky left France quickly or he would be arrested by the Nazis and shot or sent to a concentration camp and Nell might face the same fate.

Nell begged Nina to come to Paris for a farewell dinner and stay the night but realised this was impossible. Nina had no car so Nell decided to pack an overnight bag with essentials, drive to Longchêne for that farewell dinner and stay overnight. They would then return to Passy and load the car with their suitcases and the boxes she had already packed. She planned that after crossing the French-Spanish frontier they would drive to Bilbao and take a ship to New York.

Nell hoped that in America she would be able to write Kerensky's biography so had packed two boxes with their personal papers and diaries to help her do this.

On the night of 11 June 1940, Nell and Kerensky were dining with

Nina and her husband at Longchêne when they switched on the radio and were horrified by the news that German radio-controlled tanks and soldiers had overcome the ill-equipped French troops guarding the road to Paris. The announcer warned that the Germans would be in command of the city by midnight. It was too late to return to Passy and pick up their luggage and their money.

The shocking news that they could not return to Passy to pick up their possessions or their money meant Nell, normally cool and collected, burst into tears. Fortunately their passports and visas were already in the glove department of the car. They would try to get a few hours sleep at Nina's house before they left for the main highway.

At dawn on 12 June, Nell put the overnight bags they had taken with them into the Citroen and said a fond goodbye to Nina and her partner. Nina gave them a picnic basket with food and bottled water for the journey. Nell embraced her friend who had become as close as a sister. She worried about how Nina would cope when the Germans invaded, unaware that she would never see her again.[51]

Initially with Nell at the wheel the Citroen made good progress on the small country roads from Nina's house. But once they reached the main highway south they found it gridlocked with cars and farm carts in a line that stretched for over twenty miles.

The big black Citroen became part of a mass exodus of cars, farm carts loaded with children and grandparents, bedding and chickens in coops heading for the Spanish frontier. Belgian and northern French farming families were desperate to escape the German army, remembering how badly they had been treated in the previous war. The Kaiser's army had confiscated their harvests, killed their livestock and left them virtually starving. Young men were taken to work in German factories so fear had motivated farmers and Jewish families to head south to escape from the Germans.

All hotels and inns along the highway were closed as their owners had fled. Nell spent an uncomfortable night in the car with Kerensky grumbling about how stiff he had become and how his medication for his remaining kidney had been left behind in Passy.

They drank the last of Nina's coffee at dawn. The sky grew dark again as German planes appeared, dropping bombs onto the road and causing chaos among the gridlocked traffic. Frightened horses reared, farm carts overturned and cars crashed into each other, killing and injuring drivers and passengers.

The German bombers were soon replaced by small fighter planes.

Nell was horrified to see young German pilots flying low overhead using cars, livestock and people as targets for their machine guns, riddling them with bullets, demonstrating that the Germans, losers in the last war, were now the victors.

Gridlocked in traffic, the cars and farm carts proceeded at a snail's pace. A car journey meant to take two days stretched into a week with the horror of German planes bombing the column of traffic each morning just after dawn.

Nell and Kerensky slept uncomfortably in the car. Just before it was light, Nell would help her ailing husband out of the car and into a ditch as bombs landed on the road. They emerged from their ditch when the planes had gone to find the grass verge littered with corpses riddled with bullets.

On the highway were dead horses and shattered limbs of bodies blown apart by bombs. The road stank of death as the sun rose and beat down on them. Many cars had been reduced to twisted wrecks and had to be pushed out of the way before the procession could start again. Nell drove past women howling beside the bodies of dead husbands and children. Dogs whose owners had been killed wandered disconsolately through the traffic.

On the second day of their journey, as they walked back to their car, Nell saw two small girls dragging the corpse of their father over to the grass verge to bury him in a ditch. The little girls were attempting to scrape earth over the body with their bare hands. Nell went to talk to them and helped the little girls bury their father under a shallow layer of earth and leave a notification of his name. She helped bring the body of their dead mother from the passenger seat of the wrecked car and laid it beside their father, hoping the police would find the bodies and take them to the nearest mortuary.[52]

Taking the little French girls by the hand she cleared a space in the back seat of the Citroen and they climbed into the car as the long convoy slowly once again moved off.

The little girls were in shock but explained to Nell that they had an aunt who lived in a town some forty kilometres away but off the main road. Going there would have meant the German army would overtake them. Nevertheless Nell turned off the highway to the nearest small town hoping to find a police station who could trace the relatives of the orphaned children. She found the police station and the police promised to find their relatives. In the town they were able to fill the car with petrol and their water bottles with clean drinking water.

Nell remembered her father telling her that in most rural areas in France, the water was polluted with typhoid. She hoped this water was safe but there was no bottled mineral water for sale even at black market prices. It took a further two hours before they were admitted back into the long line of farm carts and cars that inched slowly forward.

All hotels and restaurants on the main highway south were deserted. Their owners had fled taking their food and bottled mineral water with them as mineral water had become more precious than gold.

The following day finding unpolluted drinking water was still a problem. Notices in public lavatories said, '*Eau non potable*' and warned of the dangers of drinking tap water as typhoid was endemic in the area. The food Nina had given them was finished and they were hungry and desperately thirsty.

In the blistering summer heat they spent a miserable day without food or water with Kerensky unwell and short-tempered. Finally Nell was so thirsty she broke into a deserted house. In the kitchen she found a bar of chocolate and two precious bottles of mineral water which they drank.

The next day, while foraging in another deserted farmhouse, Nell found a loaf of stale bread and some Brie cheese but no bottled water. Raging thirst in the summer heat forced Nell to drink more polluted tap water. She unselfishly gave Kerensky the last of their bottled mineral water. Nell worried that with only one kidney he was more likely to succumb to typhoid or blackwater fever than she was.

In another dawn bombing raid in which the Germans showed the French that they were now the victors, it was too dangerous to leave the ditch for several hours. Thirst forced Nell to use her empty water bottle to scoop up water from the ditch. This resulted in violent stomach cramps and an attack of gastroenteritis during another uncomfortable night. .[53]

Mercifully the German planes ceased their daily dawn attacks. Nell and Kerensky drove on slowly for another day, cramped, hot and uncomfortable after sitting and sleeping in the car for so long. Nell decided that Kerensky could not take this for much longer and turned off the main highway. On a side road they found a deserted barn where they managed to rest up for a couple of days before they rejoined the long procession on the main highway. Lacking his medicine, Kerensky was in pain and grumbling about the heat and lack of food and water.

In contrast Nell never complained and regarded it as a miracle they were still alive.

On one occasion when they sighted a detachment of German soldiers demanding identity papers, Nell was able to make a quick turn onto a side road. Once again she saved Kerensky's life when she threw herself on the mercy of a kindly Frenchman who hid them from the Germans in his cellar. Amazingly he had recognised Kerensky from a newspaper photograph and as a devoted Socialist offered to help the man he hailed as the real leader of the Russian people.

The memory of her father's warning about polluted water haunted Nell but there was nothing she could do about it as the summer heat was increasing. She reminded herself that her father could not have envisaged the situation in which she found herself.

After a nightmare journey they passed through the French border controls at Hendaye on the French side and entered the town of Irun on the Spanish side of the frontier. Kerensky's Russian passport and the Spanish visa Nell had purchased and filled in was scrutinised and accepted.

At Irun their car was inspected by Spanish border guards and the armed Guardia Civil in their grey uniforms and black patent leather hats. Unlike Nell's previous visit as a single girl with her cousin, this time there was no laughing or joking with the border guards.

Nell climbed out of the car and spoke in a mixture of French and Spanish to the gun-toting Guardia Civil. She explained they only intended to pass through Spain en route to America or South America as soon as they could find a ship to take them there. She showed them her British passport as Australia did not issue passports when she had left in 1926.

Nell was told to wait and after a considerable time was informed that Kerensky's name was on a list of those banned from entering Spain by Generalissimo Franco, whose brutality Kerensky had recorded in his newspaper during the Spanish Civil War. They were escorted back to their car by two Guardia Civil who watched them like hawks as Nell turned the car around and drove back into France.

Over the car radio Nell learned the southern part of France was now under joint control of the French police and the German army. The French police were arresting anyone they considered an enemy of Nazi Germany. Nell was certain this would include Kerensky so they must leave as soon as possible. Fortunately, she had the forethought to place a roadmap of France and a pocket Michelin guide in the glove pocket of the Citroen and was able to follow minor roads where petrol stations still had fuel for sale.

By now they had been on the road for eighteen days on a journey that would normally have taken two full days and one night. As their only shower had been in the house of the kind Frenchman, everything they owned was crumpled and stained. They badly needed to wash themselves and their clothes which reeked of perspiration due to the summer heat.

Nell drove back along the route they had just come, hoping that in the fashionable resort of Biarritz or the smaller picturesque port of St Jean de Luz, they could hire a French fishing boat to take them to England. By now their money was running out and all the petrol stations they passed had signs indicating they had no petrol.

Enquiries in the elegant resort of Biarritz produced information. There were no fishing boats to take them to England. The sea was mined and the voyage too dangerous. In desperation Nell drove on to the small fishing port of St Jean de Luz where in 1926 she had enjoyed a brief stay with her cousin. She hoped that in a smaller place a fisherman might be induced by the offer of money and the gift of their car to take them to England.

Nell remembered the attractive fishing port as picturesque and tranquil. Now it was full of frightened British villa owners and holiday makers desperate to escape the German enemy and return home.

The port was crowded with rows of Polish soldiers in grey uniforms and black berets. They spoke no English but good French and told Nell they were on their way to join General Sikorski's Free Polish Army in England. They feared the French police who were working closely with the Nazis might arrest them as enemy aliens.

The same fear had infected the English tourists. Wealthy people, used to buying their way out of trouble, were fighting each other for places in the queue which snaked along the harbour wall.

Nell's only hope of finding a fishing boat to take them to England was to enter a bar where she was told the fishermen drank. It was now early evening and the bar would be full. Amid a chorus of wolf whistles and lewd remarks, Nell defied the convention that respectable women did not enter waterfront bars alone as they were the preserve of prostitutes.

Nell threaded her way through a crowd of leering jeering men and asked the barman to point out any owners of French sardine boats. The barman said that many English people had come with the same idea asking to be taken to England and had been refused but pointed out one boat owner. Desperate, Nell pulled out her purse and implored the owner of a sardine boat to take her and her husband to safety at any English port he named. Although she did not have a lot of money left in her purse she offered the owner all the money it contained and the Citroen.

He shook his head. Nell took off her gold Rolex and offered it as an added inducement. The boat owner was polite and told her in French, '*Madame, je suis désolée* I have refused two fortunes already from *les Anglais*. I have a wife and children and must stay alive to protect them from *les salles Boches* (filthy Germans)'.

Nell returned to their car with the disappointing news to find Kerensky, not having had his medication for his kidney problems which been left behind in Paris, visibly weakening and grumpy. She had to get him to Britain as soon as possible or the consequences could be fatal.

She continued to ask the locals for any possibilities of getting to England and was told by a French sailor on the quayside that the British were sending a warship to St Jean de Luz to collect Madame Alice Keppel, mistress of the late King Edward VII and her husband to take them to England.[54]

Ahead of Nell were English people who resided in France laden with luggage surging towards one single counter where a pair of British Customs officials were inspecting their belongings. More well-dressed people kept arriving by car to join the long queue of those desperate to escape.

Elderly people in wheelchairs or carried on stretchers were being turned away to the distress of their relatives, some of whom were offering bribes to French officials to get to the head of the line.

Eventually reaching the counter Nell politely insisted that she was the wife of the former Prime Minister of Russia. He was ill with kidney disease and Churchill would want to see him as he had important information about Britain's enemy, Stalin, for the Foreign Office. She showed her British passport and demanded to see the captain of the British warship who was to take Madame Keppel to England. He hesitated but Nell refused to take no for an answer. She smiled sweetly and he let her onto the quayside where the British warship had just arrived. Sailors in uniform were coming down the gangway.

Nell offered all the money in her purse to one petty officer telling him about her husband and claimed she was a relative of the ship's captain and she had to see him urgently. It did the trick.

When Nell was admitted to the captain's cabin she showed both their passports. She explained that her husband was the former Prime Minister of Russia and had information that Churchill and members of his Cabinet would value. Kerensky having spoken out against Hitler was on the Nazi death list.

The captain was moved by Nell's words as well as by her looks and charm and allowed them to board his ship. Once again, Nell's quick wits and her flair for drama had saved Kerensky.

Aware they could not take the car with them Nell tossed the keys to a peasant driving a donkey cart. Nell told the startled driver the car was now his. The amazed peasant found himself the owner of an expensive motor car. He shook them by the hand and thanked Nell and Kerensky profusely for their magnificent gift.

It was dusk by the time Nell and Kerensky finally boarded the British warship. Exhausted, hungry and thirsty, they looked forward to clean sheets, drinkable water and a good dinner.

However a British steward in a white uniform informed them that no cabins were available, not even for the former Prime Minister of Russia. This was a warship not a passenger ferry. The only free cabin had been reserved by the Prime Minister's office for Mrs Alice Keppel and her husband. As a journalist Nell was aware that Mrs Keppel was the mistress of the late King Edward VII and had left England under a cloud after he died and went to live in Italy on money given to her by the King. She would be a trump card for the Germans if she was captured, being able to divulge information about the British royal family which could be used against Britain.

Nell told the steward with irony that she quite understood that a former royal mistress outranked a former Prime Minister.

Nell and Kerensky spent an uncomfortable night sitting on the hard metal deck eating a plate of stale cheese sandwiches. Kerensky, lacking his medication, was still bad tempered and did not thank Nell for saving his life. He sat, cold and sullen, on the deck, furious that Mrs Keppel had the only cabin he considered should have been given to him.

Nell consoled herself by thinking that at least they had clean water to drink although it was served in tin mugs. She kept to herself the fear that they could be blown sky high by a mine or torpedoed by a German submarine.

Alice Keppel. Mistress to King Edward VII

On their arrival at Dover, Nell cherished the hope that someone from the Foreign Office might meet them, but no one did. As Alice Keppel and her compliant husband were driven away from the docks in a gleaming Rolls Royce, Nell laughed and said that Alice Keppel's royal treatment in biblical terms could be called the wages of sin.

She and Kerensky caught a third class train to Victoria Station as their money was running out. Kerensky left Nell in a cheap hotel while he visited Putney to see his adult sons, Oleg and Gleb, at the home of their mother. He met Oleg's young wife and his first grandson, young Oleg. He was able to make phone calls to his good friends Mr and Mrs David Soskice, who arranged to collect them the following day and pay their hotel bill.

Kerensky's reunion with his divorced wife was difficult. Olga was still aggrieved over the fact that marriage to Kerensky had caused her to be imprisoned by Lenin in the Lubianka jail. She still blamed him after so many years for his love affair with her cousin Lilya.

Angrily Olga told him the details of her imprisonment. She and their young sons were held in a small cell which at times contained 50 prisoners. They were kept short of food and water and each night two or three prisoners would be taken by the guards for interrogation and many were tortured. Some of them never returned and they heard the sounds of shots being fired The effect on their sons had worried her but they had recovered and had done well at school and university.

In their first reunion for many years Olga, even though divorced from Kerensky, demanded half the money from all future sales of Kerensky's manuscripts in compensation for being jailed. This led to a bitter argument. Olga knew several American universities were competing to buy Kerensky's research material and manuscripts for his books, *The Prelude to Bolshevism, The Catastrophe* and *The Crucifixion of Liberty.*

The London office of Bougerau et Bougerau, Kerensky's French divorce lawyers had already told Olga during the divorce proceedings her demands for half the money for Kerensky's manuscripts and research notes and diaries were unreasonable. Kerensky cited their reasons to Olga which made her angry and meant they parted on bad terms.

Kerensky returned to Nell at their hotel upset by his difficult meeting with Olga but happy to be on good terms with his sons. Nell could see how much Kerensky loved his boys and how proud he was of their achievements at university where they had both qualified as engineers. He had helped pay for their education after they had fled with their mother to Britain.[55]

In London they met Kerensky's good friend Dr Jacob Gavronsky and his wife. The Gavronskys were pleased about his second marriage though they had worried that Nell was so much younger than Kerensky having seen a few elderly friends marry gold-diggers who were only after money. They were relieved to learn that Kerensky's charming wife was an heiress with a trust fund who could support him financially until he found suitable employment.

But what impressed the Gavronskys most was Nell's evident love for Kerensky, her concern for his welfare and her intelligence and sense of humour. They also admired her for the bravery she had shown in rescuing Kerensky from the Nazis and felt he had been lucky to marry an attractive talented woman twenty years his junior.

Nell's remarkable escape from Paris interested the press and she gave a lively account of her nightmare journey at the headquarters of the BBC in Langham Place. Nell made an hour long BBC broadcast about their hair-raising escape from the Nazis. She refused to answer the interviewer when he asked the name of the kind Frenchman who had sheltered them, fearing the Germans would arrest the man who had saved them. [56]

In London they stayed with Dr David Soskice who had been a member of Kerensky's staff when Kerensky had been Prime Minister in the Provisional Government and managed to escape from Russia. His son Frank Soskice, a lawyer and Labour politician and his son's English wife Susan were also delighted to see that Kerensky was happily married. They welcomed Nell and Kerensky to their elegant London home. Susan Soskice, daughter of Sir Cloudesley Hunter had inherited tea plantations in Ceylon from her wealthy father and was an accomplished, charming and well-travelled young woman. [57]

Susan and Nell found they had much in common and spent an enjoyable time together while their husbands made plans for Kerensky's future. Kerensky did not manage to get an appointment to see Churchill but was interviewed by senior officials at the Russian desk of the Foreign Office. The Foreign Office made sure the Kerenskys had ration books, clothing coupons and enough money to keep going before Nell's father sent money from Australia. They discovered that all the money in their French bank accounts had been confiscated by the Nazis.

They had long discussions with their supporters as to whether they should stay in London or aim to return to New York, where due to the enormous number of *émigré* Russians, Kerensky had a very large and enthusiastic group of supporters.

Nell and Kerensky had arrived in London during 'the Blitz' when Londoners lived with the daily threat of being bombed by German planes. Most theatres and cinemas closed. Food was rationed although The Savoy and The Ritz managed to serve three course meals with delicious food bought from what were now called 'spivs' on the black market. Clothes could only be bought with clothing coupons. With a book of these supplied by the Russian desk at the Foreign Office, Nell was able to buy a new wardrobe. In the interim she had been forced to borrow clothes and underclothes kindly loaned by Susan Soskice.

Nell's father sent money via bank transfer and with this and the clothing coupons Nell visited Harvey Nichols and Harrods. No imported Chanel suits were available in wartime as Chanel had closed her fashion house. Had Nell known that Coco Chanel was living in the Ritz as the mistress of a German officer she would never have worn Chanel clothes again. Instead she bought clothes from British designers for herself and a couple of suits, a black dinner jacket, trousers and new shirts for Kerensky. He had seen a doctor and had been given medicine for the pain in his remaining kidney and was feeling much better.

At a party at the house of Sir Frank Soskice, Nell, who had heard about the broken love affair of Bruce Lockhart and Moura from Nina, was intrigued to meet the womanising but charming Lockhart who would be present.

Lockhart had been asked to submit his resignation to the Foreign Office on his recall from Moscow over the fiasco of the plot that now bore his name in Foreign Office archives. He was seen as an embarrassment to the British government who denied any knowledge of funding a plot to kidnap and kill Lenin.

Nell was interested to learn that Lockhart was writing a novel about his years in Moscow and had found a publisher. Lockhart's book concentrated on the love affair of a young diplomat with a beautiful Russian countess, obviously based on his affair with Countess Moura, Budberg. In Lockhart's romantic fiction, Lenin was not to be killed but merely humiliated by having his trousers removed and made to walk naked through the streets of Moscow. Nell thought this plot device seemed ridiculous but it was all in another life that she had left behind.

The book she wanted to concentrate on researching and writing was a biography of her husband.

During the evening Lockhart told Nell in confidence that he and MI6 agent George Relinsky (aka Sidney Reilly, the man who gave a pistol to Fanny Kaplan to assassinate Lenin) had both been declared enemies of Russia and sentenced to death *in absentia* while the unfortunate Fanny Kaplan had paid the price for believing in the charming Sidney Reilly.

Reilly had returned to Russia in 1925 intending to pull off a lucrative arms deal but had been captured and shot by the Russian secret police. As much as he had enjoyed some of his time in Russia, Lockhart told Nell he would never go back. However she found the opportunity to eventually meet Lockhart fascinating as he updated the story Nina had learned from Moura. Nell considered it had been a most interesting evening.

Travelling first class on a luxurious transatlantic liner like the SS Normandie and dining in evening dress was a very different experience from Nell and Kerensky's nightmare journey of escape from the Nazis.

On arrival in London, Kerensky had been debriefed by a member of the Russian desk at the Foreign Office and asked them to make contact with their opposite numbers in America, explaining his difficult financial position and asking if there was a possibility of government employment in Britain or America.

The American Government agreed to pay for Kerensky and his wife to travel first class on a passenger liner to New York. They and the CIA wanted information from Kerensky on how to handle Stalin, at that time America's enemy. There was a suggestion that Kerensky would be found a position as advisor on Russian affairs to the American Government.

Kerensky's Australian Wife

Thrilling Flight Through France

From COLIN WILLS
Australian journalist now with the B.B.C. in London

LONDON, Wednesday.

The British press and BBC interview turned Nell into a heroine escaping from the Nazis.

However what was meant to be a luxury voyage across the Atlantic on a transatlantic liner, dining in full evening dress each night with French food and wines, turned out to be fraught with danger. German submarines patrolled the Atlantic with instructions to torpedo all Allied vessels. Lifeboat drill made Nell realise that they could be spending cold nights at sea before being rescued. Nell and Kerensky had anxious moments when German submarines came too close for comfort. One German submarine was sunk by the British destroyer which was escorting them. They were glad to arrive in New York alive.

CHAPTER TWENTY-ONE

Treated like Royalty in America

The American press made a big fuss over the arrival in New York of Kerensky and his glamorous wife. Flash bulbs clicked when they descended the gangway as their arrival had been announced in *The New York Times.* After being escorted through customs as VIPs Nell and Kerensky found themselves surrounded by excited crowds of Russian émigrés, some of whom brought Nell gifts of flowers or traditional wooden Babushka dolls with smaller dolls inside them.

Friends and loyal supporters, aware the Kerenskys had lost everything they owned when they left Paris, raised money to help them move to a rented apartment at 1060 Park Avenue, an elegant area of New York.

Kerensky was consulted by American Defence Department officials who were concerned with Russia and had received secret information that Stalin was disillusioned with Hitler. They wanted to discuss with Kerensky the possibility that if Stalin was handled tactfully, he might change sides and join America and Britain in the war against Hitler. The Defence Department and President Roosevelt hoped doing this would change the balance of power and bring the war to a speedy end.

That summer Kerensky's Russian-Jewish friends, Simeon and Manya Strunsky, invited them to stay in their charming holiday cottage in the attractive residential area of New Canaan, in Connecticut, some 40 miles north-east of New York.[58]

Nell greatly enjoyed her visit and became close friends with Manya Strunsky. Simeon Strunsky, recently retired as editor of *The New York Times,* was known as one of the wittiest men in America. Nell, with her keen sense of humour loved Simon Strunsky who was also known for ironic comments like 'People who want to understand democracy should spend less time in the library with Aristotle and more time on buses and in the subway.'

Nell loved New Canaan with its old-world farmhouses, beautiful mansions, an attractive main street with small but elegant shops, a good lending library and proximity to the sea. America's leading writers and publishers including Max Perkins, editor to Hemingway at Scribners, his actress wife and several members of the Russian ballet in exile lived there and Nell made new and interesting friends.

Kerensky was commissioned to write articles for several journals and had discussions with publishers about a new book on the Russian revolution. They were so happy in New Canaan that they planned to spend the summer there the following year to avoid the heat of New York as it had an excellent train service. It was a happy time for both of them. Nell was still in good health, working as her husband's translator and press secretary and organising his speaking engagements on his America-wide tours. [59]

Stalin surprised everyone by changing sides after Hitler attacked Leningrad (the former St Petersburg). The fact Stalin was now America's ally brought demands for more talks by Kerensky on Russian history and he travelled all over America. Nell wrote a few short stories for American magazines with a Russian theme and they wrote a booklet together about the Romanov dynasty. Nell was too busy working with her husband to pursue an independent literary career or start writing her proposed biography of Kerensky.

New Canaan, the Connecticut rural retreat for successful people in the worlds of literature, art and publishing was a place of attractive homes. In a converted clapboard farmhouse similar to this one, Nell and Kerensky were happy here from 1941-1944.

Kerensky's three well-researched books on Russia, *The Prelude to Bolshevism; The Catastrophe, Kerensky's Own Story of the Russian Revolution* and *The Crucifixion of Liberty* were still selling well so he received good royalties. This enabled them to rent a holiday house for the summer among their new friends in picturesque New Canaan.

By 1942, Kerensky's books and their booklet on the Romanovs had made them enough money to buy a traditional clapboard farmhouse, recently renovated on the border between New York State and Connecticut. Here Nell's artistic talent and her background of interior decorating learned from her parents' department store, helped her create a beautiful home which was featured in several American women's magazines.

Tatiana Pollock, (a Russian ballet dancer married to an American) who Nell had met in Paris and resumed contact with in New York became a frequent visitor. In her memoirs Tatiana recalled how idyllic the Kerenskys' married life appeared. She admired their home filled with books, antique furniture, Persian carpets and Russian ornaments. Tatiana described the beautiful dining room where dinner parties were held in winter. At summer house parties Nell served tea to visitors on the lawn under the trees with games of croquet for those who enjoyed it.

Nell enjoyed acting as hostess for her husband. Her innate good manners, warmth of personality and social confidence ensured she was good at entertaining important visitors and foreign ambassadors at dinner parties. She also enjoyed organising parties for members of the various Russian ballet companies who had regrouped in America in wartime.

World War Two had greatly reduced Nell's income from her family trust but even when she was wealthy, Kerensky would never consider living off his wife's money, and they kept separate bank accounts.

The fact Soviet Russia under Stalin was now an ally of America resulted in a demand for more knowledge about Russian history. People wanted to know more about the Tsars, the Provisional Government and Kerensky's role in the Bolshevik revolution. Kerensky's fees for his lectures increased considerably as he was seen as the best speaker in America on topics connected with Russia.

Nell gave her husband English lessons and translated the speeches he wrote in French into colloquial English so he could give radio talks to American audiences. She corrected his pronunciation of difficult words in English and for some radio talks made a phonetic transcript to help him overcome the language problem.

While Kerensky was on an extended speaking tour of Texas and the southern states of America, Nell received a letter from her husband written entirely in English, which, until now, he had always avoided when writing to her. The fact Kerensky had benefited from her English lessons pleased Nell enormously.

In her reply Nell congratulated him on writing to her in perfect English, telling him, 'I loved your letter, it was like having a new beau.' Simeon [Strunsky] was very impressed and said, 'you'll probably come back with an American accent wearing a ten-gallon cowboy hat!'[60]

When touring America, Kerensky telephoned Nell every day and she wrote him affectionate letters in French. In a loving and very revealing letter she told him, *'Avec toi, mon amour, j'ai bu de la fontaine de la vie'* (With you my love, I have drunk from the very fountain of life).

Nell felt her second marriage was a great success. It had brought her happiness and a fascinating life in America with a circle of amusing and talented friends. At last she was living the life she had hoped to have when she left Brisbane all those years ago.[61]

Kerensky returned from one of his lecture tours in time to celebrate Easter 1944 with his wife. Nell had gone to great pains to create a traditional Russian Easter and organised a house party for Russian friends from New York. Using stencils in bright colours she painted Russian designs on eggs to enjoy on Easter Sunday, and baked a *paska,* the traditional rich spicy Easter bread.

In his radio talks, Kerensky had been warning America that Stalin, although he had showed leadership in the fight against the German siege of Leningrad, was still an evil dictator like Hitler. Stalin had ordered the deaths of huge numbers of his subjects. Communist Russia was not and had never been the paradise for workers that Stalin's propaganda machine proclaimed.

The previous year, 1943, Kerensky's warnings about Stalin had been confirmed by Viktor Kravchenko, a military officer who had defected from Soviet Russia. Captain Kravchenko confirmed the horrors of Stalin's brutal regime with its millions of deaths which Kerensky had hinted at for years, based on smuggled information supplied by sources in Russia.

Captain Kravchenko had worked in military intelligence before being posted to Washington where he defected. He wrote a best-selling book called *I Chose Freedom* that informed American and British readers of the brutality of Stalin's *gulags* where the unfortunate prisoners had built steel works and factories which made it possible for Stalin to wage war. He revealed the enormous numbers of Russians who had been shot on the orders of Stalin and the brutality of his secret police. Kravchenko also revealed details about the assassinations and poisonings Stalin had authorised to be carried out in foreign countries.

After publication of his best-selling book, Kravchenko had to go into hiding as Stalin had ordered his assassination by SMERSH, the latest name for Russia's secret police (made famous by Ian Fleming in his James Bond novels and films).

Victor Kravchenko's book revealed to a shocked world that millions of Ukrainians had been starved to death between 1932 and 1933. This was the Holodomor, the Ukrainian Great Famine that the young British journalist Gareth Jones had written about. He was subsequently killed on the orders of Lenin for exposing the awful truth. Jones documented that over a million Ukrainians had starved to death, their grain sent to wartime Russia.

In Ukraine itself, Russian soldiers guarded the grain silos, refusing to allow desperate Ukrainians access and watched on impassively as they died of starvation.

Kravchenko's book had opened American and British eyes to Stalin's duplicity and cruelty. Stalin took his revenge. Kravchenko's relatives in Russia were shot in the same way Stalin had ordered the execution of Kerensky's lawyer brother, Fyodor, and his sister, Dr Elena Kerensky a distinguished paediatrician.

Kravchenko's book received wide publicity. The fact he had been part of Stalin's secret service gave it the ring of authenticity which convinced readers he had told the truth about Soviet Russia. There was a tragic sequel. When in hiding from Soviet vengeance, he died under mysterious circumstances with a bullet wound to the head.

****

One of Nell's pleasures living in Connecticut had been her long daily swim at the Roton Point Beach Club in Rowayton. In the summer of 1944 she noticed when swimming long distances that her strength had declined. After exercise she began to have palpitations of the heart and felt weak and nauseated. It was the beginning of a reaction to the polluted water she had drunk on her nightmare journey through

Southern France.

The escape from the Nazis had affected Nell in other ways. She had nightmares in which she saw the corpses they had to remove from the highway and German planes riddling cars and farm carts with bullets as she and Kerensky crouched in ditches to avoid being killed. She hoped the bad dreams would go away but this did not happen.

Kerensky, accustomed to Nell doing everything to keep his home and office functioning perfectly while he worked on his lectures and another book, showed little sympathy. He had become used to his young wife being a tower of strength. He imagined that as he aged she would be caring for him, rather than the other way round. He thought Nell was just being neurotic when she complained of feeling weak and having palpitations. Only after Nell told him she had consulted doctors in New York who confirmed that her underlying condition was severe, with damage to her kidneys and liver, did he finally become worried.

They moved to a much smaller house at Rowayton, for Nell to be closer to her New York doctors. The house was easier to manage for Nell and she was helped by more domestic staff, but devoted to Kerensky, she remained the organiser of his many popular lecture tours.

However the winter of 1944-45 was exceptionally harsh and Kerensky was often away on extended lecture tours. Nell became increasingly miserable, spending weeks alone at Rowayton feeling unwell. She worried that Kerensky's lecture tours were now their only source of income as her family trust fund had been greatly depleted due to the war.

Kerensky was worried about the future and hoped to obtain a tenured university professorship which would give them financial security. He had discussions with Stanford, one of America's leading universities, for a special appointment to teach Russian history. The academic board of Stanford liked the idea of having Kerensky on their university staff but advised it would take some time for them to reach a decision.

Meanwhile Nell, ill with the cold in winter, longed to return to the warmth of her childhood in Queensland. Warned by medical specialists in New York that her kidneys were failing and this problem could affect her heart, they advised they could do no more for her. (There were as yet no kidney or heart transplants.) Nell realised important decisions about her future had to be made.

Her doctors suggested if she wanted to see her parents and family, now was the time to leave for Queensland and spend the rest of the American winter in a warmer climate.

Nell decided to take their advice. She made plans for a return trip alone by sea to Australia. Kerensky, who had many advance lecture bookings was unwilling to cancel them as this was their main source of income.

Shortly before her departure, Nell suffered a mild heart attack. She was advised by her New York specialists she needed extensive bed rest, so it was unwise for her to travel alone. This convinced Kerensky that he must return to Queensland with Nell as he was alarmed at how serious his wife's medical condition had become.

CHAPTER TWENTY-TWO

Return to Brisbane as a War Heroine

Not until October 1945 was Nell deemed well enough to cope with the return journey to Australia with Kerensky accompanying her. They embarked at New York on a British liner called the *SS City of Durham* with a stateroom filled with flowers sent by American friends.

The voyage was pleasant and relaxing and Nell was feeling much better when, in November 1945 they arrived in Melbourne.

Still looking elegant although her heart attack had taken its toll Nell was interviewed by *The Melbourne Argus* and several other papers. She gave journalists an account of their harrowing escape from the Nazis, and her happy years with Kerensky in Paris and Connecticut. Wisely she refused to answer any questions about her divorce or the current whereabouts of her first husband, aware it would upset her parents if the press traced Nikolai to a sanitorium for alcoholics.[62]

Nell and Alexander Kerensky photographed as a celebrity couple on a domestic Australian flight.
(Photo courtesy Mrs Lavinia Tritton)

She told the press she was happy to be back in Australia, and said nothing about her deteriorating health, as she did not want to distress her parents.

They stayed in a hotel in Melbourne's Collins Street for a few days. Having heard nothing from Stanford University, Kerensky, encouraged by Nell, had applied for a post at the University of Melbourne which was establishing a brand new Russian Department. They were advertising a post for head of department. Clearly Kerensky was a highly suitable candidate with degrees in history and law from the University of St Petersburg, the author of three books on Russian history and his integral role in the Russian revolution.

Nell's cousin Corbett Tritton was now Private Secretary to Robert Menzies who at that time was the leader of the Australian Liberal Party and would become Prime Minister again in 1949. Corbett Tritton supported Kerensky's application to head the new Russian Department at Melbourne University. He was delighted to think that Nell would return to live in Australia permanently and in his supporting letter, described how impressed he was by Kerensky's credentials for the post of professor.[63]

After his tuition in spoken English from Nell, Kerensky believed that his interview, conducted in English and Russian, had gone well. His CV was impressive and friends were convinced he would be appointed to the chair at Melbourne University. Nell left Melbourne for Brisbane feeling optimistic that Kerensky would get the job. They had a stop-over in Sydney so Nell could show her husband the beauty of Sydney Harbour on his first visit to Australia.

Nell wanted to show her husband Elizabeth Bay where she had lived as a young journalist, the city centre and the art gallery. As she was feeling much better they enjoyed a boat trip around the harbour.

The celebrity couple were photographed and interviewed on arrival at Brisbane airport. But by the time they had driven to *Elderslie,* Nell was exhausted. She was thrilled to see her parents again and introduce her husband to them. But all the excitement had taken a toll. Their general practitioner was summoned and informed Nell her blood pressure was elevated. She must rest or this could increase the damage to her kidneys which were already compromised.

Nell rested but her weakened heart and kidney disease meant she was always tired. She spent part of the day resting in what had been her childhood bedroom with a veranda facing over the garden.

Sadly there could be no visits to the Glasshouse Mountains,

Redcliffe or Surfers Paradise, areas she had loved during her teenage years. Nell spent much of the day resting but was delighted to catch up with school friends from Somerville House and several Tritton family members when they visited her at *Elderslie.*

Nell still had enough strength to give an interview to a journalist from Brisbane's *Courier-Mail* but played down the dangers of her escape from the Nazis, not wanting to alarm her parents. However they had already read the interview she gave in Melbourne. They realised what she had endured in France and were proud of her. *The Courier-Mail* headed its article praising Nell's courage *'Our Heroine's Nightmare Ordeal in France.'*[64]

Replying to questions, Nell told her interviewer that after she had married Kerensky, she was conscious of always being followed by Communist agents in Paris so always took a bodyguard with her as her husband still feared they would try to kidnap or kill her.

It was a bleak day for Nell and her husband when Kerensky received a letter from the Registrar of Melbourne University informing him that his application for the post of Head of the Russian department had not been successful. Kerensky was angry and humiliated to learn that the successful candidate was young Nina Christensen whose father was Russian. But the young academic had never lived in Russia and lacked the many scholarly publications Kerensky had written.

Nina Christensen (born Maximoff) was a pleasant woman, married to Clem Christensen, editor of the literary journal *Meanjin*. The couple were known for their left wing Labour Party connections. Kerensky, always a moderate Socialist, subjected to years of vilification from the extreme left, felt that his rejection for this important academic post had been made on political grounds and was justifiably angry.

Nell was devastated and embarrassed by the University of Melbourne's decision. She could scarcely believe her husband had been denied a post for which many people working in the field of Russian history regarded him as the ideally suited. She was convinced that a clique of Australian writers who were Communist sympathisers had influenced members of the University Academic Appointments Committee to reject her husband's application.

This setback affected Nell's heart condition which continued to deteriorate despite the efforts of Brisbane's best medical specialists called in by Nell's father. Fred Tritton would have paid anything in the world to prolong the life of his favourite daughter. But, just like the doctors Nell had seen in New York, medical specialists in Brisbane were unable to do anything for her. They gave similar advice to her in New York physicians. Nell should rest during the day and go to bed early. Fred Tritton, normally a workaholic, took time off so that he could be with Nell.

At intervals throughout the day and into the night, Kerensky paced the wide verandas of *Elderslie,* revolver in hand guarding his wife. He could not forget the brutal assassination of Trotsky in Mexico. He worried that if Stalin could send a trained assassin to Mexico City he could also send one to Brisbane.

Kerensky wondered what he would do without Nell who had been such an essential part of his life for a decade. Kerensky was depressed that doctors were unable to help his wife. He had become resigned to the fact that her strength was declining and she had at best only a few more months to live.

Elderslie in 1945. Nell's parents with Nell who is showing signs of illness. Kerensky is standing behind her. (Photo courtesy Lavinia Tritton)

The rear veranda of Elderslie today where Kerensky patrolled, revolver in hand, fearing an assassin sent by Stalin might be lurking in the garden.
(Photo Vanessa de Vos)

The front door of Elderslie in 2020.
(Photo Vanessa de Vos)

To protect Nell from danger, Kerensky slept on the veranda outside his wife's room aware she was in pain and conscious that there were no drugs to help her.

Aware of her impending death, Nell worried about her husband and feared he must feel isolated in Brisbane with no Russian friends to speak to. Accordingly she invited her former Russian teacher, Captain Maximoff to tea to meet her husband. It was unfortunate that Captain Maximoff was the father of Nina Maximoff who had just been appointed as the new Professor of Russian at Melbourne University.

As a former Tsarist supporter Captain Maximoff disliked Kerensky and initially had no wish to meet him but. Nell was unaware of this. However, Captain Maximoff, realising that Nell was dying and because he was fond of her, agreed to visit *Elderslie.*

As a supporter of the murdered Tsar he conquered his distaste of Kerensky's political views and the two men shook hands and talked about the old days in St Petersburg before Captain Maximoff took a sad farewell of Nell who by now was now confined to bed.[65]

Early in February 1946, Nell suffered a massive stroke. Her speech became confused and she needed professional nursing day and night. In order to be close to his beloved wife, Kerensky continued sleeping on the verandah outside Nell's room.

He could see that Nell was dying and felt guilty he had not been kinder to her when she first told him of her health problems. He realised how much he loved her but felt he had not adequately expressed his love and gratitude for saving his life.

Mistakenly he had believed the great love of his life was Lilya, who had been temperamental and selfish while Nell had been loyal and loving to the very end.

Just as the doctors had predicted when she was a child, Nell's life was curtailed as her immune system had been damaged in childhood. Unselfish as always she had given Kerensky all their bottled mineral water and she had drunk polluted water which had had a slow but lethal effect on her kidneys.

Her life ebbed away at *Elderslie* on the night of April 11, 1946. Kerensky was devastated by her death, having expected that he and Nell would be together into old age. For almost ten years she had been his faithful companion and supporter and he could not imagine life without her.

The undertakers had dressed Nell in white and made up her face to look serene and beautiful. As Kerensky's grandfather and uncle had been Orthodox priests he followed the traditions of the Russian Orthodox Church and kept an all-night vigil beside Nell's open coffin.

She lay on an elevated bier, surrounded by long white candles and hundreds of red roses, the symbol of love he had given her on their first dinner at the *Kalinka* Russian restaurant. Kerensky regarded this as his way of showing his in-laws how much he had loved and appreciated Nell.

Although as a radical revolutionary Kerensky had flirted with atheism after being deposed by Lenin, he had reverted to the Orthodox faith of his parents and grandfathers. He still wore a small icon on a chain round his neck which he believed had protected him when hiding from Lenin and from Stalin's attempts to assassinate him.[66]

In accordance with her parents' wishes Nell's funeral took place in an Anglican church rather than in Brisbane's only Russian Orthodox place of worship. Kerensky made no objections.

After an Anglican funeral ceremony, Nell was cremated and her ashes placed in a grave in the Dutton Park Cemetery on Annerley Road, in the same grave as her brother Charles and her sister Lillian. The marble headstone ordered by her parents was inscribed with her full name of 'Lydia Ellen Kerensky'. In front of it is a stone cross ornamented with carved flowers.[67]

In the confusion and misery after Nell's death a mistake was made and her age was cited as 45 rather than 46 on her headstone. (Photograph Jake de Vries)

Nell's bedroom as it is today. Visitors can stay in a luxurious private suite in the former Tritton home situated on the outskirts of Brisbane. Details of short stays at Elderslie are on Airbnb under Pullenvale, Brisbane, Queensland. (Photo courtesy Vanessa de Vos)

EPILOGUE

Fred Tritton, in his eighties, was badly affected by Nell's premature death and died the following year. *The Methodist Times* in his eulogy called him Brisbane's most successful businessman. Nell with her good looks, charm and vivacious personality was Fred Tritton's favourite child. He asked to be buried beside her and his two eldest children at Dutton Park Cemetery in South Brisbane.

Nell's mother outlived her husband by many years. She died at 97 and was buried in the Tritton family grave.

Nell bequeathed all the money in her bank account to her beloved husband although she was no longer a wealthy heiress. The money in the Tritton family trust and Nell's savings had been depleted during World War Two and as a result Kerensky received only a relatively small bequest from the wife who adored him.

Lack of shipping due to American troops returning home at the end of World War Two forced Kerensky to spend six more months at *Elderslie,* the Brisbane home of his in-laws, with whom he had little in common. Kerensky was befriended by Nell's well-travelled cousin, Corbett Tritton.

As Kerensky had enjoyed visiting the Tritton's beach house and aware that Kerensky needed a break from his in-laws, Corbett arranged for Kerensky to stay with his family at the house in Surfers Paradise. [68] On this visit Kerensky confided to Corbett his fear that Stalin would have him killed in Australia since he had sent an agent to assassinate Trotsky in Mexico City a couple of years previously.

When he finally secured a passage back to America, Kerensky wrote an account of his life with Nell, her dedication to him and his ambition to preserve freedom and democracy and fight tyranny.

He described how Nell had saved his life on several occasions and the courage with which she had faced her premature death. He read a loving tribute to Nina Berberova who had finally managed to obtain a working visa to work in America after her relationship with a French artist ended.

Nina Berberova, Nell's best friend, finally achieved her aim at the end of World War Two and became an academic at Princeton University. Nina finally had her award-winning literary novels translated into English as a result of the enthusiasm of Jacqueline

Kennedy, who, when working for Doubleday in New York, recommended their translation into English which ensured Nina's talent was recognised.

Kerensky never remarried. He was made a professor at the Hoover Centre at Stanford University, had brief liaisons with divorced wives of university colleagues and had a close relationship with his Russian secretary who was devoted to him. With her help he catalogued his papers which were presented to the Hoover Humanities Research Centre at the University of Texas Austin. Other papers were donated to the Kerensky archive at Stanford University in California.

As a widower Kerensky was devastated by Nell's premature death. He decided he could no longer live in their former matrimonial home at Rowayton in Connecticut as the memories were too painful. He sold the house and donated the money from the sale to Russian displaced persons lacking passports living in refugee camps in Germany and Austria. Consequently he was left homeless.

Residing and working at the Hoover Institute of Stanford University, Kerensky gave seminars in Russian history and donated his papers to the university's archive. His lectures delivered in English were well received by students and fellow staff as was this his final book.

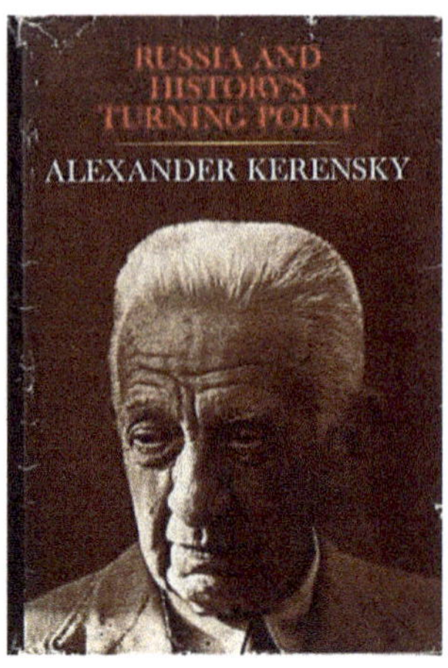

Cover of Kerensky's book, 'Russia and History's Turning Point' compiled when he was a Professor of Russian History at Stanford University.

During his years in America Kerensky worked with the distinguished historian Robert P. Browder on a three-volume anthology about the Russian revolution entitled *Russia and History's Turning Point*. Kerensky, now in his eighties and with his eyesight failing, was determined to write Russian history as well having made it.

Having sold his home to benefit Russia's displaced persons in need of financial help but unable to buy another home in his retirement, Kerensky divided his time between good friends in California and New York. He spent his final years as a guest of the widow of his friend Senator Kenneth Simpson on 91st Street, New York, cared for by her Japanese butler.

****

In 1967 Stalin's daughter Svetlana, who had sought asylum in America after falling out with her father, telephoned Kerensky. [69] She expressed her admiration for his book *Russia's Turning Point* and his other books on the Russian Revolution which pleased Kerensky enormously.

Kerensky, who believed in telling the truth, was furious when, after the Soviet invasion of Czechoslovakia, UNESCO honoured the brutal Lenin as a 'prominent humanist and humanitarian'. As the main speaker at an international Socialist seminar in Finland, Kerensky called Lenin a 'bigot and mass murderer', and his description produced cheers from his left-wing audience.

Kerensky successfully interceded with Eleanor Roosevelt to stop Stalin's secret agents intimidating displaced persons from the Soviet Union who had managed to reach America from refugee camps in Germany and Austria.[70] Unlike Stalin, Kerensky never amassed great wealth. He always lived modestly and spent little money on himself apart from buying books as he was a great reader.[71]

Kerensky was one of the last surviving major participants in the events leading to the Bolshevik Revolution of 1917.

In 1970 Kerensky was admitted to a New York hospital with a cracked pelvis. He was already suffering from arteriosclerotic heart disease and stomach cancer.

His grandson, Stephen Kerensky, claimed that Tsarist nurses caring for his grandfather cruelly refused to administer the pain relief prescribed by Kerensky's doctor for his cracked pelvis and a subsequent attack of shingles so that his death in hospital was slow and painful.[72] Death came as a merciful relief on 11 June.

Kerensky's memorial service was held in front of a large crowd on Madison Avenue. His coffin was flown to London. Both Russian Orthodox Churches in New York were wary of having a former revolutionary leader buried in their graveyard, fearing it would be desecrated by thugs on the orders of Stalin. This had already occurred in New York when the graves of other émigré Russians had been vandalised.[73]

After much argument Kerensky was buried in Putney Cemetery beside Olga, his first wife and mother of his sons. Perhaps it would have been more suitable to bury him in Brisbane beside the wife who adored him.

This joint biography of Nell and Kerensky is the result of a French collector showing the author Nell's diaries, one of which recorded Nell's purchase of a painting by Marie Bakshirtskeff. Nell's diary was used by the collector to provided 'provenance' or pedigree for this painting as well as valuable information about Nell and Kerensky's life in Paris.

Author Susanna de Vries visited the home of this French collector of works by Renoir and other Impressionists when researching her book *Impressionist Masters from Private Collections.* She was shown Nell's diaries, bought as provenance for the valuable painting by Marie Bashkirtseff, *The Girl with a Bunch of Lilacs* that Nell had owned. The painting had been left in Paris when Nell and Kerensky fled from the Nazis.

A glimpse of Nell's diaries intrigued the author and made her determined to write Nell's biography. In 1992, there were no such things as smart phones to photograph her diaries. The elderly collector whose collection of art she had come to study did not possess a photocopier so De Vries spent what time she could committing to memory as much of the diaries as possible before concentrating on the paintings she had flown from Australia to see. She was short of time as she was due to fly to New York to see more Impressionist collections to include in her forthcoming book *Impressionists Revealed, Masterpieces and Collectors.*

The elderly collector in Paris promised De Vries she could study Nell Tritton's diaries in depth when she returned to that city. She had no idea her architect husband's fatal illness would delay her planned return to Paris. Some years later when she was able to return from Australia, her home for the second half of her life, she discovered the collector who owned Nell's diaries had died. The entire collection including the diaries had been bought by a Russian oligarch with a house in Spain.

Aided by Spanish friends from her university days, De Vries located the Russian oligarch (whose name for legal reasons is withheld) who had left Marbella for a villa in S'Agaró, a luxury resort between Barcelona and the French border and friends took the author in their yacht from San Feliu harbour to S'Agaró. They came ashore at a beautiful bay in this closely guarded enclave of the international super-rich.

A security guard with a rifle and a snarling German Shepherd dog was posted at the massive wrought iron gate of the villa. The guard said the Russian owner was not in residence. De Vries' request for a forwarding address was refused and when she asked more questions the guard became hostile. Spanish friends warned her not to pursue the matter mouthing the words 'Russian Mafia'.

Back in Brisbane the author had a lucky break. She was giving classes in art history to mature age students at the Continuing Education Department at the University of Queensland. One of them had purchased *Elderslie,* the colonial home where Nell Tritton grew up after Tritton descendants had sold *Elderslie* to a property developer. The developer moved the entire weatherboard home (a common practice in Queensland) from Adelaide Street in Clayfield to acreage in Pullenvale, a beautiful rural area on the outskirts of Brisbane. The new owner of *Elderslie* and her husband had worked for the United Nations before deciding to settle in Brisbane and she shared her information she had accumulated on Nell.

A Brisbane friend introduced De Vries to Mrs Lavinia Tritton, wife of one of Fred Tritton's grandsons who showed her newspaper articles and family papers and explained how Tritton's department store failed financially when cheap chipboard furniture replaced Tritton's' furniture made from Queensland timbers in their own factory. Today the headquarters of Brisbane City Council libraries stands on what was once the site of Tritton's Department Store which occupies the entire block Tritton's once occupied on the corner of George and Adelaide Streets.

Another motivation for de Vries, biographer of some 22 significant women, was the fact Richard Abrahams, the American author of a lengthy, 500-page biography of Kerensky, devoted only one page to Nell Tritton Kerensky. He ignored the fact Nell had devoted ten years of her life to working with Kerensky in pursuit of freedom. She unselfishly gave her life for her husband giving him the bottled water and had to drink polluted ditch water when hiding from German planes on the 'road of death' from Paris to the Spanish border. Nell saved her husband several times from Stalin's assassins and then from the Nazis driving him on the 'road of death' and securing them a place on a British warship bound for London.

Wealthy Flora Solomon had been responsible for introducing Nell to Kerensky and saw herself as Kerensky's soul mate, spiritual wife and occasional lover. The fact that Kerensky was almost twenty years older than Nell made Flora ignore the possibility Nell and Kerensky could fall in love.

Flora, one of London's wealthiest women, was convinced she and Kerensky were soul mates and she was his 'spiritual wife' and was one of the backers of his first newspaper for Russian exiles. She regarded Nell as a social butterfly so was happy to recommend Kerensky employ Nell as his English translator with the result they fell in love and married in America.

In her memoir, *From Baku to Baker Street,* Flora described her shock when in *The New York Herald Tribune* she read the announcement of the wedding of Nell and Kerensky. Flora's son Peter Berenson, a lawyer and founder of Amnesty International, made things worse by pointing out that his mother had only herself to blame as she had recommended Kerensky employ Nell which had led their marriage.

Flora's rage and jealousy was such that she refused to include Nell's name in her memoir, calling her *'Kerensky's typist'* and *'an Australian divorcee'* and wrote of Nell's marriage to her former lover as *'something I thought I would never see. I cannot pretend it did not sadden me'*.[74]

Kerensky's biographer, Richard Abraham, believed Flora Solomon's comments that Nell was nothing more than Kerensky's typist. He failed to realise jealousy motivated her opinion of Nell so gave Nell only one page in his biography of Kerensky, ignoring how many times she saved her husband's life.

Nell Tritton Kerensky was a pioneer journalist, champion rally driver, author of short stories and articles published in American magazines. She tutored Kerensky in English for his America-wide speaking tours, helped run his office when he was away, acted as his social hostess when they lived in Connecticut and kept him grounded.

Nell raised money for victims of Stalin and Hitler and Spanish women and children who survived the bombings of the towns of Guernica and Santander in the Spanish Civil War and saved Kerensky's Russian Jewish staff from the Nazis obtaining them forged visas to enter Spain. She was heroic during their escape from Paris when Nazi planes repeatedly and ruthlessly bombed the long line of civilians travelling south to the Spanish border.

Nell Tritton accomplished a great deal in a life cut short in what her writer friend Nina Berberova called 'a Tolstoyan tragedy.' She deserves to be remembered as a brave and generous humanitarian at a time when women's activities were rarely recorded.

Nell's heroism and generosity is an inspiration to young women everywhere.

There are similarities between these two courageous Russian civil rights lawyers, Alexander Kerensky and Alexei Navalny. Both these brave men told the truth about dictators in Russia which resulted in attempts to assassinate and silence them.

Alexei Navalny was poisoned with Novochok at an airport, although this was denied by the Russian Government. Novochok is a Russian made poison used in the alleged attempted murder of two Russian defectors in the English cathedral town of Salisbury by members of the Russian secret police. Navalny was saved from the effects of a poisoned cup of tea in an airport café by being flown to Berlin where he was treated by German doctors.

In the period between the two World Wars Kerensky survived attempts to poison him by Russian agents sent by Stalin and was threatened by armed gunmen from the Russian secret police. He was saved by his wife, Nell Tritton, a former rally driver in a nail-biting car chase across Paris which has led to film interest in this exciting story.

NELL is the only biography of Australian born Nell Tritton, journalist, translator and champion rally driver who married Alexander Kerensky, the former Prime Minister of Russia. The book has gained new relevance with the current imprisonment of Alexei Navalny who, like Kerensky dared to reveal a great deal about Russian corruption in high places.

List Of Main Characters

Lydia Ellen (Nell or Nellé) Tritton, divorced wife of Nikolai Nadejine and second wife of Alexander Kerensky.

Frederick and Leila Tritton, Nell's parents, owners of Tritton's department store and a furniture factory in Brisbane.

Charles and Lillian Tritton, Nell's elder siblings died in the Spanish flu epidemic, their immune systems weakened by a lead lined water tank and pipes.

Ida Jane (Idie), Cyril and Roy Tritton, Nell's other siblings.

Marie Bakshirtskeff born in Ukraine, died in Paris in 1884, painter and author of the published diary which inspired Nell to visit Paris.

Nina Berberova, Russian émigré, biographer of Tchaikovsky and Tolstoy, later Professor of Russian Literature at Princeton and novelist. Nina Berberova disliked Moura and after her death was able to release her biography, *The Dangerous Life of Moura Budberg* for publication without fear of legal action.

Captain Nikolai Nadejine, former officer in the Tsar's Imperial cavalry and Nell's first husband.

Countess Yevgenia, Nikolai's aunt, widow of a Tsarist general.

Alexander Kerensky, Nell's second husband, barrister, Justice Minister, War Minister and then Prime Minister of Russia in exile.

Olga Baranovskaya Kerensky, Alexander Kerensky's first wife and mother of his sons.

Gleb Kerensky, younger son of Alexander Kerensky, as a student translated two of his father's books into English and became an engineer.

Dr Oleg Kerensky, CBE, FRS, elder son of Alexander and Olga Kerensky famous designer of bridges, worked on the construction of the Sydney Harbour Bridge.

Fyodor Kerensky, younger brother of Alexander Kerensky, lawyer and public prosecutor in Tashkent, shot in 1918 on the orders of Lenin.

Dr Elena Kerensky, elder sister of Alexander Kerensky, consultant paediatrician at the Obukhov Hospital in Petersburg, shot on Stalin's orders in 1930.

Lilya (Elena) Biriukova, wife of General Biriukova and lover of Alexander Kerensky, medical student.

Flora Benenson Solomon, widow of Brigadier Solomon, Kerensky's financial benefactor and secret lover.

Robert Bruce Lockhart, British diplomat in charge of British Embassy in Moscow accused of plotting against Lenin and jailed. Saved Kerenskys life at the Gatchina Palace during the Russian Revolution and smuggled him aboard a Swedish merchant ship.

Colonel Edouard Berzin, commander of the Latvian Rifle Regiment in charge of guarding Lenin.

Lenin, Vladimir Ilyich (Ulyanov), seized power from Kerensky in the October Revolution.

Fanny Kaplan, attempted to assassinate Lenin in August 1918 allegedly as part of a plot by MI6.

Georg Relinsky spied for the British and his alias was Sydney Reilly. When sent by MI6 to Moscow he gave Fanny Kaplan a pistol to assassinate Stalin.

Maxim Gorky, the Communist revolutionary writer, owner of a Berlin residence used as a writers' commune where Nina Berberova and Moura Benckendorff-Budberg met.

Moura Benckendorff-Budberg, wife of a diplomat, lover of Bruce Lockhart during the Russian Revolution.

Compton Mackenzie, prolific author, friend and mentor to Nell Tritton, former MI6 secret agent in World War One. He was prosecuted and fined as the author of *Greek Memories* as the novel infringed the Official Secrets Act. Compton persuaded Nell to abandon her spy novel *To Moscow with Love,* warning her she would also be prosecuted and could be fined as much as £1,000,000 or jailed.

Josef Stalin (Dzhugashvili) terrorist in Baku, editor of Pravda, and Soviet dictator who authorised several attempted assassinations of Kerensky.

Leon Trotsky, (Bronstein) Chairman of Petrograd Soviet, Commissar for Foreign Affairs, exiled by Stalin in 1924, assassinated in Mexico.

Ramon Juan Mercader, born in Spain, assassinated Trotsky and was decorated when released from a Mexican prison and given a pension by the Russian Government.

Author's Acknowledgements

Many thanks to Andrew Farrell, director of Ebook Alchemy, my on-line publisher for his technical skills in getting this book on-line. Warmest thanks to Bernard Milford of Bernard Milford Consulting and Photography who designed the eye-catching cover for this book.

Thanks for help with editing from Marusia McCormick, Lois Nichol and Carole Castle and to Justine Tarplett as proof reader. Maureen Millar did valiant work with publicity after the launch of a print version of Nell at the former Tritton home had to be cancelled due to Covid-19 precautions. The talented Jill Richardson who provided photographs taken in Paris and help with editing and Vanessa de Vos who provided the photographs of *Elderslie.* Mrs Lavinia Tritton, Brisbane, was enormously helpful with family history.

Many thanks for technical help provided by Wayne O' Connor, director of Bonza IT and Shawn Hillhecker, director of Brisbane Photocopiers. Sources of material included the French National Library, Paris; the John Oxley Library, the State Library of Queensland; Kenmore Library, Brisbane. Elizabeth L. Garver at the Harry Ransom Centre at the University of Texas kindly provided a portrait of Kerensky and a story about him in the Winter Palace.

Author Details

Born in London with Scottish and Irish roots, Susanna de Vries studied art history at the Sorbonne in Paris and in Madrid. She arrived in Australia in 1975. She has written extensively on heroic women and was awarded an Order of Australia (AM) 'for services to art and literature'. Women writers nominated Susanna as the 'Australian writer whose work has made a distinguished and long-term contribution to literature'.

The story of Nell Tritton is the last in her series of biographies of outstanding Australian women. Her readers say she has the gift of making history as exciting as a novel.

Other Books

Historic Sydney as seen by its early artists. 1983 (Susanna Evans).
Historic Brisbane and its early artists. 1985 .
Pioneer Women Pioneer Land – Yesterday's Tall Poppies. 1987.
The Impressionists Revealed: Masterpieces from Private Collections.
Conrad Martens on the Beagle and in Australia. 1993.
Strength of Spirit: pioneering women of achievement from first fleet to federation. 1995.
Ethel Carrick Fox: Travels and Triumphs of a Post-Impressionist. 1997.
Strength of Purpose: Australian Women of Achievement from Federation to the Mid-20th Century. 1998 .
Historic Sydney: the founding of Australia. 1999.
Blue Ribbons Bitter Bread, the Story of Joice Loch, Australia's Most Decorated Woman. 2000.
Great Australian Women: From Federation to Freedom. 2001.
The Complete Book of Great Australian Women: 36 Women Who Have Changed the Course of Australia. 2003.
Historic Brisbane: convict settlement to river city. 2003. This book was co-written with her husband Jake de Vries.
Heroic Australian Women in War. 2004.
Great Pioneer Women of the Outback. 2005.
To Hell and Back. 2007.
Desert Queen: The Many Lives and Loves of Daisy Bates. 2008.
Trailblazers and Females on the Fatal Shore. 2008.
Females On The Fatal Shore. 2009.
The Complete Book of Heroic Australian Women: Twenty-one Extraordinary Women Whose Stories Changed History. 2010.
Trailblazers: Caroline Chisholm to Quentin Brice. 2011.
Royal Mistresses of the House of Hanover-Windsor. 2012.
Australian Heroines of World War One: Gallipoli, Lemnos and the Western Front. 2013
A Royal Love Triangle: Diana Remembered, Camilla Revealed. 2013.
Historic Sydney: The Founding of Australia. 2014.
To the Ends of the Earth: Mary Gaunt, Pioneer Traveller: Her Biography. 2014.
Royal Marriages - Diana, Camilla, Kate and Meghan and Princesses Who Did Not Live Happily Ever After. 2018.

ENDNOTES

[1] Frederick Tritton's elder brother Charles, (after whom Frederick named his eldest son) was offered employment in Sydney where he enjoyed a successful career. Another brother went north and became a leading grazer and it is this branch of the family after whom Queensland's Lake Fred Tritton is named. Information provided by Mrs Lavinia Tritton.

[2] Information supplied by Doug Tritton and Mrs Lavinia Tritton.

[3] The Tritton building has been demolished and its corner site on George Street and Adelaide Street is now the headquarters of Brisbane's City Council Library who put on a function to celebrate publication of this book.

[4] Brisbane architect Ron Baker restored the former Queen Alexandra Home which is now a community centre. His description of the children's home is at www.Queen Alexandra Home Coorparoo: Ron Baker.

[5] Details from Professor John Tyrer, *History of the Brisbane Hospital,* Boolarong Publications, Brisbane, 1993, page 197.

[6] For details of the 1919 pandemic see *Spanish flu pandemic in Australia,* a University of Sydney publication on line published by the Macleay Museum.

[7] Charles Tritton's son never inherited Tritton's. The younger sons of Fred Tritton took over the company after Frederick Tritton's death in 1947.

[8] After Freda's death her relatives sold the love letter from the deceased Prince of Wales to Freda Dudley Ward to the State Library of New South Wales. The Prince's attack of mumps with an orchitis or swelling of the genitals while at Dartmouth Naval College was kept from the press as it was feared this could have affected the virility of the heir to the throne. The story of the Prince of Wales and Freda Dudley Ward is related in Susanna de Vries, *Royal Mistresses of the House of Hanover-Windsor,* Boolarong Press, 2012 and subsequent editions.

[9] Susanna de Vries, *Royal Mistresses of the House of Hanover-Windsor,* Boolarong Press, 2012.

[10] Many years later, WFW writing on about Nell's marriage to Alexander Kerensky described Nell in the *Sidney Morning Herald* as 'dazzlingly attractive and a talented writer' but his full name was never revealed.

[11] Quotations from the journal of Marie Bashkirtseff are at Project Gutenberg www.org.author /Bashkirtseff, Marie.

[12] The Julian Academy operated in various locations on the Left Bank and closed in 1968. Pupils included Australians Will Ashton and Walter Withers; and Americans John Singer Sergeant and the adventurous Fanny Vandergriff, the future wife of author R.L. Stephenson who after painting in France accompanied RLS to the South Seas.

[13] After her premature death many of Marie Bashkirtseff's paintings remained in Paris and Nice, a few stolen by the Nazis were destroyed in World War 2. More than 60 are now in private and public collections in Europe, Ukraine and Russia. The artist's most widely reproduced oil is *The Meeting* now in the Musée d'Orsay in Paris, Marie's journal appeared in print three years after her death and was only the second journal by a woman published in France. It was widely admired by contemporary writers including George Bernard Shaw. Marie's' journals are held in the Bibliothèque Nationale or National Library of France.

[14] Bashkirtseff's most famous oil, *The Meeting,* hangs in the Musée d'Orsay in Paris, purchased by the French Government but was in the small museum and art gallery at the western end of the Luxemburg Palace when Nell saw it in Paris. (the museum is shown on the Baedeker map see page xxx. Other works by Bakshirtskeff are in the Petit Palais in Paris,

the Jules Cheret Gallery in Nice and galleries in Russia and the Ukraine. A website pays homage to Marie Bakshirtskeff at www.jose.mito@bashkirtseff.com.ar compiled by Argentinian admirer with reproductions of Marie's best paintings citing their current locations.

15 Thanks to Nell's research, Tritton's began selling household goods by mail order. A copy of their 1936 catalogue was recently advertised for sale by Booktopia and another copy is in the State Library of Queensland.

16 This street is unique in Montparnasse with its handsome mansions turned into apartments. Today it is called the rue de Regard and in Nell's day was the rue du Regard.

17 *Mentioned in Passing: the story of Nell Tritton,* a blog of the John Oxley Library Brisbane in which Tony Brett Young describes his English relative the author Francis Brett Young and his wife Jessica sharing a holiday villa on Capri.

18 These paintings are now in the Musée d'Orsay as part of the Caillebotte Collection when it was at the Luxembourg Palace with details in Susanna de Vries *Impressionsts Revealed: Art Masterpieces in Private Collections and Collectors,* Random House USA and Little Brown, London, page 161.

19 An account of this meeting is in Nell's Paris diaries held in a private collection in France, formerly owned by a major collector of Impressionist art. The diaries were later sold to a Russian oligarch with homes in Paris and Spain who now refuses access to his collections.

20 Included in the large collection of papers and photographs of Alexander Kerensky in the Harry Ransom Centre of the University of Texas at Austen, mainly after he moved to America is a portrait photograph of Nell at the time of her wedding to Kerensky and a box of manuscripts of Nell's poems and her short stories published in American magazines. Other materials on Kerensky and his wife are held at the Hoover Institute Archives at Stanford University.

21 Stella Bowen struggled to bring up her daughter by painting portraits. In World War Two she was appointed an official Australian war artist in London. She painted a series of brilliant portraits of the crew of an Australian air force plane which crashed soon after she had painted them. Today Stella's portraits hang in the Australian War Memorial in Canberra and her self-portrait is in the State Gallery of South Australia and other paintings are in important private collections.

22 At this period the Russian secret police were called the Cheka.

23 The title was later proved by Nina Berberova to be a fabrication by Moura.

24 Reilly and Lockhart were tried in absentia in Russia and sentenced to death and in 1925 Reilly/Relinsky was enticed back to Russia and shot by the Cheka.

25 When H.G. Wells died he bequeathed Countess Moura Budberg a large sum of money which enabled her to buy an apartment in Cromwell Road, Kensington. She established herself as a London literary and film agent. Once Moura was dead and could not sue for libel, Nina Berberova wrote an unflattering biography of Budberg, exposing the fact she was not born with a title. Nina also exposed how Moura had been responsible for the deaths of many Russians by taking the suitcase of letters addressed to Gorky to Moscow and giving them to her controller in Stalin's secret police.

26 The copy of Nell's published poems is in Fryer Library, University of Queensland.

27 Address cited on a letter from Nell to Gladys Edds (formerly Tritton) held by Mrs Lavinia Tritton.

28 For details of the persecution of Jews in Russia under the Romanovs see award winning historian Simon Sebag Montefiore, *The Romanovs.* Weidenfeld and Nicholson, London, 2016.

29 Michael B Miller, *Shanghai on the Metro Spies* and *Intrigue in France between the Wars,* University of California Press, 1994.

[30] *Mentioned in passing, The Story of Nell Tritton,* John Oxley Library, Guest blogger. Tony Brett Young describes Nell's first stay on Capri with the writer Francis Brett Young and his wife Jessica when she was introduced to the large colony of writers on the island, including Compton Mackenzie, former actor and British secret agent turned author.

[31] At Compton's trial at the Old Bailey Sir Thomas Inskip, the Attorney General asked for the maximum punishment, ten years in jail and a fine of £1,000,000. The judge heartily disliked St Thomas Inskip and they argued fiercely over points of law and this saved Compton. To spite of the Attorney-General the judge did not jail Compton Mackenzie and only fined him £200,000 plus legal costs. The fines and fees of senior barristers meant Compton had to sell his villa on Capri but continued to return to the island to holiday in a rented villa. Compton wrote two more novels about Scotland which became best sellers, *Whiskey Galore* set which on the Isle of Sky and *Monarch of the Glen* which takes place in a Scottish castle whose owners are virtually bankrupt. This became a very successful TV series. Compton Mackenzie died in 1972.

[32] Divorce laws for wives wanting to divorce their husbands were not changed until 1937 when it was decided wives could gain a divorce on grounds of adultery without cruelty but this important amendment came too late to help Nell.

[33] Flora's memoir *From Baku to Baker Street, Collins, New York, 1984* claimed only six miners at the Lena River mine were killed by Russian soldiers in April 1912. Official figures at the trial at which Kerensky defended the miner's widows were 200 miners killed and over 100 badly injured. See Richard Abraham, *Alexander Kerensky,* Colombia University Press, New York 1987 pages 54-67.

[34] See the Wikipedia account of the actual storming of the Winter Palace rather than the legend put out by Lenin and continued by Stalin.

[35] Valentin Zuboz described how he foiled the assassination in a memoir titled, *Stradny gody,* Moscow, 1929. More details were revealed in Galina Stolyarova, 'Gatchina, St Petersburg's Unknown Palace; *The Moscow Times,* July ,2018.

[36] The suicide and Corporal Belenky's plan to disguise Kerensky as a sailor wearing an aviator's mask is from Richard Abraham in *Alexander Kerensky,* Columbia University Press, page 323.

[37] Cambridge University did not grant women degrees until 1948.

[38]Mark Galeotti, *A Short History of Russia,* Ebury Press, London 2021.

[39] Geneviève Dreyfus-Armand author of *L'Exil des republicains espagnols en France: De la Guerre civile à la mort de Franco* (Spanish Republicans in Exile in France: From the Civil War to the Death of Franco).

[40] Alan Sennett, *Revolutionary Marxism in Spain,* 1930-1937 Haymarket Books, Chicago, 2015

[41]Nicholas Whitlam, *Four Weeks One Summer,* Australian Scholarly Publishing, North Melbourne, 2016. Ken Lacey, *Aces of the Condor Legion,* Osprey Publishing and the personal accounts of Salvador Vila, recounted to Susanna de Vries in the 1950s when she was a student in Spain where the events of the Civil War were still raw.

[42] Flora Solomon. *From Baku to Baker Street,* page 174-175.

[43] Richard Abraham, *Alexander Kerensky,* Columbia University Press , page 167 mentions that the theft of Kerensky's papers was followed by the equally mysterious burglary of Trotsky's private papers which Kerensky was convinced was carried out by Russian secret agents.

[44] Simon Sebag Montefiore in *Stalin, The Court of the Red Tsar,* Weidenfeld & Nicholson, London, 2003 revealed the debauchery and murderous cruelty of Stalin at which Kerensky had mentioned in editorials without knowing the full extent of the Stalin's flawed character. Stalin's cruelty to former friends, foes as well as to his own children was kept hidden from the public. After *glasnost* Simon Sebag Montefiore carried out research in Russian archives in order to write *The Young Stalin* and *The Red Tsar.* Lenin's

body continues to be taken out his tomb periodically for restoration and is viewed like some medieval Christian relic by true believers. It is believed Stalin's body was moved from the central courtyard to a wall on the periphery.

[45] Fyodor Raskolnikov, former Bolshevik hero of the revolution wrote to Gorky confiding he was worried about Stalin's mental health and was thinking of fleeing to the West, unaware that Gorky whose royalties had declined to almost nothing was being bribed by Stalin with honours and money to return to Russia. Raskolnikov 'letter of denunciation of Stalin was published in full in Russian in editions of *New Russia* in March and April 1936. In 2020 it was translated into English on Google but was soon taken down at the request of persons unknown

[46] *The Lockhart Plot: Love, Betrayal, Assassination and Counter-Revolution in Lenin's Russia,* Jonathan Schneer, Oxford University Press, 2020. Professor Schneer's book revels hidden details of the British Government's involvement in the plot to assassinate Lenin and Trotsky in September 1918 which is alleged to have cost Britain over £1,000,000 and made the British look foolish for losing the gold to the Russian secret police. The British Government feared the story, if published in the press, could cost the government led by Lloyd George the next election so ordered relevant files destroyed. The Official Secrets Act was used to prevent journalists writing about it but the fact they had done this proved that the Lockhart plot had credibility.

[47] *The Australian Dictionary of Biography* cites the dates of Nell's visit as March to June 1939 but my source of information claims Kerensky's telegram arrived in Brisbane in July of that year.

[48] Cited by Richard Abraham, in his biography, *Alexander Kerensky,* page 367.

[49] Juan Mercader was eventually awarded a Lenin medal by Stalin. His mother was given a Soviet pension and an Order of Lenin while her son was in jail in Mexico. When released he fled to the Communist Cuba of Fidel Castro and died there in 1978. His body was taken to Moscow where he received a hero's burial in the Kuntsevo Cemetery.

[50] Nina Berberova. *The Italics are Mine.* Harcourt Brace, New York, 1969. Pages 303-305.

[51] 11 July 1940 was the date cited for Nell and Kerensky's escape from the German invasion in the entry on Lydia Ellen Tritton in *The Australian Dictionary of Biography.* In *The Italics are Mine,* Nina Berberova cited the date of their departure from her country home as June 12, 1940 as they spent the night at Nina's house.

[52] From *Privations in France,* a BBC interview with Nell Kerensky in, London, broadcast on 17 July 1945 about her escape with Kerensky in June 1940.

[53] Nell's press interviews, the first given in London to the *Daily Telegraph* date unknown on arrival in London in 1940 and the second in Brisbane to the *Courier-Mail* dated 18 November 1945 were headed 'Nightmare Ordeal in France' Nell revealed the full horror of dismembered limbs littering the road after the Germans bombed cars and strafed people with bullets. She repeated this account to the widow of Kenneth Simpson and other American friends when they arrived in New York.

[54] Alice Keppel, the final mistress of the late King Edward VII, received a handsome bequest from her lover and used it to buy a villa on the outskirts of Florence where she was living when the Germans invaded France. Mussolini turned hostile to British residents so the Keppels contacted the Foreign Office and a naval vessel was despatched to collect them at St Jean de Luz, aware the late king's mistress would have been used for propaganda purposes had Hitler managed to get hold of her. See Susanna de Vries, *Royal Mistresses of the House of Hanover-Windsor,* chapter on Alice Keppel.

[55] Oleg Kerensky, Olga and Kerensky's elder son was born in 1907. After studying engineering at a British university Oleg joined the British Army serving with the Royal Engineers and later worked for the English Electric Co. Gleb Kerensky translated his father's books as an engineering student and he would eventually work for Dorman

Long, a major engineering company involved with the design and building of the Sydney Harbour Bridge and would become a renown designer of significant bridges.

[56] Nell's BBC radio interview was titled *Privations in France and is in the archives of the.* BBC.

[57] Information from Richard Abraham, *Alexander Kerensky.* Columbia University Press, New York, 1987 Page 482.

[58] Richard Abraham, *Alexander Kerensky,* page 372 New Canaan was where Maxwell Perkins, Hemingway's brilliant editor lived but there is no record of Nell meeting him.

[59] The author has been unable to trace a copy of this pamphlet.

[60] Kerensky Papers, folio 191, University of Austin, Texas. Cited in Richard Abrahams' biography of Kerensky page 372.

[61] Some of Nell's letters to her husband, catalogued under the initials LK, (Lydia Kerensky to AK, Alexander Kerensky are held in the library of the University of Texas at Austin.

[62] *The Hobart Mercury,* 6 August 1945 announced the impending visit of Mr and Mrs Kerensky *The Melbourne Argus* interviewed Nell on 9 November 1945.

[63] Corbett Tritton who had worked for the BBC and his career in Australia is cited in *A History of ABC Broadcasting* by Kenneth S. Inglis. Corbett Tritton, the son of J.W. Tritton. Later Corbett became Private Secretary to Australian Prime Minister Robert Menzies.

[64] *The Courier-Mail,* 18 November 1945 article titled 'Nightmare Ordeal in France' records an interview with Nell at her family home.

[65] Meeting described in a letter from Clem Christesen to writer Joan Priest dated 25.1.80. Fryer Library of Australian Literature, University of Queensland.

[66] Richard Abraham, *Alexander Kerensky,* page 375.

[67] Nell's gravestone is in Section A3 of the South Brisbane Cemetery, the former Dutton Park Cemetery.

[68] Nell's parents owned a beach house at Redcliffe, named *Pevensey.* Before World War Two, Redcliffe was considered an ideal place for Brisbane families to have a holiday home before the Gold Coast became popular. Information from Mrs Lavinia Tritton and Mr Doug Tritton.

[69] Alliluyeva, Svetlana. *Twenty Letters to a Friend,* London, 1967.

[70] Meeting cited in Julius Epstein, *Operation Keelhaul, The Story of Forced Repatriation from 1944 to the Present,* Greenwich Press, 1973 and Kerensky Papers, folio 217.

[71] Kerensky Papers, folio 190, Harry Ransom Humanities Research Centre, University of Texas at Austin have the notes he made in his retirement.

[72] Interview for BBC programme *The Conversation* between Stephen Kerensky and Professor Michael Hughes, Professor of Modern Russian History at Lancaster University.

[73] Richard Abraham's *Alexander Kerensky* Columbia University Press, New York, 1987 only devotes half a page a page to Nell Tritton, but a great deal of new information has emerged since Abraham's biography of Kerensky was published.

[74] The incident in the Plaza Hotel was cited in Flora Solomon, *From Baku to Baker Street,* London, 1984.

www.ingramcontent.com/pod-product-compliance
Lightning Source LLC
LaVergne TN
LVHW060932110826
845147LV00029B/753

* 9 7 8 0 9 8 0 6 2 1 6 7 9 *